THE NATIONAL GEOGRAPHIC TRAVELER

BOSTON & ENVIRONS

THE NATIONAL GEOGRAPHIC TRAVELER

BOSTON & ENVIRONS

WITH THE CAPE, PROVIDENCE & NEWPORT

Paul Wade & Kathy Arnold

Contents

Page 1: Stained glass design,
Massachusetts State House
Pages 2–3: View of Post Office Square
through dome
Left: Memorial Chapel on
Harvard Square, Cambridge

How to use this guide

See back flap for keys to text and map symbols

The *National Geographic Traveler* brings you the best of Boston & environs in text, pictures, and maps. Divided into three main sections, the guide begins with an overview of history and culture. Following are seven city-area chapters and four regional chapters, each with featured sites selected by the authors for their particular interest. Each chapter opens with its own contents list.

The selected areas within Boston and the surrounding regions, and the sites within them, are arranged geographically. A map introduces each chapter, highlighting

featured sites. Walks and drives are plotted on their own maps. Features and sidebars are used to give intriguing detail on history, culture, or contemporary life.

The final section, Travelwise, lists essential information for the traveler—including pre-trip planning, special events, getting around, and emergencies—together with a selection of hotels, restaurants, shops, and entertainment.

To the best of our knowledge, all information is accurate as of the press date. However, it's always advisable to call ahead when possible.

Color coding

106

Each region is color coded for easy reference. Find the region you want on the map on the front flap, and look for the color flash at the top of the pages of the relevant chapter. Information in **Travelwise** is also color coded to each region.

Visitor information

Trinity Church

- Map pp. 106–107
- Copley Sq.
- 617/536-0944
- $
- T: Copley, Back Bay

Practical information for most sites is given in the side column (see key to symbols on back flap). The map reference gives the page number of the map and grid reference. Other details are address, telephone number, days closed, entrance charge in a range from $ (under $4) to $$$$$ (over $25), and nearest T-stop for sites in Boston. Other sites have information in italics and parentheses in the text.

TRAVELWISE

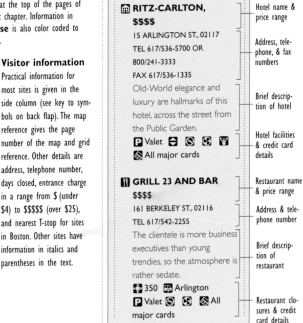

BOSTON COMMON & BACK BAY — Color-coded region name

RITZ-CARLTON, $$$$ — Hotel name & price range

15 ARLINGTON ST., 02117
TEL 617/536-5700 OR
800/241-3333
FAX 617/536-1335 — Address, telephone, & fax numbers

Old-World elegance and luxury are hallmarks of this hotel, across the street from the Public Garden. — Brief description of hotel

Valet ▢ ▢ ▢ ▢
All major cards — Hotel facilities & credit card details

GRILL 23 AND BAR $$$$ — Restaurant name & price range

161 BERKELEY ST., 02116
TEL 617/542-2255 — Address & telephone number

The clientele is more business executives than young trendies, so the atmosphere is rather sedate. — Brief description of restaurant

350 Arlington
Valet ▢ ▢ All major cards — Restaurant closures & credit card details

Hotel & restaurant prices

An explanation of the price bands used in entries is given in the Hotels & Restaurants section (on p. 241).

AREA MAPS

Point of interest

Important featured sites

- A locator map accompanies each regional map and shows the location of that region in the country.
- Adjacent regions are shown, each with a page reference.

WALKING TOURS

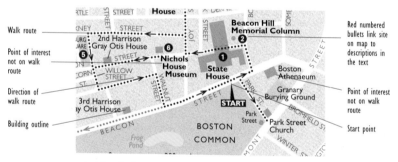

Walk route

Point of interest not on walk route

Direction of walk route

Building outline

Red numbered bullets link site on map to descriptions in the text

Point of interest not on walk route

Start point

- An information box gives the starting and ending points, time and length of walk, and places not to be missed along the route.
- Where two walks are marked on the map, the second route is shown in orange.

REGIONAL MAPS

Road number

Important point of interest

Map reference

Important featured town

Point of interest

- An information box provides details including starting and finishing points, time and length of drive, and places not to be missed along the route, or tips on terrain.

THE NATIONAL GEOGRAPHIC TRAVELER

BOSTON & ENVIRONS

WITH THE CAPE, PROVIDENCE & NEWPORT

About the authors

Kathy Arnold and Paul Wade are an Anglo-American couple based in London, England. Both are freelance writers and broadcasters, with some 30 books on travel and sports to their names. Kathy went to college in Boston, and Paul also studied in Massachusetts. Both are frequent visitors to New England, as keen to explore side roads as to visit the highlights.

Over the years, they have written in-depth articles on the inns of New England for magazines such as *Gourmet* and *Essentially America*. Their books on the region include *Charming Small Hotel Guides: New England* and *New England's Best-Loved Driving Tours*. As reporters, their experiences have been broadcast on the BBC, while their articles are published in national newspapers in the U.K., such as the *Daily Telegraph* and *The Express*. Winners of major writing and broadcasting awards, Kathy and Paul specialize in reporting on France, Great Britain, and the United States.

History & culture

A period interpreter, Plimoth Plantation

Boston today

BOSTON IS A GALLERY OF AMERICAN MEMORIES, LINED WITH ICONS OF THE world's first democratic republic. Colonial Boston's protests against British bullying were America's protests, expressed through events such as the Boston Massacre and the Boston Tea Party. Crowds at Faneuil Hall affirmed that there should be "no taxation without representation"; lanterns high above the Old North Church signaled the start of the American Revolution; the "shot heard 'round the world" rang out at nearby Concord.

The capital of Massachusetts, and the unofficial capital of New England, Boston was founded by English Puritans in 1630. Today, it is a city on a human scale, one that feels European with its narrow, wriggling streets, small cars, and wide-ranging MBTA public transportation system, known as "the T." With its brick town houses, broad green parks, and leafy avenues, the cityscape is easy on the eye. Boston is compact, safe, and relatively flat, making it easy to walk. Landmarks make orientation simple: Just look for the gold dome of the State House or the blue shaft of the John Hancock Tower.

Despite its beauty and sense of history, Boston is a red-blooded, forward-looking all-American city. The area has long been a hotbed of invention; think of the telephone, anesthetics, microwave ovens, even frozen fish sticks. Boston's professional sports teams were founding members of their leagues, with many Boston-based players among the country's greatest heroes. And the city continues to take a leading role in shaping the future of not just the United States, but the world. Some of the wizards behind the Internet are based in Cambridge, just across the Charles River.

ON THE TRAIL

There is so much to see and do in Boston that one visit is never enough. And there are additional rich layers of history and culture, along with glorious landscapes, all within a two-hour drive. First-timers, however, whether from the United States or abroad, must start by following the Freedom Trail in downtown Boston. This 2.5-mile (4 km) route traces the early history of the city, which parallels the beginning of the Republic. Marked by a line of red bricks or paint on the sidewalk, it links 16 significant historic sites, including the Paul Revere House, the Old North Church, the Old State House, and Faneuil Hall. Soak up the details of the struggle for liberty, then visit the nearby towns of Lexington and Concord, where local Minutemen came face to face with British soldiers in 1775. Explore further to discover more about the region's seafaring legacy, the Pilgrims, or its industrial heritage.

There is always good music, good sports, good beer, and good shopping. No other city in the United States offers such variety in such a compact area, with so much else to see nearby. All you need is a comfortable pair of walking shoes.

A 21ST-CENTURY CITY

Boston sells its history vigorously, but this is no living museum. Rather, it is a 21st-century city playing, along with Cambridge, a major role on the world stage in several fields. No metropolis has better hospitals or a more significant record of medical breakthroughs and innovative techniques, thanks to its outstanding research laboratories. Financial services, too, are prominent in Boston's economy. The mutual funds business is the fastest-growing sector of the 7.5-billion-dollar financial services industry in Massachusetts. In all, financial services account for some 47,000 jobs and a payroll of 3.2 billion dollars, and they generate jobs in supporting fields such as telecommunications, computer technology, printing, advertising, and law. Entrepreneurs also turn to Boston, one of the nation's major sources for venture capital.

The impact of travel and tourism has grown by over 30 percent in the last decade, with nearly 30 million visitors a year adding more than 17 billion dollars to the economy.

Nothing in Boston evokes the city's past more than Beacon Hill, with its cobbled streets and historic brick houses.

Students are a mainstay of the city's finances, with some 250,000 enrolled at the 65 or so colleges and universities within a 30-mile (48 km) radius of Downtown. Also in this sector are world-renowned consulting and research firms providing information-based solutions to companies and governments. Last but certainly not least are the region's high-tech employers. Hardware and software, instrumentation, telecommunications, and biotechnology are big business.

NEIGHBORHOOD CHARM

Boston's neighborhoods are the result of 370 years of growth. Cut off from Downtown by the steel and concrete slash of the John F. Fitzgerald Expressway is the North End. The first stop for most immigrants over the years, this is still home to many Italian families. The warren of lanes is one of the most vibrant parts of the city. In the Downtown area, new and old coexist: Skyscrapers crammed with city officials, lawyers, and business executives

overshadow such famous buildings as the Old State House and Faneuil Hall (pronounced to rhyme with Daniel), the original centers of commerce and government in the Colony. The most popular draw in the whole city is right here: Quincy (pronounced QUIN-zy) Market, or the Faneuil Hall Marketplace. The successful transformation of a run-down marketplace into a complex of shops, restaurants, and entertainment, it serves as an example for urban renewal projects around the world.

A feature of Patriots' Day celebrations since 1897, the Boston Marathon is the oldest annual marathon in the world.

Another area to benefit from renovation is the South End. From Clarendon Street West, 19th-century brick town houses to the north and south of Tremont Street have been gentrified. A mixed community, with a strong gay scene, the buzz comes from bars, restaurants, and artists' studios.

As the nation's oldest major city enters the third millennium, the most exciting changes are along the wharves and piers of the Waterfront, where obsolete warehouses are being recycled as museums, restaurants, and housing. Other areas to benefit from facelifts include the Theater District and Downtown Crossing, once just a stop on the subway system, but now a catch-all name for a pedestrian-only shopping zone. Change is everywhere Downtown. Even Boston's Chinatown, one of the largest Chinese communities in North America, is now also home to immigrants from other parts of Asia.

The most elegant neighborhood of all is Beacon Hill. With gas lights, brick sidewalks, and handsome homes, it looks like a film set for a costume drama. A stroll up and down the narrow streets is right at the top of the list of things to do in Boston. From the time of the Revolution, this has been the most exclusive address in town. When Boston ran out of land for new housing in the 19th century, the city fathers filled in the tidal Back Bay and Fenway marshes and created a grid pattern of streets, boulevards, and parks. The people who live in Back Bay's town houses have boutiques, restaurants, and art galleries at their doorsteps. And in minutes they can be over at the Fenway, where Huntingdon Avenue has been dubbed the Avenue of the Arts, thanks to its concentration of concert halls and museums.

On the north side of the Charles River is Cambridge, a city in its own right, with its own place in history, and home to Harvard University and Massachusetts Institute of Technology (MIT). Here, Harvard Square is another must for visitors, who delight in the coffeehouses and bookstores of what some consider Boston's version of Paris's Left Bank.

A MELTING POT

Boston is often characterized as consisting of three tribes: the descendants of the original English colonists, the Irish, and the Italians. But there are more than three ingredients to the Boston stew. Dating back to colonial times, Boston has one of the oldest black communities in the United States, and the African–American

Heritage sites on and around Beacon Hill are now receiving the recognition they merit. Over the past 150 years, immigrants have flooded in from every country in Europe, from Russian Jews to Portuguese fishermen. Joining the melting pot more recently are the newer immigrants from Asia and Latin America. But immigrants are not the only new Bostonians. Many students who come to college stay on after graduation, unable to leave one of the country's most lively and sophisticated cities.

A FAMILY-FRIENDLY CITY

Boston is regularly voted as one of the best cities for vacations with children. The Children's Museum, one of the world's oldest, offers plenty of hands-on activities. Also on the Waterfront is the Boston Tea Party ship, where youngsters can clamber aboard *Beaver II* and hurl fake tea chests into the harbor. Nearby, the New England Aquarium gives an excellent overview of the region's wildlife beneath the ocean. In 1999, the Computer Museum moved to the Museum of Science, Boston's biggest draw. Nearly two million visitors a year flock to see the electrifying old favorite, the Van de Graaff generator, which at regular intervals cranks out the world's biggest artificial lightning bolt.

All museums are child-friendly. The Museum of Fine Arts has regular programs to help youngsters enjoy and learn about its world-class collections. Most fun, however, is the MIT Museum, with its Hall of Hacks, explaining the best of the ingenious pranks played by techie students over the years. For those with excess energy, there are wide open spaces, particularly Boston Common and the neighboring Public Garden, with its swan boats. And there's always entertainment on the Charles River, where a good spot to watch crews rowing by is the pedestrian-only Weeks Memorial Bridge. When you need a quick break from the city, pack a picnic and take a ferryboat to one of the Boston Harbor Islands for a day's beachcombing or bird-watching.

FOUR SEASONS

Boston has year-round appeal. It is rightly regarded as the gateway to New England, and the ocean and the mountains are within easy

The Boston skyline soars above the peaceful Public Garden.

reach. A summer highlight is the Fourth of July, when some locals boat down the Charles River to join the thousands on the riverside listening to the Boston Pops outdoor concert at the Hatch Shell. Summer is also the time for ethnic festivals (see p. 258). And if the weather gets too hot, you can escape to the beaches of the North Shore or Cape Cod and the islands.

Fall brings the crisp, clear days that are perfect for walking around the city. New England's glorious seasonal colors touch the trees in nearby towns such as Concord and Lexington. The students are back, ready to cheer their football teams as they renew century-old rivalries. October brings the Head of the Charles Regatta, attracting hundreds of rowers and thousands of spectators to the riverbanks. Nowhere is Thanksgiving more significant than in the region where European settlers first celebrated their survival.

Winter in Boston can be harsh, but it also has a certain romance, with thousands of little

white lights in the trees. The custom of putting candles into windows at Christmas originated in Beacon Hill's Louisburg Square. The end of the year, and the start of the next, is marked by First Night, a Boston institution now copied across the country. Hundreds of thousands enjoy the citywide entertainment that culminates in fireworks over the harbor. Snow is welcomed by skiers, both downhill and cross-country, who can reach well-groomed trails in a couple of hours.

Organizers claim that the annual Head of the Charles Regatta in mid-October is the world's largest rowing event.

Spring brings two of the most flamboyant celebrations. In March, the city goes green for St. Patrick's Day, especially in Irish South Boston. That same date—March 17—also marks Evacuation Day, when British troops retreated from Boston in 1776. On Patriots' Day, in April, the events of April 19, 1775, are

In Back Bay, elegant Newbury Street is an attractive mix of shops, galleries, and cafés.

reenacted and celebrated on Boston's very own holiday. Part of the day's fun is the renowned Boston Marathon. Run every year since 1897, this is the world's oldest annual marathon.

PARKS & GREEN SPACES

Boston is relatively flat, which is part of its appeal as a walking city, although this is the result of landscaping and landfill rather than nature (see p. 34). Much of the city's appeal, however, stems from enlightened cooperation with Mother Nature. You are never far from the water, either the sea or the Charles River.

Boston is also very green. No other city in North America has so successfully retained its "common," the original open space in the heart of town, dedicated to the ordinary citizen, around which the city grew up. More than 150 years ago, its rough grass and trees were complemented by the adjoining, more formal Boston Public Garden. Running off this are the tree-lined boulevards of Commonwealth Avenue and Newbury Street. Other significant additions in the past century include the landscaped esplanade alongside the Charles River

and the "Emerald Necklace," a string of parks looping out to the southern suburbs (see pp. 122–23). The Arnold Arboretum in Jamaica Plain (see p. 123) and Mount Auburn Cemetery in Cambridge (see p. 162) are beautifully landscaped areas that provide a haven for birds. Today, new patches of green are being stitched on to the city's tapestry, with projects including Post Office Square in the Financial District and Christopher Columbus Park by Long Wharf. When the "Big Dig" (see p. 33) transport and landscaping project is finally finished, a further 150 acres of new parks and open spaces will have been created.

THAT'S ENTERTAINMENT

Boston is home to the world-famous Boston Symphony Orchestra, and its sibling, the Boston Pops. The Boston Ballet dominates the dance scene, while the Boston Lyric Opera is building a fine reputation. Theater relies heavily on pre-Broadway shows, although there are several repertory companies. The city, once a hotbed of rock and folk/rock, enjoys a burgeoning club and pub scene.

The Boston Pops' annual Fourth of July concert takes place at the Hatch Memorial Shell.

Lovers of the arts spend hours at a time in the Museum of Fine Arts, where must-sees include the Asian treasures and the French Impressionists. A few steps away is the delightful Isabella Stewart Gardner Museum. Harvard University is the haunt of connoisseurs who appreciate museums that range from A to Z (art to zoology). Little more than an hour away is the Peabody Essex Museum in Salem, one of the region's gems.

Thanks to television and the movies, Boston is familiar to viewers around the world. They have seen the Bull and Finch pub in *Cheers!* and the swooping shots of the Charles River, the Bunker Hill Monument, and the State House's gold dome at the start of *Ally McBeal*. A grittier Boston appeared in *Good Will Hunting* (1997). Written by and starring Bostonians Matt Damon and Ben Affleck, it contrasted tough South Boston with academic Cambridge. It's people, not scenery, that make Boston tick. Locals have a wry sense of humor, demonstrated by stand-up comedians such as Paula Poundstone and talk-show host Jay Leno. Others get their message across through music. Singers such as Joan Baez, Tracy Chapman, and Bonnie Raitt first made their voices heard in local clubs. Perhaps the most unlikely nationally known personalities are two brothers from Cambridge. Tom and Ray Magliozzi host the *Car Talk* show on National Public Radio, which attracts callers from across the nation.

Bostonians are known for their much-mimicked Bah-ston accent. The jokes may revolve around "pahking cahs in Hahvahd yahd," but the reality is that parking is very difficult all over the city. Locals laugh about this, much as they do about pushy Boston drivers. They even take a perverse pride in the misleading signs, which ensure that out-of-towners "can't get there from here."

Most Bostonians love to talk, particularly about politics and the weather. They also love to complain. They'll moan about the latest Red Sox defeat and the disruption caused by the Big Dig. They can afford to be critical, however, because underneath they believe that theirs is one of the most beautiful and livable cities in the world. ∎

Boston fare

WHEN IT COMES TO FOOD, THE SPECIALTIES OF BOSTON AND NEW ENGLAND are truly all-American. Turkey, venison, squash, and wild blueberries have been served since the Pilgrims landed. They put oysters into stew, added clams to chowder, and turned corn into bread. Local chefs today are just as inclined to absorb new influences, creating new dishes that combine flair with a sense of tradition and locale.

The first English settlers started the culinary ball rolling by copying the Native American clambake, which involved cooking shellfish in a pit over hot stones, with layers of seaweed and corn. In 1633 observers noted that both the Native Americans and English settlers ate cranberries, "boyling them with Sugar for Sauce to eat with their Meat, and it is a delicate Sauce."

Molasses imported from the West Indies was an essential ingredient for both Boston brown bread (which is traditionally cooked by steaming) and the original recipe for baked beans, Boston baked beans. In 1625, William Blaxton planted an orchard on Beacon Hill. After moving to Rhode Island in 1635, he developed the United States' first native apple variety, the Sweet Rhode Island Greening. Apples have been a New England staple ever since, used for pies, juice, and cider. In the fall, farm stands throughout the region overflow with baskets and bags of the fruit, including traditional varieties such as Roxbury Russets, Maiden Blush, and the Cox's Orange Pippin.

Boston and seafood go together. Lobsters may no longer be as large as the 30-pound (13.6 kg) whoppers that one British visitor described in the 19th century, but they are still readily available; you can even buy them live at Logan International Airport to take home! Bostonians' insatiable appetite for fish and shellfish has formed the basis for the Legal Sea Foods empire. What was just a small fish outlet in Cambridge in 1950 has now become a local institution and is currently expanding to other states.

However, some traditional dishes have almost disappeared from today's menus. Colorfully named desserts such as Cape Cod berry grunt and apple slump are now rarely seen outside the home. But Bostonians and their fellow New Englanders continue to indulge their sweet tooth by eating more ice

cream per person than anywhere else in the United States. Even in freezing midwinter, you'll see Bostonians licking ice-cream cones. If you mention Steve's, you'll be told that local ice-cream maker Steve Herrell was in the vanguard of the current craze for adding ingredients such as crumbled cookies and candy to ice cream.

In the last two decades, the Boston restaurant scene has changed dramatically. Local ingredients are being used to create quintessentially New England dishes by well-known and influential chefs such as Gordon Hamersley, Deborah Hughes, and Jasper White. Their menus often credit the producers of the ingredients and feature specialty beers supplied by some of the microbreweries that have been at the forefront of the beer and ale revival that has swept the United States.

When it comes to influencing the nation's eating habits, two Boston women have lead the way. Over a hundred years ago, Fannie Merritt Farmer (1857–1915) published the *Boston Cooking School Cook Book*. Her use of level measurements and notes on nutrition, or "the principles of diet," as she called them, set a new standard for modern cookbooks. Today, Cambridge's Julia Child (born 1912) is famous across the country, thanks to *The French Chef*, a television program that originated at Boston's WGBH television station. ∎

> "Here are grapes, white and red, and very sweet and strong also; strawberries, gooseberries, raspas etc; plums of three sorts, with black and red being almost as good as damson."—
> Edward Winslow, December 11, 1621 ∎

A favorite New England delicacy, clams gathered from the shore are eaten steamed, fried, or in chowder.

Boston history

BOSTON IS UNIQUE. THE CITY HELPED TO SHAPE THE NATION, PASSING ON ideals and education, thrift and culture, pride and vision. Over the course of nearly four centuries Boston has established itself above all as a hotbed of ideas, whether they be the ideas that led to the creation of a new country or the foundations of Nobel Prize-winning scientific advances.

There is little record of local life before the Europeans arrived in 1620, apart from some artifacts excavated on the North Shore. Bubonic plague wiped out most native tribes before the Pilgrims landed, so settlement was relatively easy. However, Native American tribal names survive as place names: the Massachusett and the Nauset, the Narragansett and the Pautucket. European explorers John Cabot and Giovanni Verrazano sailed past in 1497 and 1524 respectively, noting the vast bay, but it was John Smith (1580–1631), a first-class realtor, who reported that he saw "paradise" in 1614.

17TH CENTURY & THE PILGRIMS

Back in England, King James I (*R*.1603–1625) approved the Plymouth Company's charter to exploit New England, an area stretching from Newfoundland to Virginia. Smith's supposed paradise appealed to a group of dissident English Protestants. In 1620, 102 men, women, and children set sail aboard the *Mayflower* from Plymouth, England. On November 21, they anchored near present-day Provincetown at the tip of Cape Cod. Since the bleak spit of land proved inhospitable in midwinter, they sailed on across Cape Cod Bay to found the Plymouth Colony, eloquently re-created at Plimoth Plantation today. Only half of the settlers (not until later were they called Pilgrims) lived through the first harsh winter. Thanks to a fruitful summer, and Native American help, the colony survived. Over the next 20 years, 75,000 further settlers arrived in the Great Puritan Migration. Some 14,000 landed in the Bay Colony of Massachusetts, many setting up home in present-day Salem.

The first European in what is now Boston was a hermit, William Blaxton. In 1625, he arrived on the small Shawmut peninsula, virtually an island with just a narrow neck connecting it to the mainland. Five years later, 150 Puritans led by John Winthrop bought land from Blaxton, calling the settlement Tramount, or Trimountain, after its three central hills. They soon changed the name to Boston, after their hometown in England. Today's Tremont Street is an echo of that original name, while Beacon Hill is now the only surviving hill.

As early as 1636, settlers recognized the importance of education. Rather than send youngsters to school back in England, they set up Harvard College in Cambridge. Far from the old country and its Civil War (1642–1651), the colonists thrived. But this was no new paradise. Strict rules governing daily life suppressed merrymaking and smoking in public. Ruled by zealots, only white Puritan males could vote in this "Bible Commonwealth," where Governor John Winthrop (1588–1649) considered democracy the "meanest and worst" way to govern. All settlers paid taxes, vote or no vote. If religious intolerance was bad in Europe, the Puritan regime was worse, persecuting Baptists, Quakers, Indians, and Jews. As early as 1648, women were hanged as witches. Roger Williams (1603–1683), a friend of the Native Americans and an advocate of the separation of church and state, was banished. He founded Providence in present-day Rhode Island, where the principle of religious tolerance was paramount.

EARLY COLONIAL DAYS

The century-long conflict over taxes between the Mother Country and her New World offspring began in 1660. After the monarchy was restored in England, King Charles II (*R*.1660–1685) needed to refill the royal

As this Revolutionary War map shows, the original settlement was virtually an island; today's Boston sits on reclaimed land.

Gen. Washington's
Revolutionary Campaign War Map

Publisher, A. O. Crane, Boston, Mass.

Statute Mile

coffers. Navigation Laws were introduced to raise money from the Colonies by restricting trade. All their raw materials had to be shipped to England (rather than rival European nations), and they could import only British-made goods. In 1684 the Bay Colony's charter was revoked and a new Dominion of New England established under direct rule from London. The first governor was Sir Edmund Andros (1637–1714). Backed by British troops, he established authoritarian rule, raising taxes and commandeering land. The seeds of unrest were sown. Used to running their own affairs, the colonists quickly came to resent interference from London. Even though Protestant rulers William III and Mary II replaced the Catholic King James II (R.1685–1688), the state of Massachusetts remained under direct rule as a Royal Colony with a new charter. Voting, however, became a privilege of every property-owning man, diminishing Puritan influence. As yet more

settlers continued to arrive in New England, internal tensions began to increase between the various social and religious groups. It was during this period that the excesses of Puritan law culminated in the witchcraft trials of Salem in 1692.

Boston was, by now, part of the infant British Empire. Britain's rivalry with France was fought worldwide, including on North American soil. In 1690 the French in Canada and their Native American allies attacked the

Plimoth Plantation, south of Boston, re-creates everyday life in a Pilgrim settlement of 1627.

British Colonies. For the next 73 years, the French and Indian Wars were fought off and on as the leading nations in Europe continued to vie for world supremacy. It was the enormous cost of these wars that eventually brought arguments to a head between Britain and her North American Colonies.

INTO THE 18TH CENTURY

By 1700, Boston was well established as the capital of the new Royal Province of Massachusetts, which included the Bay and Plymouth Colonies, plus present-day Maine. However, the city still had narrow streets, wooden houses, and no sanitation, so fire and disease were everyday hazards. Smallpox

Bostonians dress up as British soldiers for annual reenactments of colonial revolt.

epidemics restricted the population to 15,000 for the first half of the century. Despite these setbacks and constant friction with the governors, affluence grew on the back of the infamous triangular trade routes. As well as shipping dried cod to southern Europe's Catholics, New England sea captains carried rum to West Africa, exchanging it for the slaves who were transported to the West Indies to work the plantations. The fruits of their labors, sugar and molasses, were shipped back to Boston to make more rum. This system became known as triangular trade. As commerce thrived, so did Boston's shipyards.

Once again, however, London wanted a share of the prosperity and, in 1734, passed the Molasses Act, a tax on West Indian sugar products. Little revenue was raised because the seafaring New Englanders were adept at smuggling. Once more, war in Europe involved the

Colonists. Fighting for the king, they celebrated their first success in 1745, capturing a fort in French Canada. In recognition of this, London sent financial compensation, but this did little to assuage the complaints about taxation. Nor did it end the smuggling.

In 1760 frustrated customs officials demanded greater powers. By now, the city enjoyed a sophisticated system of courts and lawyers, so Boston's merchants engaged James Otis to argue against the Writs of Assistance, or search warrants. In a four-hour speech he argued that they were unconstitutional. Years later, John Adams (1735–1826), second president of the United States, recognized it as a seminal moment: "Then and there the child Independence was born."

The reasons for the Revolution are often oversimplified: The Colonists were oppressed by King George III (R.1760–1820), and the level of taxation, with no representation, was intolerably high: So they rebelled. The arguments were in reality more complex.

In only 150 years, America's Colonies had developed a degree of independence and democracy undreamed of in Europe. When Britain pushed France out of North America in 1763, it became the world's leading colonial and naval power. But London still had bills to pay. For a start, there was the 10,000-strong garrison in North America. The Colonists were expected to pay for one-third of the cost of this standing army, sent for their protection. In came more taxes, including the now notorious 1765 Stamp Act, a direct tax on some 50 items ranging from marriage licenses to playing cards. Boston politician Samuel Adams (1722–1803) called on the 13 Colonies to unite against them. Nine delegations met in New York City in October 1765 for the Stamp Act Congress, but their petition to the Crown fell on deaf ears. When the Stamp Act went into effect, bells in Boston tolled as if for a funeral. Much as the Colonists felt aggrieved, notes American historian Thomas A. Bailey, they expected "the rights and privileges of Englishmen, without the duties and responsibilities of Englishmen."

THE PROTEST GROWS

With a cry of "Liberty, Property, and No Stamps," a group of businessmen calling

Paul Revere's engraving of the Boston Massacre of 1770 helped to stir up anti-British feeling.

themselves the Sons of Liberty led a boycott of British goods. The Stamp Act was repealed in 1766, only to be replaced by the Townshend Acts. Named for British government minister Charles Townshend (1725–1767), the taxes covered vital imports such as glass, paper, and tea. At the time, a million Colonists drank tea twice a day, so the three pence a pound tax was significant. The riposte was more boycotts, and more smuggling. In one year, taxes raised only £295, while the defense of the Colonies cost £170,000. Crowds flocked to Faneuil Hall and the Old South Meeting House, where Samuel Adams and James Otis (1725–1783) now advocated independence. In 1768, George

III responded by sending 4,000 troops to patrol a city with a mere 16,000 inhabitants.

Incidents such as the Boston Massacre of March 5, 1770, fueled patriotic propaganda. Eyewitness John Tudor wrote, "This unhappy affair began by some boys & young fellows throwing snow balls at the sentry placed at the customhouse door." British soldiers came to help, panicked and opened fire, killing three men. The Paul Revere engraving (1770) of the incident exaggerated the facts and fanned local outrage. In a demonstration of democracy in action, two staunch patriots, John Adams and Josiah Quincy (1744–1775), defended the soldiers in court and won their acquittal.

A statue of Samuel Adams stands by Faneuil Hall, where he made many fiery speeches.

December 16, 1773, brought another incident: the Boston Tea Party. To save the near-bankrupt British East India Company, Parliament awarded them the trade monopoly for New England. Not only was their tea cheaper in Boston than smuggled Dutch tea, it was even cheaper, tax-paid, than tea sold in Britain. But still the Colonists objected to the tax. When three ships arrived, carrying 342 chests of tea, locals refused to unload it. Dressed up as "Indians from Narragansett," about 120 Sons of Liberty boarded the vessels and dumped 60 tons of tea overboard. The incident is cited as one reason coffee is North America's preferred hot beverage. Today, visitors can throw fake tea chests over the side of a reconstruction of a Boston Tea Party ship, moored at the Congress Street Bridge.

To punish Boston, Parliament sent in more troops, banned public meetings, and, most punitive of all, closed the port. "The Dye is cast: The people have passed the River and cutt away the Bridge," wrote Samuel Adams. With its trade links cut, Boston's economy collapsed. In response, fellow Colonies called the first Continental Congress in September 1774. As discontent simmered, militia, called Minutemen, who could be ready at a minute's notice, were drilled in villages across New England. In February 1775, London declared that Massachusetts was in a state of rebellion.

THE SHOT HEARD 'ROUND THE WORLD

On April 18, 1775, the British military governor, General Thomas Gage (1721–1787), ordered 700 troops to confiscate an illegal stockpile of arms in Concord, 20 miles (32 km) west of Boston, and to arrest two prominent agitators, politician Samuel Adams and merchant John Hancock (1737–1793). Where Adams's articles and speeches promoted independence, John Hancock's money funded the cause. News of Gage's plan reached fellow patriots Paul Revere and William Dawes, who galloped off to warn Adams, Hancock, and the Minutemen. Revere is glorified in Henry Wadsworth Longfellow's famous poem, "Paul Revere's Ride"; Dawes, another messenger that night, is ignored.

As the redcoats marched inland in the early hours of April 19, "Alarm guns were fired, and the drums beat to arms." On what is now Battle Green in Lexington, the British forces

Boston-born Benjamin Franklin signs the 1783 Treaty of Paris.

confronted militiamen and, in a sudden skirmish, ten Minutemen died, shot by the king's troops. The British pressed on to Concord. At the North Bridge, shots were again exchanged. Three British soldiers were killed. (A moving memorial service to the dead of both sides takes place at the bridge each year on Patriots' Day, April 19.) The redcoats retreated to Boston, where they were besieged by a force of 20,000 armed Colonists. Although the participants did not realize it at the time, the American Revolution had begun.

The Siege of Boston lasted nearly a year. In June, the Colonists seized Bunker Hill, and although the British recaptured the position, their losses were heavy. It was a psychological victory for the rebels. Enter 43-year-old George Washington (1732–1799). In July, he arrived in Cambridge to take command of the Continental Army. Even at this stage, the Colonists were divided. One-third were Loyalists (also called Tories), one-third were neutral, but the remainder sought independence. As the siege dragged on through the bitter winter, the Colonists' argument was enunciated by the English-born activist Thomas Paine (1737–1809). His pamphlet

"Common Sense" sold an astonishing 120,000 copies. Part propaganda, part popular journalism, Paine's work exhorted fence sitters to establish the world's first independent, democratic republic.

Thanks to cannon captured months before at Fort Ticonderoga and hauled all the way from New York state, the siege finally ended in March 1776. Set up on Dorchester Heights under cover of darkness, the guns were trained on the British, trapped on the Boston peninsula. Next morning, General Howe gave the order to evacuate by ship. Along with the redcoats went a thousand pro-British Bostonians. March 17, Evacuation Day, is still a holiday in Boston.

The Revolution dragged on for seven years. Although the city saw no further action, Bostonians continued to play major roles in the establishment of the new nation.

John Adams and Boston-born Benjamin Franklin (1706–1790) negotiated the 1783 Treaty of Paris, by which Britain formally recognized the independence of the United States. Boston's economy was rejuvenated, and trade routes opened up to the Baltic and as far as Asia. A new 1,503-foot-long (458 m) bridge

joined Boston with Charlestown. By 1800, the population of the burgeoning city had grown to reach 25,000, out of a total in Massachusetts of 500,000.

INTO THE 19TH CENTURY

In Europe, Britain and France, under Napoleon Bonaparte (1769–1821), were at war. The United States did not want to take sides, but it found that its ships were targets for both belligerents, who seized cargoes and crew at random. In 1807, President Thomas Jefferson (1743–1826) pushed through the Embargo Act, boycotting all foreign ports. This was a disaster for Boston, Salem, Nantucket, and Newport. No wonder there was little support in New England for the War of 1812 against the British. Massachusetts even discussed seceding from the Union.

As trade slumped, the resourceful New Englanders kick-started another revolution, this time industrial. The first factory where

cotton fiber was both spun and then woven into cloth under one roof opened in 1813, in Waltham, near Boston. Decisive battles at New Orleans and Waterloo in 1815 ushered in an era of peace, and industrialization spread rapidly. New England's rushing rivers powered the machines, manned mainly by young women drawn from the region's farms.

Boston witnessed dramatic changes. As well as organizing police and fire departments to serve the population of 43,000, dynamic

Italian *festas* are celebrated with typical Latin energy in the North End, where European traditions are kept alive.

mayor Josiah Quincy put in a sewage system, the nation's first (1823). Railroads were laid (1835) to Providence, Lowell, and Worcester. Boston also led the way in social reforms: the American Temperance Movement, the Abolitionist Movement, and the New England Anti-Slavery Society. As secretary of the

Massachusetts Board of Education, Horace Mann (1796–1859) laid the foundations for the country's public school system, insisting on properly trained and paid teachers, books, and decent schoolhouses. In the 1840s, the Massachusetts Supreme Court recognized the rights of labor unions.

In the middle of the century, Boston, like New York, became a gateway for wave upon wave of European immigrants. During the Potato Famine of the 1840s, some 37,000 Irish immigrated to Boston alone, joined by Italians and Jews from Germany and Eastern Europe. By 1860, half of the 136,000-strong population was foreign born. Politicians courted the immigrant vote. When Hugh O'Brien won the 1884 mayoral race, he was the city's first—but not the last—Irish mayor.

This era also saw the city's development as a national financial hub, which, then as now, centered on State and Devonshire Streets. The second bank in the nation had opened in 1784 (today's BankBoston). By the middle of the 19th century, the Boston Stock Exchange was at the heart of a business district that had 40 banks and insurance companies. Nationally known stockbrokerage Paine Webber opened in 1865, investing in mills, factories, and the telephone company of Boston-based Alexander Graham Bell (1847–1922). In 1897, Boston introduced the nation's first streetcar subway. The "T," today's efficient transport system, was born.

THE 20TH CENTURY & BEYOND

By the turn of the century, the population hit 560,000 after swallowing up neighboring Roxbury, Dorchester, West Roxbury, and Brighton. For better or worse, Boston's reputation for political chicanery also grew. For the first half of the century, the Irish-American politician James Michael Curley (1874–1958) dominated the scene. His flamboyance and corruption exacerbated the natural struggle between his power base among the workers and the old establishment in the State House.

An even more serious question of morality was the case of Sacco and Vanzetti. World War I had triggered a wave of nationalism, while the Russian Revolution produced an anti-Communist scare. In 1921, two poor Italian immigrants, shoe factory worker Nicola Sacco

(1891–1927) and fishmonger Bartolomeo Vanzetti (1888–1927), were together accused of murder. Their six-year-long trial became a landmark case in the judicial history of both Massachusetts and the United States. Found guilty, both were executed, though more for their atheist and anarchist beliefs than for their alleged crime, which was never conclusively proved.

Despite the temporary stimulation of two world wars, Boston's overall economic decline continued, hastened by the Crash of 1929 and the subsequent Depression. Shipbuilding and manufacturing industries moved to other parts of the United States where costs were lower. Fortunately, the second half of the 20th century saw a halt to the downward spiral.

The regeneration project around Fanueil Hall and Quincy Market has successfully blended historic and modern architecture.

Brand-new industries were stimulated by breakthroughs in computer research at Harvard and MIT. Once more, Boston was a major player on the world stage. In a new spirit of optimism, major redevelopment, not always successful or aesthetic, swept away Downtown slums in the 1960s. A decade later, the Quincy Market (or Faneuil Hall Marketplace) project exemplified a more sympathetic style of urban regeneration.

If there is any single venture that proves that Boston has faith in its future, it is the huge Central Artery/Tunnel Project, more commonly known as the Big Dig. Incredibly ambitious and mind-bogglingly expensive, this decade-long civil engineering plan is the largest and most complex highway project under way in the world today and the largest ever in United States history.

The idea is to bury the old elevated section of the I-93 by creating a tunnel under the Downtown area. When it is finally completed—the most recent estimated target is 2005—the North End and the Waterfront will once again be linked with the rest of Downtown by a series of new parks and walkways. This expensive facelift will ensure that the oldest major city in the country remains one of the most beautiful and will once again allow unimpeded views of Boston Harbor. ■

Arts & sciences

BOSTON HAS AN ENVIABLE CULTURAL AND INTELLECTUAL DIVERSITY. ITS architectural tapestry forms a fine backdrop for a community embracing world-class talent in fields as diverse as music and medicine. Thanks to the Boston Symphony Orchestra, the Boston Pops, and the acoustic perfection of Symphony Hall, music is a major draw. Art lovers can choose from museums large and small—the enormous Museum of Fine Arts for Impressionists, the smaller Isabella Stewart Gardner for Rembrandt, and the smaller-still Busch-Reisinger for hard-edged German Expressionists— while any city in the world would covet the collection at the Peabody Essex Museum in Salem on the North Shore. When it comes to intellectual life, what other city can match Boston's collection of colleges and universities? In the field of medicine, the hospitals and research programs are renowned. But perhaps the first aspect of the city to strike the visitor is the architecture.

ARCHITECTURE

Today, it is hard to imagine that Boston's first inhabitants settled on what was virtually an island. What they called the Shawmut Peninsula, connected by a slender "neck" to the mainland, was dominated by a ridge of three hills. Over the centuries, these were lowered (only Beacon Hill survives, albeit reduced in height), and the earth was used to fill in the coves, bays, and ponds around the peninsula to create more land for housing. More than half of the Boston we see today is built on top of landfill.

No city in the United States can match the four centuries of architecture that has graced Boston since those early days. What is more, the surrounding towns and countryside also have fine examples of domestic and public buildings. Architecture critic Ada Louise Huxtable points to the town of Marblehead on the North Shore, for example, for its "clapboard-to-clapboard sequence of Colonial, Federal, and Greek Revival houses of stern simplicity in the best New England tradition…Things have remained crowded, austere, and beautiful for several hundred years."

Colonial

The settlers' first proper houses, on the Shawmut Peninsula, were built of wood and covered with clapboard or shingle. Renovated it may be, but Paul Revere's house in the North End is the only 17th-century wooden building surviving in the city. When the national hero bought it in 1770, the dark gray frame house on North Square was already 100 years old. With its narrow Elizabethan staircase and overhanging upper story, known as a jetty, it gives an idea of how affluent Puritan merchants would have lived back in early colonial times. Less grand were the saltbox houses. Small wooden cottages one-and-a-half rooms deep, with a lean-to at the back to allow snow to slide off, they took their name from the shape of the boxes used for storing salt by the fire to keep it dry. The 1686 Jethro Coffin House on Nantucket is a classic example. Another design that is still reproduced today is the Cape Cod house, a two-story cottage with dormer windows, a large central chimney, and single-story wings.

Georgian

With wood readily available, it was some time before more-expensive brick became common. However, after a devastating fire in 1711, well-off colonists rebuilt in brick, replicating the English Georgian design. Next door to the Paul Revere House, the Pierce/Hichborn House has all the hallmarks of this style, with strictly symmetrical doors and sash windows, a low hipped roof, and decorative, lateral courses of brick between each of the three floors. Instead of churches, the Puritans built meeting houses, which were used both for religious services and town meetings. Plain and

The Boston area boasts a rich architectural heritage. In Cambridge, Harvard University has some of the city's handsomest buildings.

rectangular, they usually had galleries on three sides, with the pulpit for the fire and brimstone sermons on the fourth. Once the Puritan theocracy was broken, New Englanders copied the elegant Anglican London churches of Sir Christopher Wren (1632–1723), with their needle-sharp steeples. Imitated right across New England, these dazzling white wooden spires are the region's trademark.

Federal

In the late 18th century, after the Revolution, the new Americans still drew on British design, especially the London houses built by the Adam brothers, Robert and James. Embraced by Charles Bulfinch (1763–1844), the country's first recognized architect, this was dubbed "federal" style. Bulfinch changed the face of Boston, with urban planning projects that included streets, houses, and public buildings. His gems can be seen all over the city, but particularly on and near Beacon Hill, with the new State House (1795) and the three Harrison Gray Otis Houses. In Salem, Samuel McIntire (1757–1811) has a historic district named for him. More carpenter-builder than architect, McIntire lived and worked in the seaport all his life, designing handsome, well-proportioned homes for wealthy sea captains and merchants, including the Hawkes House on Derby Street. Down in Rhode Island, Joseph Brown set the standard in Providence. The home on Benefit Street that he designed for his merchant brother, John, was built in 1786, and described by John Quincy Adams as "the most magnificent and elegant private mansion that I have seen on this continent."

As merchants grew ever richer in the early 1800s, so architects added more flourishes for their patrons. Front doors boasted semicircular fanlights and sidelights, while set above them were solid porticos, crowned with elegant balustrades.

19th-century revivalist

The next influence to arrive in New England was Greek Revival, between 1820 and 1840. With the Greeks battling with the Ottoman

Trinity Church's ceiling epitomizes the Richardson Romanesque style popular in 19th-century Boston.

Empire for their liberty, there was an upsurge of interest in things Hellenic. The result was that everything from courthouses to private houses looked like Greek temples, with their bold line of columns marching across the front of the house.

When Boston needed to expand, the city fathers filled in the marshy bays around the crowded peninsula. Now, railroads shipped in enough gravel and earth to double Boston's land area by 1900. The newly created Back Bay and South End were planned neighborhoods for the rising middle class. Back Bay reflects French urban design, with a practical grid pattern, broken up by neat gardens and broad boulevards. In the South End, the street plans are more English, rather like Beacon Hill, with tall, comfortable brownstones with copious wrought ironwork and characteristic bow fronts that extend to the top of the house.

Architecture was still a new science in the second half of the 19th century. When MIT opened its school of architecture in 1868, it was the first in the United States. As Boston expanded, homeowners still preferred to look to the past with a variety of styles that come under the general heading of Victorian. As well as reviving memories of colonial and Tudor times, there was also neoclassic, a heady mixture of Georgian, Adam, and Greek Revival. Gothic Revival, with its turrets and battlements, pointed-arch windows and elaborate stone carving, was another fashionable import from Britain. As suburbs grew, new churches were often Gothic, as were buildings on the new college campuses. When mimicked in wood, with "gingerbread" detail, Gothic Revival is dubbed Carpenter Gothic, and still survives in seaside summer homes. The Queen Anne Revival was also popular toward the end of the century. Often built from patterns, these generously proportioned houses boasted grand wraparound porches. The elegant pillars and balustrades were precut and easy to assemble, thanks to modern construction techniques that offered everything from machine made nails to steel frames.

Public grandeur

Public buildings reflected late 19th-century affluence. The influence of architect Henry Hobson Richardson (1838–1886) can be seen

all across the country in churches, city halls, and libraries. In 1877 his Boston masterpiece—Trinity Church on Copley Square—was hailed as the greatest building in the United States. The solid Romanesque style, labeled Richardson Romanesque, drew on France and Spain for inspiration, but was uniquely American, with warm stone and red-brick facing, massive rounded arches, and a gravity that reflected the seriousness of the era.

Across Copley Square, Italian buildings were the inspiration for the architectural firm of McKim, Mead, & White, when they designed the monumental Boston Public Library (1888–1895). A Richardson protégé, Charles McKim (1849–1909) later went on to design Harvard's football stadium and a host of other university buildings in Cambridge. He designed the Symphony Hall, part of Boston's new cultural hub on Huntington Avenue, which also included the Museum of

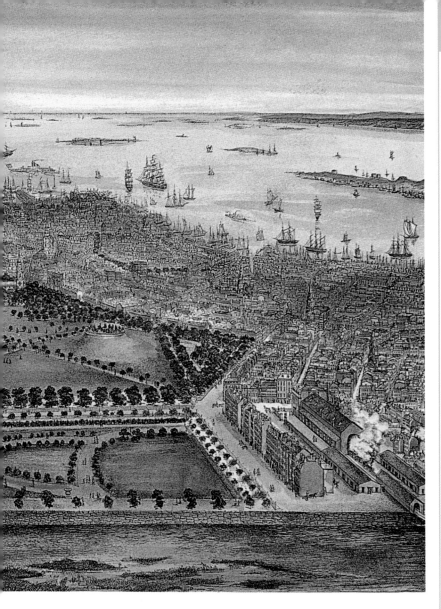

Fine Arts, the Boston Opera House (which has since been demolished), the Horticultural Hall, and the New England Conservatory of Music's Jordan Hall. Always the individualist, Boston socialite Isabella Stewart Gardner (1840–1924) brought a touch of the romantic to the city. Fenway Court, her exotic combination of home and museum, reflected the Venetian palazzo style favored by many wealthy patrons of the arts in North America in the early 1900s.

This "Bird's Eye of Boston" by J. Bachman shows the flourishing and developing city in the mid-19th century.

Down the coast in Newport, Rhode Island, even richer families were doing their best to mimic the lifestyles of the rich and famous members of Europe's aristocracy. A graduate of the École des Beaux-Arts in Paris, Richard Morris Hunt (1828–1895) was employed to turn their grandiose ideas into opulent reality.

Inspired by the old palaces of Italy and France, he built The Breakers and Marble House for the Vanderbilt brothers. Costing millions of dollars, these New World palaces were the most expensive summer cottages the world had ever seen.

Dawn of the high-rise

By the end of the 19th century, new construction techniques resulted in changing skylines in cities across the United States. Both Chicago and New York expanded upward with the first of the skyscrapers. Boston, however, was prevented from joining the architectural revolution by a local law limiting buildings to a 125-foot (38 m) maximum. Only federal projects could ride roughshod over local legislation, and in 1911, a 16-story tower was added to the Custom House. Now dwarfed by gleaming office blocks, it is hard to imagine that at the time, it was the tallest building in New England.

Architects of the modern era

When the modern movement in 20th-century architecture did arrive in Boston, it came from Germany. After the Nazis came to power in the 1930s, Walter Gropius (1883–1969) fled to Harvard, where he was installed as head of the Graduate School of Design. The director (before he fled the Nazis) of the Bauhaus, the most important architecture and design school of the 20th century, he was an early advocate of modern materials such as steel,

The ballroom at the Marble House, in Newport, Rhode Island, exemplifies Gilded Age splendor.

concrete, and glass. At Harvard, he influenced an important generation of architectural students, and his legacy can be seen across the United States today. Three Finnish architects also left their mark on Boston. On the ever expanding MIT campus, Finnish architect Alvar Aalto (1898–1976) designed the

undulating Baker House dormitory (1949); fellow Finns Eliel Saarinen (1873–1950), and his son Eero (1910–1961), planned the striking Kresge Auditorium and chapel (1955).

As it did in other cities through the second half of the 20th century, urban renewal in Boston sparked controversy. Wholesale clearance of old railroad yards in Back Bay and the red-light district downtown resulted in two of the city's least-loved buildings: the 52-floor Prudential Center tower (1959) and the concrete complex of the Government Center (1968). Later projects, such as the restoration of Quincy Market (Faneuil Hall Marketplace), were more traditional.

I. M. Pei (born 1917), one of the best-known architects in the United States today, has a special relationship with Boston. Not only was he educated at MIT and Harvard's Graduate School of Design, where he studied under Gropius, he also taught and received his first commissions in the city. Later, two Boston landmarks established his reputation: the John Hancock Tower (1975) and the John F. Kennedy Library and Museum (1977). Often attributed to Pei, the John Hancock Tower was in fact the work of a team headed by Pei's partner, Henry Cobb. As New England's tallest building—788 feet (240 m)—it is ten floors taller than the Prudential Insurance Company's rival skyscraper. Shaped like a parallelogram and covered with a shiny skin of reflective glass, the Postmodernist tower is cleverly set at an angle to Copley Square, minimizing its impact on its dowager neighbors. The John F. Kennedy Library is at Columbia Point, south of Downtown. Although it is inconvenient to get to, architecture buffs make the journey to tour the eye-catching black-and-white building overlooking the water.

PAINTING & SCULPTURE

The Boston region has been a powerful magnet for both painters and sculptors over the centuries. The earliest of these artists to make his mark was John Smibert (1688–1751), a Scot who taught local portrait artists such as John Singleton Copley (1738–1815). Although

The John Hancock Tower, completed in 1975, was one of the first skyscrapers in the world to be sheathed in reflective glass.

Copley painted the portraits of patriots Paul Revere and John Hancock, which hang in the Museum of Fine Arts, the artist fled to England after the Revolution, where he was elected to the Royal Academy. (He was also the owner of the land on Beacon Hill that was bought up and redeveloped by Harrison Gray Otis and Charles Bulfinch.)

New England artist Gilbert Stuart painted the most familiar portrait of President George Washington.

Everyone in the United States has carried a Gilbert Stuart portrait in their pocket, as Stuart (1755–1828) painted the picture of George Washington that adorns the United States one-dollar bill. The original oil painting is shared between the Museum of Fine Arts in Boston and the National Gallery of Art in Washington, D.C. His portraits of the United States' first president may have been romanticized, but the artist knew that the nation wanted to see and remember a hero, not an elderly leader with wooden teeth.

Benjamin West (1738–1820) left New England to further his career in old England,

"Lighthouse Hill" by Edward Hopper captures the essence of the New England experience.

where aristocrats were willing to pose—and pay—for their portraits. His dramatically realistic portrayal of the "Death of General Wolfe" (1771) was considered avant-garde for the time, but 20 years later, he was elected president of London's Royal Academy, succeeding Sir Joshua Reynolds (1723–1792). A century later, two famous New England artists also made their names in England: James McNeill Whistler (1834–1903) and John Singer Sargent (1856–1925). Although Sargent's decoration of the rotunda in the Museum of Fine Arts was acclaimed, his mural series in the Public Library caused controversy.

Just as Boston's writers threw off the cultural yoke of Europe, so artists such as Winslow Homer (1836–1910) found inspiration in all-American subjects. This Boston-born artist's watercolors of sea and sky, sailboats, and everyday life are still reproduced by the millions. In the 20th century, the two capes—Ann and Cod—provided inspiration for Edward Hopper (1882–1967). In the second half of the 20th century, a group known as the Boston expressionists made its name with paintings of this area. Best known are Leonard Baskin

(1922–2000), sculptor and graphic artist; Jack Levine (born 1915), social realist; and David Aronson (born 1923), founder of the School of Art at Boston University.

Sculpture

Statues abound in Boston. Most are dedicated to past heroes, some to near-forgotten names, and a few are just plain whimsical. The city's best-loved piece of public art is the straggle of bronze ducks on the north side of the Boston Public Garden. Nancy Schon's 1987 sculpture immortalizes the Boston-based children's book, "Make Way for Ducklings." Over in Copley Square, a tortoise lumbers past an overconfident hare. These charming protagonists of Aesop's famous fable are a tribute to runners in the annual Boston Marathon, whose finish line is just a few strides away on Boylston Street.

Perhaps the most familiar sculptures in the Boston area are both by Daniel Chester French (1850–1931). His much-photographed "Minute Man" stands, gun in hand, at the North Bridge in Concord, while university benefactor John Harvard sits in Harvard Yard.

Daniel Chester French's portrayal of Paul Revere is one of Boston's most popular statues.

Other popular photo opportunities include "Paul Revere," a few steps from the Old North Church near his North End home, and "George Washington," in the Boston Public Garden. Both are on horseback. "Samuel Adams" stands behind Faneuil Hall, where he made so many fiery speeches. One of the city's most significant sculptures is the memorial to Col. Robert Gould Shaw and the 54th Regiment of Massachusetts Volunteer Infantry (see p. 94). Unusual for its time, this bronze relief by Augustus Saint-Gaudens was sculpted to show the black soldiers as individuals.

More memorials to historic figures stand across Beacon Street, in front of the State House. Alongside statues of well-remembered politicians such as Daniel Webster and John F. Kennedy are some fascinating characters caught in the spotlight of history. In the 17th century, two women suffered under the Puritans for their beliefs: Anne Hutchinson (1591–1643) was exiled, and Mary Dyer (died 1660) was hanged. Modern martyr and Boston University postgraduate Dr. Martin Luther King, Jr. (1929–1968) is remembered outside the campus chapel with a flock of 50 metal doves.

A LITERATE CITY
Writers & thinkers

In 1820, the British wit Sydney Smith made the waspish comment, "Who reads an American book?" He was soon to eat his words. Of course, the early settlers were too busy cutting down trees and plowing the fields to pen great works. Although the first recorded printing press in New England stood in what is now Harvard Square, early reading material was generally limited to religious treatises, records of travels, and Thomas Paine's pamphlet, "Common Sense." Only when the city finally wrenched itself free of British influence did American writers began to flourish.

When they did, the results were dramatic. In the middle of the 19th century, Boston enjoyed a golden age of both literature and philosophy and was dubbed the "Athens of America." Local writers such as Ralph Waldo Emerson (1803–1882), Henry David Thoreau (1817–1862), Nathaniel Hawthorne (1804–1864), and especially Henry Wadsworth Longfellow (1807–1882) not only were bestsellers in the their home country but were also respected abroad. Longfellow was considered

to be the favorite poet of British Queen Victoria *(R. 1837–1901)*. Although Longfellow lived in Cambridge, the others gravitated to Concord. One hundred years after the Revolution, Concord became famous as the center of the Transcendentalist Movement (see p. 178); this cultural current was headed by Amos Bronson Alcott (1799–1888), father of Louisa May Alcott (1832–1888), the author of *Little Women.*

Boston's love affair with literature continues to this day. Russian émigré Vladimir Nabokov (1899–1977) managed to hold down several jobs here: While working as a butterfly expert at Harvard's Museum of Comparative Zoology, the author of *Lolita* was also a professor at Wellesley College and, later, he became a visiting lecturer at Harvard. The poet Sylvia Plath (1932–1963) was born and raised in the Boston area, and Pulitzer prize-winner John Updike (born 1932) studied at Harvard and then stayed on in Cambridge. Even unbookish baseball fans know of Updike, thanks to his lyrical farewell to slugger Ted Williams in 1960, beneath the newspaper headline "Hub Fans Bid Kid Adieu." But what is the best loved of all the books ever written in Boston? It could well be the 1941 children's tale *Make Way for Ducklings*, by Robert McCloskey (1914–1969).

Publishing & the media

Boston has played a powerful role in publishing since the early 19th century. In 1834, William Ticknor discovered the talents of Nathaniel Hawthorne, and, with his business partner James T. Fields, also published Emerson, Longfellow, Thoreau, and Charles Dickens from the office above the former Old Corner Bookstore. Not that Boston's editors have always managed to spot winners. When Fannie Merritt Farmer tried to interest the city's publishers in her revised version of *The Boston Cooking School Cook Book* over a century ago, Houghton Mifflin offered to bring it out at her expense. Since 1896, the recipes and advice of Fannie Farmer have been a mainstay of kitchens in the United States. By contrast,

the publishing coup of the century goes to John P. Jewett, who brought out *Uncle Tom's Cabin* by Harriet Beecher Stowe (1811–1896). This antislavery novel, which helped trigger the Civil War, sold 305,000 copies in 1852.

Bookstores As well as writers and publishers, booksellers have long been fundamental to Boston life. The Brattle Book Shop (founded in 1825) is the oldest antiquarian bookstore in the United States. It is situated downtown, a few blocks from the venerable former Old Corner Bookstore. Cambridge was, and still is, a book-lover's paradise and, with around 30 bookstores, claims to have the highest concentration in the world. Even the bookstore owners in the Boston area liked to get into print. Not so long ago, most households had a plump copy of Bartlett's *Familiar Quotations.* John Bartlett (1820–1905) brought out his first "small thin volume" in 1855, and sold it in his University Book Store. Published by Little, Brown and Company of Boston, the volume thickened over the years into a best-selling reference work. Just off Harvard Square is the Grolier Poetry Book Shop, the oldest specialist poetry store in North America. Open since 1927, it holds around 15,000 tomes of verse and hosts regular readings from young hopefuls. However, not everything here is highbrow. Nearby is Kate's Mystery Books, which is the nerve center for the thriving band of local detective story writers, which includes Linda Barnes, Jeremiah F. Healy, Jane Langton, William G. Tapply, and the most prolific and popular of them all, Robert B. Parker, creator of the craggy Boston private eye, Spenser.

The media Boston's media credentials are equally impressive. No public service broadcasting organization in the country has a better track record than WGBH. A model for National Public Radio (NPR), the WGBH radio station opened in 1951. WGBH's Channel 2 television followed in 1955, with award-winning shows that are now part of the everyday cultural life of the nation, offering the drama of *Masterpiece Theater,* the political edge of *Frontline,* the science behind the headlines of *NOVA,* and educational children's shows such as *Zoom* and *Arthur.* Practical but

Bookshops such as this one on Avenue Victor Hugo are an integral part of Boston's longstanding literary heritage.

fun programming ranges from Julia Child's cookery demonstrations to *This Old House*. The city's day-to-day appetite for reading material is satisfied by newspapers such as the *Boston Globe* and the *Boston Herald*, while the *Pilot*, established as long ago as 1829, is the nation's oldest Catholic newspaper.

PERFORMING ARTS

The Pilgrims may have banned merrymaking, but Bostonians have been making up for lost time ever since. Contemporary entertainment thrives on the energy provided by the huge student population of both Boston and Cambridge. Theater ranges from traditional to experimental and includes many pre-Broadway tryouts, while jazz vies with rock on the stages of numerous pubs and clubs.

It is for classical music, however, that the city has an international reputation. As early as 1803, pianos were manufactured in Milton, just south of the city, and since 1860, they have been sold at M. Steinart and Sons, the oldest piano store in the United States. It is still open for business at 162 Boylston Street, where the stretch between Tremont and Charles Streets was nicknamed Piano Row after the numerous piano stores and music publishers that were established here. When the New England Conservatory opened in 1867, it was one of the first in the nation, but Boston's current reputation for classical music is built squarely on the century-old Boston Symphony Orchestra (BSO), and its current music director, Seiji Ozawa (born 1935). The BSO was founded in 1881 and soon attracted the attention of European performers and conductors. During the summer season at Tanglewood in the Berkshire Hills of western Massachusetts, the orchestra is the bedrock of one of the world's most famous festivals, while, somewhat unusually, the Boston Symphony Chamber Players features principal players from the BSO itself.

With the claim to be the "most recorded orchestra in the world," the Boston Pops has been around since 1885. Fifteen years after the first Viennese-style light music concert was presented in Boston, the name Pops (for popular music) came into use, and in 1935, under the baton of the legendary Arthur Fiedler (1894–1979), the Boston Pops Orchestra

became the official title. Since then there have only been three conductors: Fiedler, the movie-score composer John Williams, and the current incumbent Keith Lockhart. The Pops, which is based on members of the BSO, stages performances in Symphony Hall from May to mid-June and again at Christmas. The Boston Pops Esplanade Orchestra, made up of local freelance musicians, is best known for its free concerts at the Hatch Shell in summer, especially on the Fourth of July. The 1976 Bicentennial performance attracted a world-record audience of 400,000.

Although the BSO hogs the headlines, the city also has five highly competitive conservatories: Berklee, Boston University, Longy, Peabody, and the New England Conservatory. Much of this strength and depth is credited to Lowell Mason (1792–1872), an important figure in the development of music appreciation. He not only opened the Boston Academy of Music (1832), but also introduced the teaching of music into the public school system (1838).

Today, there is enthusiasm for all types and styles of music. As well as a dozen ensembles that perform regular concerts of chamber music, choral singing thrives, thanks to a tradition dating back to 1815, when the country's oldest choral group, the Handel and Haydn Society, first performed. Opera is currently enjoying a renaissance in the city, thanks to one of the fastest-growing companies in the country, the Boston Lyric Opera, founded as recently as 1976. The Boston Ballet goes from strength to strength, with its annual winter performance of *The Nutcracker Suite* regularly a sellout.

IN THE GROVES OF ACADEME

Boston likes to promote itself as America's College Town. With some 65 institutions of higher learning and more than 250,000 students both living and studying in 60 square miles (160 sq km) of greater Boston, the city has no real rivals for this claim. Harvard and MIT (across the river in Cambridge) have international reputations, while other schools,

The Mapparium at the Christian Science Center spectacularly combines art and engineering.

such as Boston University, are major players on the national scene. Then there are the various graduate schools for subjects such as law, medicine, theology, and diplomacy. Some are better known abroad than they are at home: Graduates of the Fletcher School of International Law at Tufts University fill the corridors of power in Washington, D.C., and embassies around the world.

Harvard's main rival is MIT, the Massachusetts Institute of Technology. Since 1865, this institution has not only flourished as one of the world's foremost research centers, but has also shown a businesslike, practical bent by spinning off many well-known companies such as Raytheon. Mass. 128, the highway that curves around the edge of Boston, is dotted with the numerous high-tech companies set up and run by MIT graduates.

Boston College (1863) started out serving the large Irish population in the South End. With the growth in its reputation, however, this prestigious Jesuit school has relocated and is now situated in leafy, upscale Chestnut Hill.

Boston University (founded in 1869), which has 30,000 students, is the fourth largest private university in the country. It boasts a formidable array of alumni, including Dr. Martin Luther King, Jr., who received a Ph.D. from the School of Theology in 1955.

But the college system in and around Boston caters to more than just the affluent, enabling exceptional talents to be supported not by scholarships alone. Students who want to work their way through college, for example, head for Northeastern (1898), a cooperative university where academic courses alternate with work stints in the real world.

New England has long been at the forefront of women's education, with both Wellesley (chartered in 1870, opened in 1875) and Radcliffe (1879) building formidable reputations for themselves.

In 1948, Brandeis was opened to provide college-level education specifically aimed at the Jewish community.

Harvard president Abbot Lawrence Lowell (1856–1943) once suggested that "every educated man should know a little of everything and something well." On the above evidence, Boston appears to be the right place to to try to achieve that.

Medical firsts

With America's oldest medical school (Harvard, 1781) setting the trend, research breakthroughs have been, and still are, frequent in Boston. These are announced in the world's oldest medical periodical, *The New England Journal of Medicine,* which was first published in the city in 1812. Although several doctors experimented with anesthetics, William Morton (1819–1868) is given credit for demonstrating the benefits of ether in 1846. Watched by fellow physicians at Massachusetts General Hospital, Morton administered ether as Dr. John Warren successfully removed a tumor from a patient's neck. "I have felt no pain," the relieved patient is reported to have said. Fanny Longfellow, the wife of the poet, was also able to benefit from "the new-fangled anesthetic" when giving birth to a daughter.

Although he was not a medical doctor, statistician Lemuel Shattuck (1793–1859) revolutionized attitudes toward public health in the United States when his painstaking research for the Massachusetts Sanitary Commission (1850) showed that mortality rates indicated a strong correlation to variations in living conditions.

When Alexander Graham Bell's newborn son died in 1881, the inventor sketched plans for what he called a "vacuum jacket" to counteract respiratory failure. The technology was not available until 1928, when Harvard professor Philip Drinker tested the first iron lung on a polio victim at the Peter Bent Brigham Hospital in Boston.

In 1950, Professor Howard Green of MIT worked out how to grow new sheets of skin in a matter of days. This breakthrough for skin grafts was improved upon 36 years later by the invention of artificial skin, again at MIT. Other innovative techniques include the first successful kidney transplant (1954) and arm transplant (1962). In the international medical fraternity, Boston is preeminent in cardiology, with open-heart surgery first carried out at Boston's Children's Hospital in 1967.

Equally influential was the work of Dr. Gregory Pincus (1903–1967). The biologist was working at Boston University when he perfected the Pill, the oral contraceptive that went on sale in 1960. ■

Downtown Boston is a contrast in architectural styles. Gleaming skyscrapers stand on twisting lanes, with some of the oldest buildings in the United States clustered at their feet.

Downtown Boston

A colonial interpreter

Downtown Boston

BOSTON'S DOWNTOWN FEELS MORE EUROPEAN THAN NORTH AMERICAN. Streets and even avenues seem to meander in a way that confounds visitors expecting to find a logical crisscross street pattern. Business people hurrying to their appointments brush shoulders with sightseers following the Freedom Trail, a red line around the city that links 16 historic sites. At lunch time, they stand in line together for sandwiches, then vie for space on benches to eat them.

Boston began as a small settlement on an outcrop of land that was virtually an island. According to William Wood, who published the equivalent of a real estate brochure in 1634, it was safe from the "three great annoyances of Woolves, Rattle-snakes and Musketoes." A glance at the map reveals how the web of streets grew. The focus of daily life was the Old State House on State Street, which then led down to the water's edge. What is now Washington Street was the main road leading to the narrow neck of the peninsula and on to the mainland. The side and cross streets were neatly laid out, just as they would have been in the settlers' native England. Many of those original thoroughfares survive, although historians scorn the colorful theory that the curves and bends were the result of cattle being driven to and from the Common. Water was the most vital daily need, so houses were built as near as possible to the Great Spring, marked by a plaque on present-day Spring Lane. Only in 1708 were streets given official names. While Crooked Lane, Cow Lane, and Paddey's Alley are long gone, Milk and Essex, Summer and Oliver survive today. Sometimes the names of roadways altered along with the tide of politics: Great Street changed to King Street, then to the more republican-sounding State Street after the Revolution. Queen Street eventually became Court Street.

Downtown is a fascinating area, where the oldest buildings rub shoulders with the new. Stand in front of Faneuil Hall, and you can't miss 75 State Street, nicknamed the "Painted Lady" for obvious reasons. Not only is it faced with five different shades of granite, its geometric patterns glitter with gold leaf. As well as architecture, recent additions to the cityscape include sculpture memorials: to the Holocaust, to the Irish Famine, and, in 2000,

to immigrants. A few steps away from Faneuil Hall are further distinctive areas, such as the Theater District and Chinatown, guaranteeing that Boston has one of the most diverse downtown areas in the world.

Since 1991, the Central Artery/Tunnel Project has disrupted the daily life of Downtown. One of the largest and most complex highway construction projects in the world (known locally as the Big Dig), it will transform this part of the city when it is finished, theoretically in 2005. The old heart of Boston will be reunited with the waterfront and the North End, as it was before the advent of the 1954 John F. Fitzgerald Expressway. ■

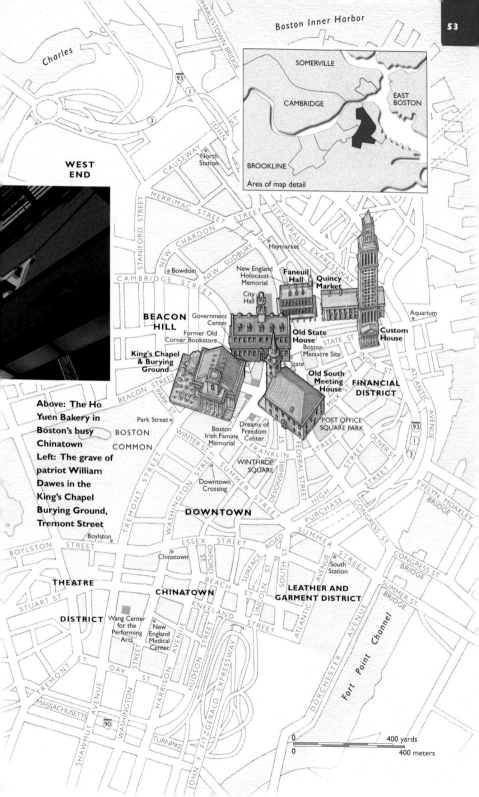

Charles

WEST END

SOMERVILLE

CAMBRIDGE

EAST BOSTON

BROOKLINE

Area of map detail

North Station

Haymarket

MERRIMAC STREET

CHARDON STREET

CAMBRIDGE STREET

Bowdoin

New England Holocaust Memorial

Faneuil Hall

Quincy Market

City Hall

Government Center

BEACON HILL

Former Old Corner Bookstore

Old State House

Boston Massacre Site

STATE ST.

Custom House

Aquarium

King's Chapel & Burying Ground

State

Old South Meeting House

FINANCIAL DISTRICT

INDIA ST.

ATLANTIC AVENUE

BEACON STREET

PARK STREET

Park Street

BOSTON COMMON

Boston Irish Famine Memorial

Dreams of Freedom Center

MILK STREET

POST OFFICE SQUARE PARK

OLIVER ST.

WINTER STREET

WINTHROP SQUARE

FRANKLIN STREET

DEVONSHIRE ST.

FEDERAL STREET

CONGRESS ST.

Downtown Crossing

SUMMER STREET

HIGH STREET

PURCHASE

DOWNTOWN

Above: The Ho Yuen Bakery in Boston's busy Chinatown
Left: The grave of patriot William Dawes in the King's Chapel Burying Ground, Tremont Street

Boylston

TREMONT STREET

Boylston

BOYLSTON STREET

ESSEX STREET

OXFORD ST.

SUMMER STREET

CONGRESS ST. BRIDGE

EVELYN MOAKLEY BRIDGE

Chinatown

BEACH STREET

SURFACE ROAD

LINCOLN STREET

SOUTH ST.

ATLANTIC AVENUE

South Station

LEATHER AND GARMENT DISTRICT

SUMMER ST. BRIDGE

THEATRE

STUART ST.

DISTRICT

CHINATOWN

Wang Center for the Performing Arts

New England Medical Center

KNEELAND STREET

HUDSON STREET

HARRISON AVENUE

DORCHESTER AVENUE

Fort Point Channel

TREMONT ST.

OAK ST.

WASHINGTON ST.

MASSACHUSETTS AVENUE

SHAWMUT AVENUE

TURNPIKE

JOHN F. FITZGERALD EXPRESSWAY

0 — 400 yards
0 — 400 meters

Old State House

IN BOSTON, TWO OF THE BUILDINGS MOST ASSOCIATED with the American Revolution are not only still standing, but also look much as they did in 1775. Cherished and preserved, both the Old State House and the Old South Meeting House still serve the public. A visit to both enables visitors to step into a world of political agitation and fiery rhetoric.

Old State House Museum

- Map p. 53
- 206 Washington St.
- 617/720-3290
- $. Rent an audio wand for more information on the exhibition.
- T: State St.

Visitor information

- 15 State St.
- 617/242-5642

Surrounded by modern skyscrapers and with MBTA trains rumbling beneath, the Old State House stands like a defiant reminder of 18th-century Boston. From 1713 until the new State House opened in 1798, this brick building was the hub of government. Behind the classic Georgian facade, James Otis argued against the Writs of Assistance in 1761 and legislators debated the Stamp Acts a few years later. On July 18, 1776, the Declaration of Independence was read out from the balcony on the State Street side. Two centuries later, Queen Elizabeth II stood on the same spot and paid tribute to the United States during the Bicentennial celebrations. You might wonder if she noticed that the lion and unicorn, symbols of the British Crown, which were torn down and burned in 1776, had been restored.

Today this, the oldest public building in the city, is an appropriate home for Boston's **History Museum.** The exhibitions on these two floors trace the political and financial issues during the colony to commonwealth period and explain what really happened during the Boston Massacre, which took place just outside. A ring of cobblestones set in the street marks the spot. Read the coroner's report on Crispus Attucks (1723–1770), the runaway black slave who was among the dead, and learn why staunch patriots John Adams and Josiah Quincy defended the British soldiers in the trial. Memorabilia include the red velvet frock coat and exquisitely embroidered waistcoat of John Hancock, who spent his money on enjoying the good life as well as funding the Revolution. There's plenty of engaging trivia as well: This is the place where you can discover why Yankee Doodle was called a "macarony."

As for the building, you have to thank the citizens of Chicago for its preservation. In 1881, when the Old State House was dilapidated and threatened with demolition, they offered to buy it and transport it to the shores of Lake Michigan, where they planned to turn it into a tourist attraction. The mere thought of this galvanized Bostonians into saving and restoring this handsome building. ■

"There is most perfect harmony in the government of this Province." —Governor Francis Bernard on his arrival in Massachusetts in 1760 ■

Left: The lion outside the Old State House Right: In front of the Old State House, traffic passes by a simple circle that marks the site of the Boston Massacre.

Old South Meeting House

As well as holding religious services, the Old South Meeting House has long served as a forum for free speech.

"THIS MEETING CAN DO NOTHING MORE TO SAVE THE country!" When Samuel Adams spoke those words to the 5,000 Bostonians crowded into this building on December 16, 1773, the Sons of Liberty went into action, heading for the harbor and three ships loaded with tea.

Old South Meeting House

🅰 Map p. 53

✉ 310 Washington St.

☎ 617/482-6439

💲 $

🚇 T: State St., Downtown Crossing

But the story of the meeting house is more than just the prelude to the Boston Tea Party. Put on the free headset, and the 20-minute "If These Walls Could Speak" audio program re-creates some of its most important moments. Puritan meeting houses were places both for worship and public debate. As the largest building in colonial Boston, Old South, as it was always known, held important assemblies, from the protest after the Boston Massacre in 1770 to abolitionist meetings before the Civil War. Built in 1729, it has the high-sided pews, central pulpit, and tall compass windows typical of the era. What you see is not original: During the Siege of Boston, the interior was virtually destroyed by British troops, who used it as a riding

school. When General Washington surveyed the damage, he expressed surprise that those who venerated their own churches should have desecrated ours. Saved from demolition in 1876, Old South became a museum, but the tradition of public speaking has continued, with the principle of free speech enshrined forever in 1929. All this is reflected in the "Voices of Protest" exhibition that opened in 2000 in the upstairs gallery, where life-size figures of influential Bostonians include Phyllis Wheatley (1753–84) and Margaret Sanger (1879–1966). Wheatley joined the congregation in 1771 and was the first African-American writer to be published in the United States; Sanger was an early 20th-century advocate of birth control. ■

Dreams of Freedom Center

ACROSS FROM THE OLD SOUTH MEETING HOUSE IS THE
Dreams of Freedom Center, which opened in August 2000. The aim
here is to focus on the long history of immigration to Boston, and
to bring it right up to date with stories about recent refugees.

**Dreams of
Freedom Center**
🄰 Map p. 53
✉ I Milk St.
☎ 617/338-6022
💲 $$
🚇 T: State St.

The **"Whispering
Wall"** tells the
story of Boston's
immigrants.

Number 1 Milk Street has long
been known as the site of Benjamin
Franklin's birthplace. A bust of the
great man peers down from a niche
above the door. Now the building is
home to the offices of the Interna-
tional Institute of Boston. This
social service organization helps
refugees and immigrants to find
jobs and housing, legal advice, and
language classes. The Dreams of
Freedom Center is on the two lower
floors of the building. First, you see
trunks and suitcases with clothes,
photographs, books, and even
bowls with chopsticks, all donated
by immigrants and their families.
Multimedia presentations feature
first person interviews with new
Boston residents, but the final exhi-
bition, in a state-of-the-art movie
theater, has the strongest message.
The 22-minute movie, complete
with multi-sensory effects such as
smells and sounds, tells the story of
various groups such as the Irish,
black slaves, and Italians. Each is

introduced by a hologram "narra-
tor": for the Irish, Patrick Kennedy,
the grandfather of John F. Kennedy,
and for black slaves author Phyllis
Wheatley (see p. 56). This is a small
museum, but it has a large message:
that the need for the United States
to offer refuge is as relevant today
as in the past. ■

Benjamin Franklin (1706–1790)

Patriot, diplomat, editor, scien-
tist and inventor: Franklin
was born in Milk Street and bap-
tized in the Old South Meeting
House. Aged 10, with only a
year's schooling, this candle-
maker's son was apprenticed to
his brother, James, a printer and
newspaper publisher. At 15, he
was already writing articles un-
der the name Silence Dogood.
Poorly treated by his brother, he
fled to Philadelphia in 1723. ■

Freedom Trail

If you have time to do only one thing in Boston, be sure to walk the Freedom Trail. This 2.5-mile (4 km) route is the world's easiest history lesson, linking 16 sites that tell the story not just of early Boston, but of the beginning of the United States itself. The trail is clearly marked on the sidewalk with red-brick and occasionally red paint. This is not a trail that you can drive along, so you need to put on a comfortable pair of shoes and head for the starting point, the visitor center at Boston Common.

The year 2001 sees the 50th anniversary of the simple but brilliant idea first proposed by *Boston Herald Traveler* journalist William Schofield. His suggestion, that the "city of Boston tie together its historic sites in one sight-seeing package," was the seed of the Freedom Trail, which came to fruition in 1958. Originally organized by volunteers, it became the Boston National Historic Park in 1974. Today, some five million visitors every year from the United States and abroad follow the red line.

Despite its title, not all the stops date from the American Revolution; nor are they in chronological order, as they would be in a theme park. You go back and forth through 200 years, from the first settler arriving on Boston Common in 1625 to the War of 1812. You also see a lot of old Boston, passing through Downtown to the North End, and across to Charlestown.

As you follow the red line, remember that there is more to see than the officially recognized sites. Reminders of other stories from Boston's past are everywhere. On Tremont Street, for example, is the Tremont Temple Baptist Church just across from the Granary Burying Ground. Organized in 1839, it was the first racially integrated church in the United States. Similarly, opposite the former Old Corner Bookstore on Spring Lane is a plaque commemorating the Great Spring that provided water to Bostonians for more than 200 years. Near Faneuil Hall is the moving New England Holocaust Memorial (see p. 66).

"How long does it take?" is a frequently asked question. That depends on how long you spend at each site. Allow about half of a day, although if you go into all the buildings (about half charge an entry fee) and explore the cemeteries, you will need a full day or more. But there are no rules: You can start and stop wherever and whenever you like.

Along the way, you may spot one of the Freedom Trail Players. Perhaps lawyer James Otis, who protested taxes, or William Dawes, who, like Paul Revere, rode to warn his fellow patriots that the British were coming. These are costumed interpreters, who are happy to talk about everyday life in colonial times. They also lead tours of the Freedom Trail during July and August, and on some holiday weekends. The guided tours led by National Park Service rangers are more frequent. The daily program runs from spring through fall, and each tour lasts about 90 minutes. Rangers also give historical talks at Faneuil Hall. As for children, there are regular events such as scavenger hunts in the Old State House, "maritime amusements" aboard U.S.S. *Cassin Young* in Charlestown, and "musical interludes" in the Old North Church that help to bring the past to life.

Visitor information centers are at Boston Common, 15 State Street (opposite the Old State House), and at the Bunker Hill Pavilion, near the U.S.S. *Constitution*. Pick up some of the free publications such as the Boston National Historical Park leaflet and "Boston's Freedom Trail," a brochure that lists the sites and also has useful information about tours, events, and public rest rooms. Visitors with disabilities should ask for the "Boston Freedom Trail Brochure," with details of wheelchair access. If you do not want to walk across the bridge to Charlestown, take the ferry from Long Wharf (next to the New England Aquarium). ∎

Freedom Trail sights

1. Boston Common
2. State House
3. Park Street Church
4. Granary Burying Ground (Tremont Temple Baptist Church)
5. King's Chapel
6. King's Chapel Burying Ground
7. Benjamin Franklin's Statue and the site of the First Public School
8. Old Corner Bookstore Building (The Great Spring)
9. Old South Meeting House
10. Old State House
11. Boston Massacre Site
12. Faneuil Hall (New England Holocaust Memorial)
13. Paul Revere House
14. Old North Church
15. Copp's Hill Burying Ground
16. U.S.S. *Constitution*, U.S.S. *Cassin Young*
17. Bunker Hill Monument

CHARLESTOWN

Bunker Hill Monument
17

N

0   300 yards
0   300 meters

WARREN STREET

MAIN STREET

WINTHROP ST.

PARK STREET

ADAMS ST.

HARVARD MALL

CITY SQUARE

CHELSEA STREET

CONSTITUTION ROAD

1ST AVENUE

U.S.S. Constitution Museum

SHIPYARD PARK

Bunker Hill Pavilion

16 U.S.S. *Constitution* "Old Ironsides"

U.S.S. Cassin Young

CHARLESTOWN BRIDGE

Boston Inner Harbor

NORTH END PLAYGROUND

COMMERCIAL STREET

HULL STREET

Copp's Hill Burying Ground
15

Old North Church
14

SALEM STREET

HANOVER ST.

NORTH END

PAUL REVERE MALL

The painted line takes visitors past Faneuil Hall.

NORTH WASHINGTON STREET

JOHN F. FITZGERALD

PRINCE STREET

PARMENTER STREET

SALEM STREET

CROSS STREET

HANOVER STREET

Paul Revere House
13

RICHMOND ST.

CLARK ST.

GARDEN COURT STREET

NORTH SQUARE

Haymarket

HANOVER ST.

MARSHALL STREET

UNION ST.

NORTH STREET

CONGRESS STREET

NORTH STREET EXPRESSWAY

New England Holocaust Memorial

Tombstones are often worth a closer look.

Medallions and bricks in the sidewalk mark the Freedom Trail.

King's Chapel Burying Ground
6

King's Chapel
5

Government Center

Benjamin Franklin's Statue
7

Old State House
10

DOCK SQUARE

Faneuil Hall
12

SCHOOL STREET

First Public School Site

Former Old Corner Bookstore
8

Tremont Temple Baptist Church

State

SPRING LANE

STATE STREET

Boston Massacre Site
11

The Great Spring

Old South Meeting House
9

WASHINGTON

MILK ST.

CONGRESS STREET

1
93
3

POST OFFICE SQUARE PARK

Church services have been held in King's Chapel for longer than anywhere else in the United States.

King's Chapel & Burying Ground

CLOSELY LINKED TO THE PILGRIMS, KING'S CHAPEL AND ITS adjoining Burying Ground date from the 17th century. The bell cast in Paul Revere's foundry in 1816 still rings out at King's Chapel. Services have been held here since 1689, although in those days it was an Anglican church, the first built in Boston.

King's Chapel & Burying Ground

🅼 Map p. 53

✉ 58 Tremont St.

☎ 617/227-2155

🕐 Closed Sun.–Fri. Nov.–May. Sun. services 11 a.m. & 5 p.m., concerts Tues. & Sun.

🚇 T: Park St.

When Sir Edmund Andros, the royal governor, arrived after the Massachusetts Colony came under Crown rule in the 1680s, he wanted to attend Church of England services. The Puritans refused to sell him any land, so he commandeered part of a cemetery and put up a wooden structure. The rich vestments, Communion silver, and altar table represented a tradition of which the Puritans disapproved.

Within 50 years the congregation outgrew the building, so in 1749 they built a new one—a shell around the original. When it was finished, they dismantled the old church and took the wood out through the windows and doors.

Today's church is the design of Peter Harrison (1716–1775) of Newport, R.I., who was inspired by St. Martin-in-the-Fields in London. When funds ran out, construction

(1809–1894). Despite changes over the years, the graceful wineglass pulpit remains. Nearly 300 years old, it is the oldest in continual use in the United States.

Many of Boston's earliest residents rest eternally at King's Chapel Burying Ground.

KING'S CHAPEL BURYING GROUND

Next door is the King's Chapel Burying Ground, the oldest in the city, dating to 1630. Here lies John Winthrop, the first governor, who believed he was founding a city upon a hill, a model Christian community. Look for headstones decorated with symbols such as wings (representing the spirit), or an hourglass (for the passage of time). On the grave of Joseph Tapping, just inside the entrance, is a grim reaperlike figure that has been snuffing out the candle of life since 1678. Mary Chilton, the only *Mayflower* passenger who left the Plymouth Colony to live in Boston, lies here, as does Elizabeth Pain. Legend has it that this minister's wife was the model for Hester Prynne in *The Scarlet Letter* by Nathaniel Hawthorne. The coat of arms on the headstone features what looks like a large "A." Find the grave of William Dawes, the second messenger sent out from Boston on April 18 to warn patriots that British soldiers were on the way. ■

Visitor information

✉ 147 Tremont St., 15 State St.

☎ 617/426-3115

of the steeple was put on hold, so the unfinished granite building looks dark and squat. Inside, however, the large windows shed plenty of light on the elegant simplicity of the gallery and double row of Corinthian columns that are typical of Harrison. George Washington sat in the canopied governor's pew in 1756 as a guest of Governor William Shirley (1694–1771). When Washington returned in 1789, he was the first President of the United States. He is said to have donated seven pounds to the portico building fund. By then, the parishioners had opted to follow the Unitarian doctrine, the first congregation in the country to do so. There is a memorial to their first minister, James Freeman, in the chancel. On the north side is another memorial, to the 19th-century writer and physician Oliver Wendell Holmes

Faneuil Hall & Quincy Market

FANEUIL HALL AND QUINCY MARKET GIVE ELOQUENT testimony to the vitality of Boston, past and present. Faneuil Hall, a crucible of free speech, has heard orators championing slavery, racial equality, and much else besides. Neighboring Quincy Market (Faneuil Hall Marketplace) is a successful 20th-century redevelopment project and a world leader in the field of urban planning.

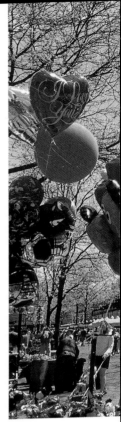

Left: A wide choice of shops, restaurants, and cafés fill the market halls.

Faneuil Hall is one of the most important sites in the Revolutionary history of Boston. Indeed, the Marquis de Lafayette (1757–1834) dubbed the site the "Cradle of Liberty." Appropriately, the statue outside the west end is of Samuel Adams, who both organized the Revolution and signed the Declaration of Independence. Today, he would not recognize this handsome building with its additions by Charles Bulfinch (see pp. 92–93). In 1805 the architect doubled the size of the hall, adding the great attic.

Souvenir shops on the first floor of the hall continue the tradition of commerce that started with the original marketplace, built and donated to the city by merchant Peter Faneuil in 1742. Before then, merchants met up in the Old State House (see p. 54), but there was no regular place for farmers to set up stalls and sell their produce. Before

accepting Faneuil's offer, the people of Boston hesitated, fearing that an official marketplace would bring with it increased regulation and taxes by the authorities. Ironically, those very topics were hotly debated here in the years leading up to the Revolution.

Today, park rangers give regular talks in the **Great Hall,** identifying the famous patriots depicted in portraits and busts. You cannot miss "Webster versus Hayne," G.P.A. Healy's enormous painting (circa 1850), which dominates the room. Statesman and orator Daniel Webster (1782–1852) is addressing the United States Senate in 1830, repudiating the theory of states' rights, arguing that it would lead to a breakup of the Union. Webster also spoke against slavery here, as did abolitionist William Lloyd Garrison (1805–1879) and ex-slave Frederick Douglass (1817–1895). But since Bostonians believed in free speech, they also flocked to hear Senator Jefferson Davis (1808–1889) defend slavery in 1858, just three years before the outbreak of the Civil War. In the 20th century, the platform has been taken by civil rights leader Dr. Martin Luther King, Jr. (1929– 1968), Archbishop Desmond Tutu (born 1931) of South Africa, and spiritual leader the Dalai Lama. Most famously, John F. Kennedy culminated his successful 1960 presidential campaign here.

Faneuil Hall

- Map p. 53
- Congress St.
- 617/242-5642
- Closed when hosting ceremonies & events. Call ahead
- T: Government Center, State St.

Above: With its outdoor stalls, pushcarts, and entertainers, the Faneuil Hall and Quincy Market area is Boston's most popular visitor destination.

QUINCY MARKET

In front of Faneuil Hall is Quincy Market, the most tourist-trodden site in Boston. Until about 1970, this was still the main wholesale market for meat and produce. Remodeled and revitalized, its stores, restaurants, and street entertainers welcome millions of visitors every year. If you can find a quiet spot, take time to admire the brainchild of Boston's second mayor, Josiah Quincy. Finished in 1826, the three buildings were part of a major development that included new streets and impressive warehouses.

To the north of Faneuil Hall, between North and Union Streets, is a muddle of small lanes. Much of Boston would have looked like this in the 18th century: low buildings, tiny alleyways, and small shops, with offices above. At 10 Marshall Street is the **Ebenezer Hancock House,** where John Hancock's brother stored the 2.5 million silver crowns donated by France to aid the colonial cause. A few steps farther on, at sidewalk level, is the **Boston Stone,** dated 1737. Used as a publicity gimmick by an innkeeper in the 18th century, it originally served as a stone for grinding paint.

On nearby Union Street is the **Union Oyster House,** the oldest continually operated restaurant in the United States. In this 1713 building, the *Massachusetts Spy,* a patriotic paper that carried Samuel Adams's rousing articles, was published. In the open space between Union Street and City Hall are two bronze figures. Both are of Irish-American Mayor Michael Curley (1874–1958), who, for the first half of the 20th century, was the city's most charismatic politician. ■

Boston's Downtown districts

BOSTON'S DOWNTOWN AREA ENCOMPASSES SEVERAL "mini-districts," each with its own distinctive character. Opting for preservation rather than urban renewal, the city authorities are helping to revitalize areas that have a mixture of historic buildings and traditional businesses, from banking to pianomaking.

State Street marks the heart of Boston's **Financial District,** and the streets radiating from the Old State House are among the city's oldest: State, Oliver, Pearl, Federal, and Devonshire. They are interrupted here and there by attractive squares, which, actually, are often triangular. Office workers settle to eat lunchtime sandwiches in Angell Memorial Park, Church Green, Post Office Square, and Winthrop Square. Liberty Square is dominated by a heroic statue, recalling the 1956 Hungarian Uprising. Drop by the lobby of the **Bell Atlantic Building** *(185 Franklin St., tel 617/743-9800)* to see the small museum housed in the original workshop of Alexander Graham Bell (1847–1922), where the Scot made his 1876 breakthrough in transmitting the human voice. Also here is the first-ever commercial telephone, made by his assistant, Thomas Watson (1854–1934).

With its eye-catching tower, the **Custom House** *(State & India Sts.)* was the focal point of Boston's Custom House District. It is hard to imagine now that the building once stood at the water's edge, near the wharves that generated the revenues. Built between 1837 and 1847, the Custom House where author Nathaniel Hawthorne worked as a weigher and gauger had a handsome dome and rotunda. In 1913 a soaring tower was added, blasting through the city's 125-foot (38 m) height limitation. As a federal building (U.S. government, not the architectural

style), it was exempt. Now late 20th-century skyscrapers dwarf the tower with its four-faced clock. Although long notorious for showing different times, the faces have been repaired and are the focus of the countdown to midnight on First Night, Boston's al fresco New Year's Eve celebrations.

At the bottom of the Financial District is the century-old **South Station.** Thanks to a massive facelift, what was the world's biggest and busiest station a century ago is once again a handsome building, its vast concourse enlivened with cafés and shops. A little farther to the west, on South and Lincoln Streets, is the bohemian **leather and garment district.** Here the factories and warehouses once used by 19th-century craftworkers have been converted into lofts for artists, with contemporary art galleries and small restaurants situated down at street level.

Although Boston's **Chinatown** is the third largest in the country, the area encompassed by Beach, Hudson, Oxford, and Tyler Streets is quite small. As well as pagoda-roofed telephone booths and Chinese street signs, you can see a 36-foot-high (11 m) traditional *pailau* (Chinese gate) and the four 3,000-pound (1,364 kg) marble foo dogs that guard Chinatown against evil spirits. In recent years, the Chinese stores, businesses, and restaurants in the area have been joined by those of Thai and Vietnamese entrepreneurs. The area

Now wedged between office blocks, the soaring Custom House tower is a reminder of Boston's maritime heritage.

is still rather rough, and at night, the atmosphere here can sometimes be intimidating.

Downtown Crossing was once little more than a T (subway) stop. Now the pedestrianized precinct along Washington Street, with offshoots along Winter and Summer Streets, is a pleasant spot to linger in, with pushcarts selling items including food and flowers. Workers from nearby offices use their lunch hours to shop in Macy's, Borders, and Barnes & Noble. Best known of all the stores in this area is the 1881 Filene's Basement (see p. 253), which is still a byword for bargains in Boston, even though it is no longer a part of the Filene's company.

The **Theatre District** is currently undergoing a much-needed revival thanks to the preservation of several of the country's historic playhouses. There is still a wealth of live entertainment to be enjoyed in the city, and Boston is one of the United States' main pre-Broadway try-out cities. As recently as a century ago, some 30 theaters, mainly situated on and around Washington and Tremont Streets, provided entertainment for approximately 50,000 patrons. Many later went on to become movie theaters, with the Tremont hosting the 1915 premiere of *Birth of a Nation* by D. W. Griffith. To soak up an atmosphere similar to the one your great-grandparents might have enjoyed, take in a show at the Colonial (1900), the Emerson Majestic (1903), the Modern (1876), the Savoy (1928), the Paramount (art deco, 1932), the Shubert (1910), the Wang Center for the Performing Arts (previously the Metropolitan, 1925), or the Wilbur (1914). ■

TELEPHONE

"Mr. Watson— Come here—I want to see you."

—The first words transmitted by telephone were spoken by Alexander Graham Bell to his assistant on March 10, 1876, at 109 Court Street. ■

More places to visit in Downtown Boston

BOSTON IRISH FAMINE MEMORIAL

At the corner of School and Washington Streets, just opposite the Old South Meeting House, is a small plaza where office workers sit, sipping coffee and munching sandwiches. In the center stand two bronze "families": One looks strong and healthy; the other is under-nourished and despairing. This is the Boston Irish Famine Memorial. Dedicated in 1998, it commemorates "An Gorta Múr," the Great Hunger of 1845–1850, when more than one million people died of starvation and disease in Ireland during the disastrous potato famine. Tablets on stone plinths spell out the role of the English absentee landlords, but they also recall both American generosity and prejudice. Although Bostonians sent 800 tons of food to Cork in 1847, signs such as "No Irish need apply" greeted the 37,000 refugees

The New England Holocaust Memorial resembles candles of remembrance.

who crossed the Atlantic aboard unseaworthy "coffin ships." The theme of "Lest We Forget" is a potent reminder that the Irish were not the only ethnic group of immigrants for whom the American Dream did not come ready-made.
Map p. 53 ✉ Corner of School & Washington Sts. 🚇 T: State St.

NEW ENGLAND HOLOCAUST MEMORIAL

As solemn and thought-provoking as the Boston Irish Famine Memorial is the New England Holocaust Memorial, a few steps from Faneuil Hall. Looking like candles of remembrance, the six glass towers symbolize the chimneys of the gas chambers and are etched with six million randomly chosen numbers. As the Holocaust Memorial takes pains to point out, Jews were not the only victims of the Third Reich. Gypsies, homosexuals, Jehovah's Witnesses, political dissidents, and mentally or physically disabled were among the nearly 11 million who died in a matter of years.

A timeline provides a "what happened when" from 1933 to 1945, but it is the quotes from survivors that chill the soul. "When the last mass grave was opened, I recognized my whole family—my mother, my sisters, and their kids. They were all in there" (Motke Zaidl, on death detail at Chelmno).
Map p. 53 ✉ Congress St. near Faneuil Hall 🚇 T: State St., Haymarket

OLD CORNER BOOKSTORE

Just across from the Boston Irish Famine Memorial is the former Old Corner Bookstore. Although the literary connection dates back to 1832, the glory years were the mid-1840s to the mid-1860s, when the shop was the office of Ticknor (1810–1864) and Fields (1817–1881). They sold and published the works of such notables as Alcott, Emerson, Hawthorne, Longfellow, and Thoreau, as well as those of British authors Charles Dickens and William Thackeray. Here, too, the *Atlantic Monthly* literary magazine was first published.

Built as an apothecary's shop in 1718, this brick building remains dedicated to books, with the Boston Globe Store specializing in books on Boston. As is typical in Boston, the story goes back even further. An earlier home on this site belonged to Anne Hutchinson, exiled from Boston in 1638 for daring to disagree with the Puritan hierarchy.
Map p. 53 ✉ 1 School St.
☎ 617/367-4000 🕐 Closed Sat.–Sun.
🚇 T: State St. ■

Boston thrives on contrast. This is most visible in the juxtaposition of the resurgent Waterfront, with its hotels, offices, and restaurants, and the narrow, atmospheric lanes of the Italian North End.

North End & the Waterfront

A sculpted relief recalls the Boston Tea Party.

North End & the Waterfront

JUTTING OUT INTO THE HEART OF BOSTON HARBOR ARE TWO OF THE CITY'S most fascinating districts—the North End and the Waterfront, where history, seamanship, and learning are suffused with the enticing aromas of the Old World. No residents of Boston are more eager to see the completion of the Central Artery/Tunnel Project than those who live and work in these areas. When finished, one of the world's biggest civil engineering projects, known as the Big Dig, will reunite the area with Downtown.

The North End has long been a neighborhood that warranted a visit in its own right, thanks to the sites along the Freedom Trail (see pp. 58–59) and the thriving Italian community. Although Mediterranean influences can be seen, smelled, heard, and tasted, the locals object to the Little Italy label that likens them to what they consider to be little more than a tourist attraction in New York. The North End is a tightly knit community, where the annual summer *festas* (saints' days) are still part of the Roman Catholic way of life. Outsiders are both attracted and welcomed by the smell of cappuccino and freshly baked cannoli and *amaretti* (pastries), and by *salumerias* (grocery stores) piled high with imports from the Mother Country. The trattorias, known for

their Italian–American pastas and pizzas, are now rivaled by more authentic restaurants run by chefs newly arrived from Italy.

In the early days of Boston, the North End was the wealthy part of town, with a small African–American community. By the time Paul Revere bought his house here in 1770, many craftsmen had moved in. They were succeeded by waves of immigrants: the Irish, Eastern European Jews, Portuguese, and, finally, Italians. Among the descendants of those immigrants was Rose Kennedy, mother of future president, John F. Kennedy. Today, some 40 percent of the 17,000 residents are Italian Americans.

The Waterfront that created Boston's past could well also be its future. Once lined with

0 _____ 400 yards
0 _____ 400 meters

Boston Inner Harbor

NORTH END
PLAYGROUND

COPP'S HILL
BURYING
GROUND

Constitution
Wharf

Battery
Wharf

Spite
House

North Bennet
Street School

Old North
Church

Lincoln
Wharf

St. Stephen's
Church

Union
Wharf

NORTH
END

Paul Revere
House

Sargent's
Wharf

North
Station

NORTH
SQUARE

Pierce/Hichborn
House

Lewis Wharf

ships, the numerous
wharves and fishing
piers are now being recy-
cled as offices and hotels,
restaurants and museums. Ferries
and water taxis buzz to and fro,
linking up the area with Logan
International Airport in East
Boston and commuter towns on the
South Shore, as well as Salem and the
new attraction of the Boston Harbor
Islands National Recreation Area. The
regeneration includes the sparkling new
Federal Courthouse, a major trade center,
and an international cruise liner terminal. ∎

Haymarket

Commercial
Wharf

CHRISTOPHER
COLUMBUS
PARK

Aquarium

Long Wharf

New England
Aquarium

Central
Wharf

India Wharf

WATERFRONT

Rowe's Wharf

**Left: Boston's
Waterfront is
a modern and
prosperous
part of the
city.**

DOWNTOWN

Federal
Court House

SEAPORT
DISTRICT

Boston Tea
Party Ship &
Museum

Children's
Museum

SOUTH
BOSTON

SOMERVILLE

EAST
BOSTON

CAMBRIDGE

Black Falcon
Cruise Terminal &
World Trade Center

BROOKLINE

Area of map detail

Convention
Center

Boston Inner Harbor

From Puritan
ministers to
members of the
black community,
the graves in
Copp's Hill
Burying Ground
reflect the city's
social and ethnic
diversity.

Copp's Hill Burying Ground

WITH HOUSES LOOMING ON THREE SIDES, IT IS DIFFICULT
to appreciate the strategic importance of Copp's Hill Burying Ground
(1660) in the events leading up to the Revolutionary War, when it
was a lookout post for 18th-century redcoats.

**Copp's Hill
Burying Ground**

🗺 Map p. 69

✉ Hull St.

🚇 T: Haymarket,
Aquarium

Look north from the highest point
of the North End and you can see
the masts of U.S.S. *Constitution*
across the water in Charlestown.
That is why British troops were
stationed among the tombstones in
1775, supposedly whiling away the
time by using headstones for target
practice. In pre-revolutionary
Boston, the North End was a
wealthy enclave. This is reflected in
elaborate headstones such as those
just to the left of the entrance.
Clearly visible is a tall, broken column. This commemorates Prince
Hall (1748–1807), a leader of
Boston's African–American community and the "first Grand Master
of the colored Grand Lodge of

Masons in Mass." He was one of the
black soldiers who fought the
British at the Battle of Bunker Hill
in June 1775. Hall believed in education, and since blacks were not
allowed to attend public schools, he
organized classes in his own home
on Beacon Hill. His school then
moved to the African Meeting
House (see p. 95). A few steps away
is the grave of Robert Newman,
sexton at the Old North Church
(see p. 71), and downhill, by a brick
table tomb, lie generations of
Mathers, including the influential
17th-18th century Puritan ministers, Increase (1639–1723), Cotton
(1663–1728), and Samuel
(1706–1785). ∎

Old North Church

Old North Church
Map p. 69

193 Salem St.

617/523-6676

"Behind the Scenes" tour & "Paul Revere Tonight" program: **$$**

T: Haymarket, Government Center

FEW SIGNALS ARE MORE FAMOUS IN MILITARY HISTORY than the lanterns that warned the colonists that "the British are coming." Placed in the steeple of the Old North Church on Salem Street by Robert Newman, the lights were immortalized by Longfellow's poem, *Paul Revere's Ride.*

On the night of April 18–19, 1775, Robert Newman took his place in history. The patriotic sexton hung lanterns in the 190-foot-high (58 m) steeple to alert the Sons of Liberty across the water in Charlestown that the redcoats were moving by sea on their way to Concord. The

Right: Lanterns on the stairs leading to the belfry of Old North Church are a reminder of the events of April 18, 1775.

Below: The old-fashioned box pews in the Old North Church promise quiet contemplation.

signal lights provided a vital backup in case his friend, Paul Revere, was captured. The Old North is Boston's oldest church, and its bells, which still ring out on Sundays, are the oldest in use in the United States. Even the 1726 clock inside is the oldest still working in a public building. The box pews were bought by families who needed to bring their own foot warmers in cold weather. In No. 25, a brass plaque marks the visit of Theodore Roosevelt on December 19, 1917. Look for a stone embedded in the wall outside by the entrance. This comes from the Guildhall in Boston, England; the bricks surrounding it were taken from a cell where the Pilgrims were once imprisoned. The ten-minute talk by docents is free. For a more authentic colonial atmosphere, attend a Sunday service or one of the monthly concerts. ■

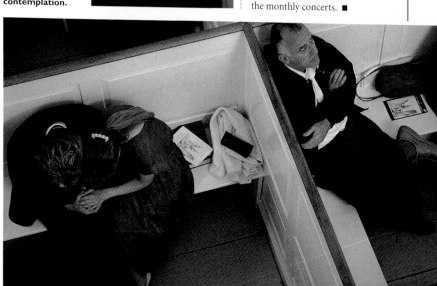

Paul Revere House

A FEW BLOCKS FROM THE NORTH CHURCH, IN NORTH Square, is the Paul Revere House, more a shrine than a museum. Built in 1680, when the town was only 50 years old, it is the oldest residence in Boston. Paul Revere would not recognize the exterior, since the structure had a third story when he lived here from 1770 to 1800. This was removed during restoration in the early 1900s.

The house where Paul Revere lived is furnished much as it would have been in the 18th century.

Enterprising and multitalented, Paul Revere (painted by John Singleton Copley) was typical of the early colonists.

Some of the interior, however, would look familiar to him, particularly the kitchen, which Revere himself added in the 1790s. Walk through to the multipurpose hall, where the simplicity of the room is typical of the 17th century. The linen cupboard on the bare floor is one of the few pieces of furniture, and the small windows (glass was expensive) let in little light, emphasizing the dark colors of the decor and furniture. Up the steep stairs, you find the master bedroom, with furniture that reputedly belonged to Revere's family. Small glass cases are used to display examples of his silverware, as well as his own account of that famous ride, which includes details of his capture and questioning by British soldiers.

Revere's first wife, Sarah Orne, died only three years after the family moved here, in May 1773, and left him with seven children. In October 1773 he married Rachel

Paul Revere (1734–1818)

The most famous messenger in American history was born in the North End to a French Huguenot family, who changed their name from Rivoire to Revere. A fine silversmith and political activist, Revere knew the value of publicity, and his engraving of the Boston Massacre was deliberately inflammatory. After the Revolution, this multitalented man was a founder member of the Massachusetts

Mutual Fire Insurance Company (1798) and ran the new Boston Board of Health. His foundry cast church bells and cannons while his copper mill made the cladding for the new State House and U.S.S. *Constitution*. Although not a surgeon dentist, he sold toothpaste, cleaned real teeth, and wired in false ones. Contrary to popular myth, he did not make a set of dentures for George Washington. ■

Walker, with whom he had another eight children between 1774 and 1787. Eleven of these 15 children grew up in this house and survived to adulthood.

Next door to the Paul Revere House is the **Pierce/Hichborn House** (pronounced hitch-born), the second oldest residence in Boston. It is run under the auspices of the Paul Revere House, but may be seen only on a guided tour. Since these may be irregular, it is important that you phone ahead to check the times. The name of the house refers to two of its previous owners. Moses Pierce, a glazier, built the house in 1711; note the numerous windows, which were a good advertisement for his skills. Nathaniel Hichborn, a boat builder, was Paul Revere's cousin. Few middle-class homes from this era survive, so this particular building is fascinating for fans of historic architecture and furnishings. The 30–40 minute tour includes four period rooms: a bed-chamber, a parlor, the hall, and the kitchen stocked with 18th-century pots and pans. ■

Paul Revere House

www.paulreverehouse.org

🅐 Map p. 69

✉ 19 North Sq.

☎ 617/523-2338

🕐 Closed Mon.
Jan.–March

💲 $. Combined ticket
includes tour of
Pierce/Hichborn
House

🚇 T: Haymarket,
Aquarium

In the lively North End, celebrations often spill out into the streets.

A walk through the North End

Although the North End is best known as Boston's Italian section, it has also been home to African Americans, Irish, Jews, Portuguese, and other immigrants. As one of the oldest parts of the city, it also boasts several sites on the Freedom Trail. You will see them on this walk, where you will also get a flavor of the various ethnic groups that once lived on this harborside hill.

Start at Faneuil Hall, cross North Street and Union Street, then follow Marshall Street, a lane whose cobblestones and old buildings are reminders of early Boston. Turn right on Hanover Street and follow Freedom Trail signs through the construction for the Big Dig to Salem Street. Suddenly, you could be in Italy. Shops have Italian names, locals chat in doorways (older people may be speaking Italian), and the sound of Verdi arias spills out from windows. Continue to **Baldwin Place,** a little alley on the left. At No. 4, on the third floor, you can just make out the Star of David and Hebrew letters. This school and a nearby synagogue were the focus of the Jewish community here a century ago. Return to Salem Street where, farther along on the right, is the **North Bennet Street School,** founded in 1885 by the well-off Bostonian Pauline

Shaw. Here she taught immigrants English and skills such as cooking. Still a school, it offers classes in bookbinding and cabinetmaking.

Walk on toward the **Old North Church** ❶ (see p. 71), whose steeple is a landmark on this side of Boston. Next door is a gift shop in the former **Chapel of St. Francis,** built with the help of Episcopalians from the Old North Church for Italian-speaking Waldensians (the first protestants to leave the Roman Catholic Church) in 1918. Turn left on Hull Street and walk up to **Copp's Hill Burying Ground** ❷ (see p. 70). Opposite, at No. 44, is the "narrowest house in Boston," sometimes known as the **Spite House.** It is supposedly named for a quarrel between two brothers: one built it to block the other's view. Farther on is a parking lot that stands on the site of the Great Brinks Robbery of 1950; at

A WALK THROUGH THE NORTH END

The spire of the **Old North Church** has been a local landmark for over a century.

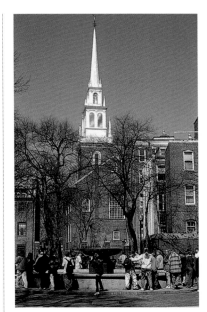

the time, the 1.2 million dollars stolen from the security company was the biggest theft of cash in United States history. The eight robbers were arrested and convicted in 1956.

Return to the Old North Church and follow the Freedom Trail along Paul Revere Mall. Known as the Prado, this Mediterranean-style promenade is home to the frequently photographed statue of Paul Revere on horseback, cast in the 1870s. Ahead is the Roman Catholic **St. Stephen's Church ❸** *(401 Hanover St., tel 617/523–1230),* where Rose Kennedy was baptized and her funeral was held in January 1995. This 1804 building, the only surviving church designed by Charles Bulfinch (see pp. 92–93), replaced the New North Meeting House of 1714.

Turn right on Hanover Street, where Eben Jordan and Benjamin L. Marsh opened the store that grew eventually into the empire of Jordan Marsh, absorbed by Macy's in 1996. Turn left on Fleet Street, then right on Garden Court Street, where No. 4 is the birthplace of Rose Fitzgerald, later Kennedy. Her father was Boston's legendary mayor, John F. Fitzgerald, nicknamed Honey Fitz.

Next comes North Square and North Street, where No. 19 is the **Paul Revere House ❹** (see p. 72–73). Next door is the **Pierce/Hichborn House** (see p. 73). From here, you can see the dome of Faneuil Hall. Try to imagine the scene in a few years' time, when the Big Dig has succeeded in putting the elevated highway underground. At Richmond Street turn right, then left on Hanover Street, and return to Faneuil Hall. ■

Ⓜ Map p. 69
► Faneuil Hall
↔ 1.4 miles (2.3 km)
🕒 1.5 hours
► Faneuil Hall

NOT TO BE MISSED
- Old North Church
- Copp's Hill Burying Ground
- Paul Revere House

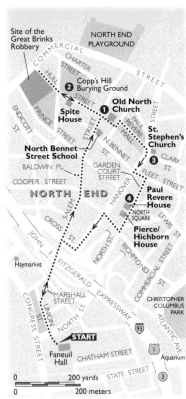

Boston Harbor

SHAWMUT, THE ORIGINAL NATIVE AMERICAN NAME FOR the Boston peninsula, means "land of living waters." Part of the city's appeal is that you are never far from the water. Significant in the city's founding and early history, the harbor has once more emerged as a vital element in Boston's vision of its own future.

The dramatic colors of Boston's night sky are mirrored in the calm waters of the inner harbor.

In the early days, no point in the city was farther than three blocks from the waterfront. Over the years, constant land reclamation has left several famous locations far from their waterside origins. Griffin Wharf, site of the Boston Tea Party, now lies buried under Congress Street at Atlantic Avenue. The Old State House was once just a block away from the water, looking straight down at Long Wharf, which once stretched a third of a mile (500 m) beyond the shore. It is considerably shorter today, one of a dozen truncated wharves, poking, like blunt fingers, out into the water. The warehouses are now long gone but names such as India Wharf, Rowe's Wharf, Commercial Wharf, and Union Wharf remain to recall the glory days of far-flung trade and wealthy merchants.

By 1970, Boston's port, once the most important in the United States, had virtually been abandoned. The docks were run down, the U.S. Navy had left, fishermen were out of work, and the water was heavily polluted. A combination of tough environmental laws and inspired redevelopment has revitalized the waterfront, bringing back much of the old bustle with museums, restaurants, condominiums, and offices. The **New England Aquarium** (see p. 78) attracts visitors to Central Wharf, while Rowe's Wharf anchors the modern grandeur of the Boston Harbor Hotel with its giant archway. Another hotel, the Marriott, bestrides Long Wharf, now reduced to a mere stub. Next to it is situated the attractive **Christopher Columbus Park,** created in 1976 to give the public more access to the water. Neighboring Long Wharf is a good spot to watch the U.S.S. *Constitution* as she takes a two-hour-long tour of the harbor every July 4. Towed by a tug, and decked with flags, she halts off Castle Island and, at noon, her cannon fire a 21-gun salute to the nation.

As Boston enters the 21st century, renewed appreciation for the city's waterfront heritage is the theme of new development. A new **Seaport District** has been invented. Alongside the Black Falcon cruise terminal is one of the city's newest landmarks, the glamorous **Federal Courthouse,** right on the water. A vast new convention center and a world trade center fulfill booming business needs. Water taxis and shuttles now ferry residents and visitors around Downtown, across to East Boston and Logan International Airport, and even to the North and South Shores. As for the pollution, you can find out just how effective the cleanup has been by taking a New England Aquarium tour, which includes experiments on specimens of harbor water.

BOSTON HARBOR ISLANDS NATIONAL RECREATION AREA

In 1996, Boston's 30 harbor islands became part of the National Park system. They may be small, but they make an unusual and fun day out,

Visitor information

- 🗺 Map p. 69
- ✉ 15 State St.
- ☎ Boston Harbor Cruises: 617/227-4321. Aquarium "Science at Sea" Harbor Tours: 617/973-5206
- 💲 Harbor Cruises: $$
- 🚇 T: Aquarium, State Street
- ⛴ Long Wharf

and are yet another place where Bostonians and visitors can escape from the hustle of the city. You may spot some of the seals that frolic within sight and sound of a major international airport!

A seasonal ferry serves 30-acre (12 ha) **George's Island.** Here, the roll of confederate prisoners who were held behind the thick walls and iron gates of Fort Warren included Alexander H. Stephens (1812–1883), the vice president of the Confederacy, who was imprisoned here in 1865. On the park rangers' tours you'll hear tales of the sightings of the ghostly "Lady in Black." In 1827, when 16-year-old military recruit Edgar Allan Poe was stationed on **Castle Island,** he heard the grisly tale of a duelist who had been walled up alive by

fellow soldiers. This inspired his chilling short story, "The Cask of Amontillado." In 1905, the duelist's skeleton was found by workmen. More cheerful is **Little Brewster,** with its Boston Light, the only remaining manned lighthouse in the United States. Choose Gallops Island for panoramic views of Boston; Grape Island for wildlife; and Lovell's Island for its swimming beach. Peddock's Island, the largest, has walking trails around a pond and wetlands.

George's Island, which is the first and main stop, has a simple café. The other islands are accessible from here by free water shuttles in high season. All are dry, so you must take your own supply of water. Some overnight primitive camping is permitted. ∎

Boston Harbor Islands National Recreation Area

www.BostonIslands.com

☎ 617/223-8666

💲 $$ (round-trip)

🕐 Ferries do not run mid-Oct.–April

🚇 T: Aquarium

🚢 Long Wharf (for ferry information, see pp. 238–39)

New England Aquarium

www.neaq.org

 Map p. 69

✉ Central Wharf

☎ 617/973-5200

💲 $$$. Reduced price
Wed., Thurs., &
4–7:30 p.m. in
summer

🚇 T: Aquarium, State
Street

New England Aquarium

IN RECENT YEARS, AQUARIUMS HAVE BECOME TRENDY: IF a city does not have one already, it is probably planning one. Built in 1969, Boston's was the first modern aquarium in the United States, showing animals in a naturalistic setting. It celebrated its 30th birthday with a program of expansion that continues today.

The showpiece of the aquarium is the four-story-high cylindrical **Giant Ocean Tank,** encircled by a spiral ramp. The temptation is to go straight there, to watch the host of aquatic creatures such as sea turtles, sharks, and sting rays swim freely in the 909,000 gallons (4,131,405 liters) of saltwater. A better approach is to explore the outer exhibit galleries, floor by floor, walking up the angled ramp. From the top, you can then descend, spiraling down around the Giant Ocean Tank itself.

The low lighting throughout the aquarium gives you the feeling of being underwater, making it easier to see species such as the flashlight fish that provides its own lighting in the depths of the ocean. Stop first at the information desk to pick up the "Daily Specials" menu of talks and presentations. Then go to the **Special Exhibits Gallery,** where the exhibitions are long

term, changing every year or two. In 2000, for example, "Nyanja! Africa's Inland Sea" opened, focusing on the earth's second largest inland body of water, Lake Victoria in eastern Africa, where 200 of the original fish species are now extinct. The displays highlight the international studies of the problem, as well as showcase the beauty of the lake itself.

Stay on the main floor to see the ever-popular penguins. Identify the African penguins by the black stripe curving across their white chests; spot the rockhoppers with a yellow tuft of hair on top of the head. The little blues from Australia and New Zealand are the world's smallest. Also called fairy penguins, they weigh only a few pounds and stand about one foot (30 cm) high. Nearby is the **Medical Center,** which cares not just for inhabitants of the aquarium, but also for animals rescued locally. You may see a penguin having a physical checkup or a fish with a deformed jaw being fitted with braces. By touching the computer screen you can call up the medical records of the patient.

A ramp leads from the Medical Center up one floor to the **Thinking Gallery,** where it is tempting to do no more than admire the brilliantly colored tropical fish. But the idea here is to think about the reasons for behavior and development. The exhibition covering habitats as diverse as New England salt marshes and tropical mangrove swamps provokes questions about man-made pollution to these important ecosystems. Education is always blended with a large dose of fun. Children ooh and aah as they pass the **Shark Wall,** where the shapes of sharks, ranging from the small, smooth dogfish to the great white, glow in ultraviolet light. On the next level, smaller but equally scary creatures, including

Above: The New England Aquarium takes pride in its environmental awareness programs for youngsters.

Right: A close-up view of an aquarium resident

piranhas and poison arrow frogs live in the **Fresh Water Gallery.** The electric eels may initially look dull and harmless, but they light up bright red when killing their prey.

The fourth level brings you to the reef at the **Top of the Giant Ocean Tank,** where intricate fiberglass brain, staghorn, and elkhorn coral provide a backdrop to the evil-looking puffer fish and

fast-paced needlefish. Make sure you are by the tank at one of the five feeding times each day, to watch scuba divers swimming among the fish. Then walk back down around the tank.

Outside the building are the California sea otters and harbor seals. Once again, see them at feeding time, when keepers explain how sea otters are related to skunks and badgers. Around the corner is the *Discovery,* a floating barge where sea lion shows take place about every 90 minutes. Although keepers tell you how they got their name (because they roar like a lion) and explain how these aquatic creatures can be trained, don't expect silly tricks and circus routines. The museum also runs excellent harbor tours and whale-watching trips. ■

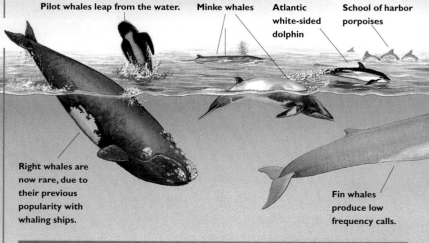

Pilot whales leap from the water.

Minke whales

Atlantic white-sided dolphin

School of harbor porpoises

Right whales are now rare, due to their previous popularity with whaling ships.

Fin whales produce low frequency calls.

The waters off Boston offer some of the best whale-watching in the world.

Thar she blows!

For many visitors, a whale-watching cruise is one of the highlights of their New England trip. These gentle giants are often found feeding at Stellwagen Bank, a marine sanctuary 25 miles (40 km) east of Boston and 6 miles (10 km) off Provincetown. The chances of seeing at least one whale are high, and knowledgeable crew members give running commentaries, pointing out the different types.

Minke whales, at 23 to 28 feet (7–8 m) in length, are relatively small, while fin whales can measure 70 feet (21 m) in length. Both are regularly seen, as are humpbacks, the ones that like to breach (leap clear out of the water). Right whales are rare. Guides explain that naturalists are able to identify individual whales by their tails, because the tail of a whale—like the fingerprint of a human—is unique.

These cruises also give an insight into the lives of whalers, whose voyages could last five years at a time. The oil they extracted from whales was used to light parlors, illuminate

Orcas (left & bottom) are sociable whales, often found in schools.

Humpback whales can be identified by characteristic behavior; they breach, show their dorsal fin and "hump" as they swim, and display their tail flukes.

THIS DIAGRAM SHOWS WHALES THAT CAN BE SEEN IN THE BOSTON AREA AND LISTS THEIR PHYSICAL AND BEHAVIORAL CHARACTERISTICS.

Just as blue whales are the biggest cetaceans of all, they are found at the lowest depths.

Sperm whales swim in deeper waters.

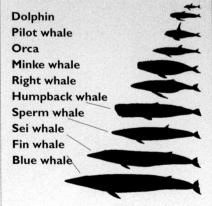

WHALE SIZES COMPARED

Dolphin
Pilot whale
Orca
Minke whale
Right whale
Humpback whale
Sperm whale
Sei whale
Fin whale
Blue whale

city streets, and run industrial machines in Europe and the United States. To while away the time, sailors carved the surface of the jaw-bones and teeth of whales. This carving, known as scrimshaw, rose to a high art form, with intricate patterns colored with ink. Museums in this region exhibit examples of scrimshaw and other whaling memorabilia, including tools such as harpoons, pikes, and throat spades, lamps used to burn whale oil, and paintings of whaling ships.

To see whales today, you can sail from Boston or nearby towns such as Gloucester, Provincetown, or Barnstable. Wear rubber-soled shoes and pack sunblock, dark glasses, and seasickness pills. Remember that even on a hot summer's day, temperatures drop sharply once you are out on the water, so bring warm clothing. For details on whale-watching trips, see page 262. ■

Children's Museum

WHILE BOSTON, WITH ITS COLORFUL HISTORY, LIVELY sports life, and tempting ice cream, is always a popular destination for young visitors, the city can pride itself in having one of the first—and most thought-provoking—museums aimed at young children.

Interactive exhibits at the Children's Museum help children learn through play.

Children's Museum
www.bostonkids.org
- 🅰 Map p. 69
- ✉ 300 Congress St.
- ☎ 617/426-8855
- 🕐 Open late Fri. until 9 p.m.
- 💲 $$$, discount admission ($) Fri. 5–9 p.m.
- 🚇 T: South Station

You can't miss the Children's Museum: Just look for the giant milk bottle outside a former warehouse at the east end of the Congress Street Bridge. Once inside, pick up a map, start at the bottom, and work your way up through the four floors. Or you might choose to plan a visit around a theme, such as the "Natural World" or "How Things Move." Free shows are presented regularly on Kidstage, where a recent favorite starred Arthur, the aardvark from the popular program on PBS television. Staff is on hand throughout the museum, to help children (and parents) get the best out of individual exhibits. Children used to the high-tech wizardry of theme parks

may consider some of the exhibits here old-fashioned, but they soon discover that there are plenty of fun things to do. They can start by working off excess energy in a specially designed two-story combination jungle gym and maze. When tiredness looms, try a low-key activity such as weaving.

SECOND FLOOR

Children have fun in the **Science Playground** without realizing that they are learning principles laid down by Sir Isaac Newton (1642–1727) at the turn of the 18th century and Galileo Galilei (1564–1642), 100 years earlier. Watch a golfball circle around a large bowl, before dropping through the hole in the center: This display, called "Motion in a Dish," is all about momentum, friction, and gravity. Experiments change regularly here, but the bubble-blowing station is always ready for parents and children to compete in blowing the biggest.

One of the most popular areas is **Boats Afloat,** at the other end of the floor. Plastic aprons help to keep clothes from becoming totally soaked while vessels of every size and shape navigate the Fort Point Channel. Named for the waterway right outside the windows, this 28-foot-long (8.5 m) tank has 800 gallons (3,636 liters) of water sloshing under four bridges. Crank the handle and change the direction of the current, then put out a pretend fire with a pump.

Next door, **Playspace** is for children four years or younger. They can clamber over a jungle gym, play in a sand box or with a train set, or invent their own make-believe world with the dolls and stuffed animals.

THIRD FLOOR

Spread over levels 3 and 4 is **Grandparents' House,** offering an excuse for the older generation to tell stories about the good old days…of 1959. Back then, when television programs were mainly in black and white, and rock 'n' roll ruled the radio, technical toys were cranked up or battery-operated. Try convincing the children of today that everyone had lots of fun without video and computer games.

Construction Zone caters to all ages. Put on a hard hat and an orange safety vest, then practice walking along a steel girder and using the hand signals that steel workers use for load up, stop, and swing load. Use wooden blocks for building skyscrapers and see information displays about Boston's own

construction project, the Big Dig. There are many safety lessons here, from the best shoes to wear on a bridge construction site to the need for hard hats. A sign reads: "Caution: This is fun and may be habit forming."

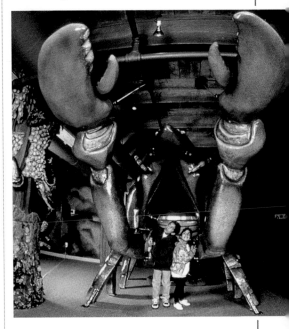

Older children will enjoy the **Japanese House.** After reading about how a traditional Japanese home is built, they take off their shoes and enter a real one, brought from Kyoto, Boston's sister city.

FOURTH FLOOR

At the opposite end of the floor above is **Teen Tokyo,** highlighting the differences between the everyday lives of Japanese teenagers and their American counterparts. Twelve youngsters from Tokyo are featured, with their pictures and biographies. The strict school rules come as a shock, particularly the dress codes. Boys can have only brown or black watchbands; girls may not wear jewelry or makeup. ∎

A favorite exhibit at the Children's Museum is "Under the Dock," which shows what's going on in Boston Harbor's waters.

Boston Tea Party Ship

Aboard the Boston Tea Party Ship, visitors can still protest the high tax on tea.

"DUMP THE TEA INTO THE SEA. DUMP THE TEA INTO THE sea!" The cry resounds from a group of visitors standing on the decks of the *Beaver II*, a reconstruction of one of the three brigs that was boarded during the Boston Tea Party. One after another, they throw chests labeled "TEA" overboard, then haul them back up by rope, ready for the next protester. This popular attraction appeals to anyone who finds the Freedom Trail rather serious.

Visitors tour the Boston Tea Party Ship and Museum in groups. You start out sitting on a plain bench, where you are invited to play the role of a Boston citizen at a town meeting on December 16, 1773. The costumed guide talks about the taxes levied by parliament in London, from the Stamp Act through the Townshend Acts, dubbed the Intolerable Acts. Much is made of the boycott of tea and other British goods; no mention is made of the profitable smuggling by Bostonians and their fellow Colonials. Audience participation is encouraged, and shouts of "hear, hear" and "aye, aye" greet the anti-British slogans. Feathers are handed out, recalling the 120 men and boys dressed as Mohawks who climbed onto the ships that night. Then everyone boards *Beaver II* and takes a turn throwing the tea into the harbor. Back in 1773, some 60 tons were destroyed in this way, enough for 23 million cups of the colonists' favorite beverage.

Once the fun is over, you can explore the ship on your own. Built in Denmark, it actually sailed across the Atlantic to Boston in 1973. The museum, much improved in recent years, gives a good background to the whole debate about tax and tea. You learn about the five different types of tea available in the 18th century, and see one of the surprisingly ornate tea chests from that era. A political time line starts with the end of the French and Indian Wars in 1763 and ends with independence. Significant dates such as that of the Stamp Act and its repeal are shown, with explanations of the role of the East India Company, which enjoyed a monopoly on sales of tea to the Colonies. ■

Boston Tea Party Ship & Museum

- Map p. 69
- Congress St. Bridge
- 617/338-1773
- Closed Dec.–March
- $$
- T: South Station

With its 18th- and 19th-century architecture, Beacon Hill is one of the most photogenic neighborhoods in the United States. The world-class Museum of Science attracts nearly two million visitors a year.

Beacon Hill & the Museum of Science

The gold dome of the Massachusetts State House

Elegant Beacon Hill is, and always has been, a desirable place to live.

Beacon Hill & the Museum of Science

BEACON HILL IS ONE OF THE BEST-KNOWN AREAS OF THE CITY. THE HANDsome State House, with its golden dome, is the center of Massachusetts politics. Flanking it gracefully on Beacon Hill are streets with brick sidewalks and gas lamps, lined with elegant houses in Georgian, federal, Greek Revival, and Victorian styles. At the bottom of the hill near the river is Charles Street, known for antique stores, boutiques, and restaurants.

The story of Beacon Hill is the story of Boston. One of the three original hills of Tramount or Trimountaine, Beacon Hill was home to William Blaxton, Boston's first settler, in 1625. For decades, the slopes were no more than meadows; John Hancock's mansion, on the site of the present State House, was one of the few houses. Boston-born painter John Singleton Copley (1738–1815) owned much of the land before he fled to England. After the Revolution it was sold off cheaply, and Beacon Hill was developed by the first significant architect and urban planner in the United States, Charles Bulfinch (see pp. 92–93).

His new State House moved the focus of the city away from the harbor, while his designs for well-off families (moved here from the North End) on Beacon Hill's south slope began the expansion of the original settlement. In the early part of the 19th century, practical legislation, often based on the amount of space required for cows to pass one another, resulted in narrow streets and alleyways. To walk these charming lanes today is to enter the world of author Henry James (1843–1916). On Chestnut Street and in Louisburg Square, the Boston Brahmins, the members of Boston's aristocracy, lived alongside writers and artists.

By contrast, the north slope of Beacon Hill has only recently been recognized for the wealth of its history. The first significant African–American community in the country was well established by the 19th century, with its own church and school. Beyond Beacon Hill is the mouth of the Charles River, once little more than a marsh. The building of a dam in 1910 transformed an eyesore into the present lagoon, one of the city's finest amenities. The dam was put to practical use as the foundation of the Museum of Science, the most popular museum in Boston today. ■

28

LAND BOULEVARD

Museum of Science

Science Park

CHARLES RIVER DAM

LEVERETT CIRCLE

93

1

JOHN F. FITZGERALD EXPRESSWAY

3

CHARLES STREET

WEST END

CHARLES RIVER BASIN

CHARLESBANK PARK

BLOSSOM ST.

WILLIAM CARDINAL O'CONNELL WAY

CAUSEWAY

North Station

MERRIMAC ST.

Massachusetts General Hospital

3

28

STANIFORD ST.

NEW CHARDON ST.

NEW SUDBURY

LONGFELLOW BRIDGE

3

GARDEN ST.

BLOSSOM ST.

CAMBRIDGE STREET

1st Harrison Gray Otis House

Bowdoin

BOWDOIN ST.

Charles/ MGH

PHILLIPS ST.

SMITH COURT

JOY ST.

Abiel Smith School

Beacon Hill Memorial Column

SOMERSET ST.

Government Center

COURT ST.

REVERE STREET

African Meeting House

MYRTLE ST.

W. CEDAR ST.

CHARLES ST.

BEACON HILL

PICKNEY ST.

Nichols House Museum

Granary Burying Ground

SCHOOL ST.

VERNON ST.

Massachusetts State House

Boston Athenaeum

EMBANKMENT ROAD

MOUNT

Bull & Finch

BEACON STREET

Park Street Church

BOSTON COMMON

2

28

Frog Pond

PARK STREET

WINTER ST.

BEACON STREET

MARLBOROUGH ST.

ARLINGTON ST.

CHARLES STREET

PUBLIC GARDEN

DOWNTOWN

BACK BAY

Boylston

TREMONT STREET

Paul Revere's headstone in the Granary Burying Ground

BOYLSTON STREET

2

0   400 yards
0   400 meters

SOMERVILLE

CAMBRIDGE

EAST BOSTON

BROOKLINE

Area of map detail

Massachusetts State House

**Massachusetts
State House**

www.state.ma\us\sec\trs

🅰 Map p. 87

✉ Entrance on Beacon St.

☎ 617/727-3676

🕐 Closed Sun., tours Mon.–Sat 10 a.m.–3:30 p.m.

🚇 T: Park St.

THE MASSACHUSETTS STATE HOUSE IS A MASTERPIECE OF architectural bravura. Until the advent of the skyscraper, its gold dome was visible from almost anywhere in the city. Even today, you can see it from as far away as Back Bay and the Cambridge side of the Charles River. This is the true center of Boston, the point from which mapmakers measure distances.

Left: The grand marble interior of the Massachusetts State House

Right: A wooden codfish hanging in the House of Representatives highlights the importance of the state's fishing industry.

When Charles Bulfinch designed the State House more than 200 years ago, the United States was a new country; over time, his noble dome set the standard for capitol buildings across the nation (see pp. 92–93). The 23-carat gold leaf, which dates to 1861, replaced the copper sheathing that was put on by Paul Revere's foundry in 1802. There are free tours available year-round, or you can walk around by yourself. Pick up a free information sheet in the lobby.

Imagine the celebrations on July 4, 1795, when the cornerstone was dragged up the hill by 15 white horses, representing the 15 states in the Union. It was laid by Governor Samuel Adams and Paul Revere. Inside the entrance is a model of the original Bulfinch structure, which was only 65 feet (20 m) wide; the wings and offices at the back are later additions. Both the pinecone on top of the cupola and the ten original columns in **Doric Hall**—each made from a single pine tree trunk—represent the lumber trade, the second most important industry in colonial New England at the time of construction. Through the **Nurses' Hall,** with its murals of historic events, and the Hall of Flags, is the staircase to the upper level. The best known of all the commemorative statues and emblems is the **Sacred Cod,** the carved wooden fish that hangs over the public gallery in the House of Representatives. According to legend, it was presented in 1784 to remind the legislature not to over-tax fishermen. Another State House tradition concerns the main doors. These remain locked, opened only for a President of the United States, or for a Massachusetts governor at the end of his or her term, when he or she takes the "Long Walk" out of the capitol and down the steps back into private life. ■

Park Street Church & the Granary Burying Ground

JUST DOWN THE HILL FROM THE MASSACHUSETTS STATE House, on the corner of Park and Tremont Streets, stands Park Street Church, with the Granary Burying Ground next to it. In 1809, William Lloyd Garrison gave his first speech denouncing slavery here, one of several firsts claimed by this white-steepled brick building.

"Since the cause of emancipation must progress heavily, and must meet with much unhallowed opposition—why delay the work?"
—William Lloyd Garrison, Park Street Church, 1829 ■

The congregation set up the first Sunday School in the United States (1817), dispatched missionaries to the Sandwich Islands (now Hawaii, 1819), and founded a prison aid society (1824). The first public rendition of "America" ("My Country 'Tis of Thee") took place on the front steps in 1831. The words were new, although the tune was already in use for the British national anthem, "God Save the King."

GRANARY BURYING GROUND

Next door, hemmed in by offices and the Boston Athenaeum, is the resting place of some of Boston's most famous names. To the right of the entrance, a large boulder marks the grave of Samuel Adams, "A Leader of Men and an Ardent Patriot." Next to it is a simple tablet commemorating the five men who died in the Boston Massacre (see p. 27). On the other side of the entrance is the grave of James Otis (1725–1783), whose legal challenge to the Writs of Assistance in 1761 was a major step toward the Revolution. The tallest monument is on the Franklin family plot, with an inscription by Benjamin Franklin (1706–1790), although he is interred in Philadelphia. Over by the church wall stands an elegant obelisk dedicated to John Hancock. With his wealthy background, love of parties, and elaborate dress, he seemed the archetypal Tory. Yet he funded the patriot cause and was right at the top of the British government's most-wanted list. At the back is the businessman Peter Faneuil (see p. 62) and Paul Revere (see pp. 72–73). ■

Above: Memorial to James Otis
Right: Park Street Church was a focal point for abolitionists.

Park Street Church
- 🅰 Map p. 87
- ✉ 1 Park St.
- ☎ 617/523-3383
- 🕐 Closed Mon. May–Sept.
- Ⓣ T: Park St.

Granary Burying Ground
- 🅰 Map p. 87
- ✉ Tremont St./Bromfield St.
- Ⓣ T: Park St.

Charles Bulfinch, architect & urban planner

If imitation really is the most sincere form of flattery, then Charles Bulfinch (1763–1844) would be a very happy man, were he alive today. Few architects have left such a visible legacy of their work in one nation. Across the United States are capitol buildings and courthouses sporting gleaming domes, columned portals, and broad flights of stone steps. Although the self-taught architect did not design them himself, he set the pattern with his grandiose hilltop landmark in Boston, the new State House (1795), which was the third state house to be built in the young republic.

Born in Boston, this affluent Harvard graduate spent a year in Europe on the Grand Tour. Whereas his mentor, Thomas Jefferson, had looked to continental Europe for inspiration, deliberately spurning anything British, Bulfinch preferred the buildings of the London-based Adam brothers. Back in New England, his adaptations of their designs founded a style that was subsequently labeled as federal.

Bulfinch came from a well-off family, so early on in his career, he designed houses for fun, drawing up plans for his friends in Boston. However, he was a poor businessman and went bankrupt in 1796; from then on, architecture was a job, not a hobby. Luckily, his creativity and energy knew no bounds. Over three decades, he transformed what was a seaport town into an elegant city. During much of this period, he was chairman of the Boston board of selectmen (1799–1817), with wide-ranging powers and influence. He laid out whole streets and parkways, built houses and schools, banks and insurance offices. Major projects included the remodeling and

expansion of Faneuil Hall (see p. 62) and construction of handsome new wharves. He designed University Hall at Harvard and, in 1817, the Pavilion and Ether Dome of Massachusetts General Hospital. From 1818 to 1829, Bulfinch lived in Washington, ordered by President James Monroe to complete the nation's Capitol building. He later built a new state house for Maine, in Augusta.

Sadly, only 20 percent of his work can be seen in Boston today; the rest has been destroyed or redeveloped over the years. Apart from the State House and the Ether Dome, there are the three houses he built for friend and business partner Harrison Gray Otis. The first, at 141 Cambridge Street, is open to the public (see p. 104). The second, considered by many to be his finest design, is a private home

at 85 Mount Vernon Street. The third, again private, is the mansion at 45 Beacon Street. Only one of his 12 churches survives: St. Stephen's in the North End, originally known as the New North Church. Today, he would be considered a town planner as well as an architect for the overall improvements he made to the city of Boston. As Josiah Quincy, the first mayor, wrote, "Few men deserve to be held by the citizens of Boston in more grateful remembrance than Charles Bulfinch." ■

Left: Portrait of Charles Bulfinch
Below left: Bulfinch's design for the
Massachusetts State House set the pattern
for capitol buildings across the country.
Below: Bulfinch lived in Washington, D.C.,
for eleven years while supervising work on
the U.S. Capitol.
Right: The Ether Dome at Massachusetts
General Hospital was designed by Bulfinch
to let students observe surgical operations
using new anesthetic techniques.

Boston African–American National Historic Site
www.nps.gov/boaf

 Map p. 87
✉ 46 Joy St.
☎ 617/742-5415
🕐 Closed Sun., tours: Mem. Day–Labor Day
🚇 T: Park St.

Boston African–American National Historic Site

BOSTON HAS A LONG-ESTABLISHED AFRICAN–AMERICAN population, which has contributed greatly to the city's—and the country's—growth and prosperity. Linking many of the historical African–American sights is the Black Heritage Trail, which focuses on the many achievements of this group. Established in 1908, the Boston African–American National Historic Site is not a single museum, but a series of sites linked by a common theme.

Political and anti-slavery meetings accompanied religious activities at the African Meeting House.

This is not a park with an entrance and exit, but a designated area on Beacon Hill that commemorates the first free African–American community in the United States. It flourished in the 19th century on the north side of Beacon Hill, where blacks owned homes, ran businesses, built churches, and set up schools. They also worked to further the abolitionist cause and sheltered escaped slaves. The 1.6-mile (2.6 km) **Black Heritage Trail** zigzags up and down Beacon Hill between some 14 sites, nearly all private homes. The best way to appreciate the story is to join one of the free tours led by park rangers in the summer. During the rest of the

year, ask at the Museum of Afro American History (see p. 95) or at the Freedom Trail visitor centers (see p. 58) for information and a self-guided map of the trail.

Directly opposite the State House is the **Robert Gould Shaw and the 54th Regiment Memorial,** designed by sculptor Augustus Saint-Gaudens (1848–1907). In 1989 the Oscar-winning movie *Glory* told the story of this Massachusetts regiment, with the first black troops to sign up to fight for the Union. More than 60 fell in the attack on Fort Wagner, part of the campaign to take Charleston, South Carolina. One of the dead was their white commander, Colonel Shaw, buried with his men on the battlefield, at the request of his family. Among the survivors was Sgt. William Carney of New Bedford, the first African American to win the Congressional Medal of Honor.

Massachusetts was the first colony to legalize slavery in the 1600s. It was also the first state to end it in 1780. One of the test cases leading to abolition was brought by Elizabeth Freeman, who sued a cruel mistress to gain her freedom and won. Thereafter, the black population in Boston was increased by escaped slaves, along with freemen and women. In the early 19th century, abolitionist sentiment was heightened by speeches such as that by Angelina Grimke (1805–1879) in the State House (see p. 89). In 1838 she told senators, "I feel that I owe it to the suffering slave, and to the deluded master, to my country and my world to do all that I can to overturn a system of complicated crimes."

Before the Civil War, the black community on Beacon Hill numbered some 2,000. After the passing of the Fugitive Slave Act of 1850,

the 13th stop on the trail, is a symbol of the long struggle by black parents to educate their children. Denied access to state schools, they set up their own until, in 1855, a Massachusetts law outlawed segregation in the public system. Nearby, at No. 8 Smith Court, is the **African Meeting House,** the oldest black church still standing in the United States, and the last stop on the trail. Dedicated in 1806, it

Museum of Afro American History
www.afroammuseum.org

◪ Map p. 87
✉ 46 Joy St.
☎ 617/725-0022
🕐 Closed Sun. Sept.–May
🚇 T: Park St.

they set up a Vigilance Committee to hide runaway slaves. The **Lewis Hayden House** (sixth stop on the trail) at 66 Phillips Street was a station on the Underground Railroad. Hayden was born a slave but escaped. In 1853, Harriet Beecher Stowe, author of *Uncle Tom's Cabin,* came here to meet a group of fugitive slaves. Some years later, abolitionist John Brown (1800–1859) arrived to recruit volunteers for the unsuccessful raid on Harper's Ferry in 1859.

The **Museum of Afro American History** covers two buildings, both open to the public. Founded in 1834, the **Abiel Smith School,** at 46 Joy Street,

was funded by contributions from all over New England and built by free black craftsmen. Church services, as well as public meetings and political debates, were held in this plain but elegant building, with 300 people crowding into the pews and upper gallery. On January 6, 1832, William Lloyd Garrison established the New England Anti-Slavery Society and predicted that "Faneuil Hall shall ere long echo with the principles we have set forth. We shall shake the nation by their mighty power."

Both the Abiel Smith School and African Meeting House are focal points for Boston's Black History Month, celebrated in February. ∎

On Beacon Street, the Massachusetts 54th Regiment memorial honors the first black regiment to be recruited in the North.

Beacon Hill walk

Ever since 1799, when the development of the south side of Beacon Hill began, this residential area has been synonymous with wealth and status. On the north slope, the Charles River side of the hill, Boston's black community lived in the 19th century (see pp. 94–95). On this scenic walk, you get a flavor of both sides of the hill.

The streets of Beacon Hill invite visitors to stroll back into Boston's past.

Start in front of the **Massachusetts State House ①** (see p. 89) and walk around the east wing, on Bowdoin Street. In the small park stands a reconstruction of the 60-foot-high (18 m) **Beacon Hill Memorial Column ②**. The original, built by Charles Bulfinch (see pp. 92–93) in 1789, was one of the earliest monuments to the Revolution. It also marks the site of the beacon for which the hill is named. The hill was dug away to fill in nearby wetlands, but the top of the monument

> 🅰 Map p. 87
> ▶ State House
> ↔ 1.4 miles (2.2 km)
> ⏱ 1 hour
> ▶ Beacon Street
>
> **NOT TO BE MISSED**
> - State House
> - Louisburg Square
> - Nichols House Museum

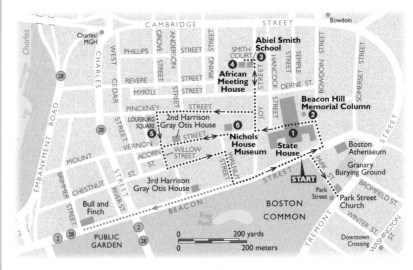

Louisburg Square displays the greenery that distinguishes Boston from many American cities.

gives an idea of the height of the original hill-top. Walk under the rear addition of the State House. Turn right on Joy Street.

Between Pinckney and Cambridge Streets was the heart of the black community. At 46 Joy Street is the **Abiel Smith School** ❸ (see p. 95); behind it, in Smith Court, is the **African Meeting House** ❹ (No. 8, see p. 95), also known as the Black Faneuil Hall. At the end of Smith Court is a small alleyway, one of many paths that were day-to-day shortcuts for locals, and also helped runaway slaves escape from slave catchers.

Return to Joy Street and walk uphill. Turn right on Pinckney Street and walk to the corner of Anderson Street, where you can see the Charles River and the Bulfinch-designed Ether Dome of Massachusetts General Hospital.

Continue to **Louisburg Square** ❺, (pronounced Lewis-burg). One of the most prestigious and expensive addresses in Boston, it was modeled on squares in London. The central park is reserved for residents, who are also entitled to two precious car spaces. Author Louisa May Alcott (1832–1888) lived at No. 10; singer Jenny Lind (1820–1887), "the Swedish Nightingale," was married at No. 20. Walk through the square to **Mt. Vernon Street,** which looks like a film set with its

uneven brick sidewalks, Victorian lampposts, and elegant houses. In the 18th century Mt. Vernon was the red light district of Boston; it was labeled "Mount Whoredom" on a map drawn by a British officer in 1775. Turn left, noting No. 85, the second of three houses designed for Harrison Gray Otis (1837–1917) by Bulfinch, who also built Nos. 51–57. The public can enter No. 55, the **Nichols House Museum** ❻ (see p. 104).

Retrace your steps, turning left on Willow Street—where poet Sylvia Plath (1932–1963) lived at No. 9—to Acorn Street, the narrowest on the hill, but wide enough for two cows to pass, as required by regulations in 1825. Continue to Chestnut Street and turn left. Look at the glass in No. 29A, whose purple color proves its historic pedigree: In 1818, a consignment of German glass was tainted with manganese oxide, which turned purple when exposed to light. Turn right on Walnut Street, where Julia Ward Howe (1819–1910) and later John Singer Sargent (1856–1925) lived at No. 13. At the bottom is Beacon Street. From here, walk uphill to Park Street and turn right for the T (subway) station, or downhill, past the third Harrison Gray Otis house (1808). At the bottom is the **Bull & Finch** pub, inspiration for television's *Cheers.* ∎

Charles River

Although the Charles River is officially 26 miles (42 km) long, from the town of Hopkinton to the dam at its mouth, boatmen stretch it to 80 miles (129 km) by measuring its meanders and bends. The only urban river in the country dedicated to recreational use, the Charles is like an aquatic park, offering a breath of fresh air to residents and visitors.

Before it was dammed in 1910, the Charles was little more than a smelly trickle, which is why the handsome houses on the Back Bay bank were built facing away from the unattractive mud flats. The dam, which also provides the foundations of the Museum of Science (see pp. 100–103), converted the river into a peaceful lagoon. Half a dozen bridges cross the river. The 1907 Longfellow Bridge, named for the Cambridge-based writer, can be identified by its pepper-pot-shaped towers. The poet regularly crossed the West Boston Bridge, an earlier bridge on this site, and even penned a poem, *The Bridge*, in its honor. Farther upstream is Harvard Bridge, where escapologist Harry Houdini (1874–1926) performed a manacled jump followed by an underwater escape in 1908. As this bridge terminates right by the Massachusetts Institute of Technology, some attempts have been made to rename it for MIT. Although this has never happened, a group of ingenious MIT students certainly left their mark in 1958. Using the unprotesting body of fellow student Oliver R. Smoot, they measured the span in what they called Smoots and declared it to be exactly 364.4 Smoots and one ear long. When the

bridge was rebuilt in the late 1980s, the Smoots were carefully repainted on the sidewalk on the downstream side. The local police even use the markings to record the location of accidents. You have fine views of the river, and of Harvard, from the traffic-free Weeks Memorial Bridge, linking Cambridge to the B-School, Harvard's world-renowned Graduate School of Business Administration.

The first link in Boston's Emerald Necklace (see pp. 122–23), the Charles River Reservation, encompasses the grassy banks and bicycle paths that flank the water. Out on the water, sailors battle with the tricky winds that gust between the buildings, while oarsmen and women benefit from the current-free course in the basin, which is only about 8 feet (2.4 m) deep. Mid-October sees the annual Head of the Charles Regatta, which organizers claim is the world's biggest rowing event. Equally animated is the Fourth of July, when

In the heart of the city, the Charles River provides year-round recreation for thousands of Bostonians.

some 400 pleasure craft join thousands of people picnicking on the river's banks for the Boston Pops concert at the Hatch Memorial Shell on the Esplanade.

To get the best out of the river, explore it riotously on a Boston Duck Tour (see p. 262), aboard a World War II amphibious craft, which begins its tour of the city on land and then plunges into the river. The Charles River Cruise boats (see p. 263) offer a somewhat more sedate alternative with hour-long tours that benefit from well-informed on-board commentaries, which are rightly considered to be educational rather than commercial. In 1999 the *Boston Globe* considered the skyline view from the deck to be the best available in the city. ∎

Museum of Science

WANT TO WATCH LIGHTNING BEING MADE? SEE PROOF that the earth turns? Eyeball a Tyrannosaurus rex? Learn how your heart works? More than 1.9 million visitors every year do all that and more in the enormous Museum of Science, the first in the world to include all the sciences under one roof.

**Museum of
Science**

www.mos.org

⬛ Map p. 87

✉ 1 Science Park

☎ 617/723-2500

🕐 Late opening on Fri.

💲 $$$

🚇 Science Park

As well as maintaining more than 600 hands-on, permanent exhibits, the museum has special temporary exhibitions plus interpreters who give regular demonstrations. You'll see parents answering young children's questions and older children patiently explaining to their parents how things work, particularly in the stimulating and sometimes challenging exhibitions from the Computer Museum, which joined forces with the Museum of Science in 1999. Add in the Charles Hayden Planetarium and the Mugar Omni Theater with its IMAX movies, and you can spend hours—perhaps even an entire day—here.

With so much to do and see, it is easy to be overwhelmed. Before you leave the lobby, pick up a list of "Today's Presentations" and a map of the three levels, color coded by area. Ask about combination tickets that include the planetarium or an IMAX movie as well as the museum. Some 4,000 school groups visit every year and if you are visiting on a weekday during the school year, be prepared for noise. They usually leave by around 2:30 p.m. Thereafter, the museum is suddenly quieter and you can pull levers, press buttons, and ask those simple questions to which any ten-year-old knows the answer.

BLUE WING

Whatever you do, don't miss one of the "Lightning!" presentations in the **Thomson Theater of Electricity.** The star of the stage is the air-insulated Van de Graaff generator. The world's largest, it stands

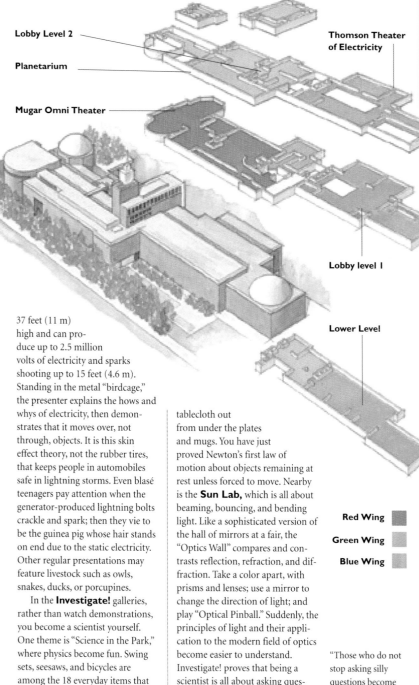

Lobby Level 2

Planetarium

Mugar Omni Theater

Thomson Theater of Electricity

Lobby level 1

Lower Level

Red Wing
Green Wing
Blue Wing

37 feet (11 m) high and can produce up to 2.5 million volts of electricity and sparks shooting up to 15 feet (4.6 m). Standing in the metal "birdcage," the presenter explains the hows and whys of electricity, then demonstrates that it moves over, not through, objects. It is this skin effect theory, not the rubber tires, that keeps people in automobiles safe in lightning storms. Even blasé teenagers pay attention when the generator-produced lightning bolts crackle and spark; then they vie to be the guinea pig whose hair stands on end due to the static electricity. Other regular presentations may feature livestock such as owls, snakes, ducks, or porcupines.

In the **Investigate!** galleries, rather than watch demonstrations, you become a scientist yourself. One theme is "Science in the Park," where physics become fun. Swing sets, seesaws, and bicycles are among the 18 everyday items that are presented as experiments in inertia, velocity, and acceleration. Try the clown's trick of pulling the tablecloth out from under the plates and mugs. You have just proved Newton's first law of motion about objects remaining at rest unless forced to move. Nearby is the **Sun Lab,** which is all about beaming, bouncing, and bending light. Like a sophisticated version of the hall of mirrors at a fair, the "Optics Wall" compares and contrasts reflection, refraction, and diffraction. Take a color apart, with prisms and lenses; use a mirror to change the direction of light; and play "Optical Pinball." Suddenly, the principles of light and their application to the modern field of optics become easier to understand. Investigate! proves that being a scientist is all about asking questions, conducting experiments, and drawing conclusions.

At the Museum of Science, new

"Those who do not stop asking silly questions become scientists."
—Leon Lederman, physicist ∎

technology has two roles: to enhance exhibitions and to be the subject of exhibitions. **Virtual FishTank** combines the two. A favorite at the Computer Museum in its days down on the waterfront, this fishtank is a virtual underwater world, ready and waiting for your experiments. Start by designing your own fish, then add it to the 50 computer-graphic species already in the huge tank. Having decided how your creation reacts to other cyberfish, what food it eats, and how deep it dives, you can watch what happens once it is in among the sharks and angelfish in the 3-D sea. Through computer simulations

such as these, scientists can conduct experiments and analyze results without making sudden, harmful changes to the real environment, which could prove to be damaging.

An instant success after its introduction in 2000, **Cahners ComputerPlace** swarms with families, encouraged by knowledgeable volunteers and staff. Start by checking what or who is appearing at "Info Bytes," a demonstration area and forum for guest speakers. If you are accompanied by children who usually balk at educational programs, you might see a change of heart in the **Best Software for Kids** gallery. As well as

Right: Lightning is generated by the Van de Graaff generator in the Thomson Theater of Electricity.

improving reading and writing skills, they can set up their own TV studio, and even create their own show. The Internet is there, along with **Creativity,** with an array of digital cameras, graphics software, and video editing facilities. Youngsters can even design their own web page.

The **Messages** exhibit is all about communication. Using computers, you can mix and match silent movie clips with different types of music. This "what happens next?" game reveals how music can signal a change of action or mood. This is the sort of exhibition that children often rush past, pushing buttons and pressing keys without waiting for the result. It takes longer to understand the points being made.

GREEN WING

One of the most popular areas is the **Human Body Discovery Connection.** You can test your eyesight, pulse, strength of grip, breath control, and senses. Ever looked closely at your tongue? Stick it out and look in the mirror: is yours round, square, or pointed? Not only do tongues differ in size, they have differing numbers of taste buds, so things taste different for different people. Test yours by trying the sample papers. Tongues and taste are individual, governed by the DNA that makes each person unique. There are 75 interactive exhibits here, designed to illustrate different aspects of the body. There are knowledgeable interpreters on hand, who explain, encourage, and even carry out a daily dissection of a sheep's lung.

You need even more time to get the best out of the nearby **Seeing the Unseen.** Here, microscopes are set up for you to see the life in a drop of water: rotifers. They are the smallest of multicelled animals, and

at the bottom of the food chain. Look at the model, then watch them in action.

RED WING

The **Mugar Omni Theater,** renovated in 1999, shows IMAX movies. Tilt your seat back so you get the full effect of the five-story-high domed screen that seems to put you into the larger-than-life picture. Stargazers should make reservations for the "Sky Tonight" program at the **Charles Hayden Planetarium.** Settle back in the ergonomically designed seats and watch a depiction of the heavens of New England on the screen above

you. Other shows follow themes such as "Comets are Coming!" or "Messenger from Mars," and there are laser images set to music.

As well as the main galleries, there are small exhibits placed throughout the museum. Walk down the **Sound Staircase** next to the Omni Theater and you create music; run, and the rhythm speeds up. The **Discovery Center** is reserved for children of five and under, with puzzles and guinea pigs, a Water Activity Area, and much more. ∎

A fantastic sensory experience awaits at the IMAX cinema in the Mugar Omni Theater.

More places to visit in Beacon Hill

BOSTON ATHENAEUM

A major renovation program to restore the elegance of this 1849 building is planned to finish in 2001. As of spring 2002, the first floor of the building will be open to the public, and it will also be possible to take guided tours.

When the Athenaeum was founded in 1807, libraries were really private clubs for the well-off and educated. Today it remains a private institution, although it is no longer reserved for the elite. Most of its original art collection was considered important enough to be transferred to the Museum of Fine Arts (see pp. 116–121), but its rooms are still filled with a variety of sculptures, busts, and portraits by, among others, John Singer Sargent (1856–1925). The **Reading Room** is one of Boston's most elegant spaces, with its high vaulted ceiling. As you look at it, you can almost imagine founding member Ralph

The dining room in the first of three homes designed by Charles Bulfinch for Harrison Gray Otis

Waldo Emerson (1803–1882) sitting there reading a book from the private library of George Washington, which is now another of the treasures housed in the Athenaeum.
🅜 Map p. 87 ✉ 10 Beacon St. ☎ 617/227-0220 🕐 Call for hours 💲 Call to check 🚇 T: Park St.

FIRST HARRISON GRAY OTIS HOUSE

Lawyer, property developer, United States congressman, and third mayor of Boston, Harrison Gray Otis was a pillar of the new Boston establishment. The first of three homes designed for him by Charles Bulfinch (see pp. 92–93), this is the only one that is open to the public. The house was notably large and luxurious for its time (1795), and its hallway alone could swallow up an entire contemporary working-class home. As you progress through the dining room, parlor, and upstairs to the private rooms, you learn about 18th-century social customs and the role of servants, and how Otis helped to develop Beacon Hill into the most beautiful area of the city. This building is also the headquarters of SPNEA (Society for the Preservation of New England Antiquities), dedicated to the conservation of important buildings and landscapes from the 17th century to the present, throughout New England.
🅜 Map p. 87 ✉ 141 Cambridge St. ☎ 617/227-3956 🕐 Closed Mon., Tues. 💲 $ 🚇 T: Park St., Charles/MGH

NICHOLS HOUSE MUSEUM

Step through the door of this early 1800s house and you enter the privileged world of the late Rose Nichols. Tour guides tell the story of her wealthy Boston family, who moved into the house in 1885. On display are the family's Chinese temple urns and Japanese prints, all souvenirs of the China Trade, as well as a number of portraits of ancestors and Rose's own embroideries. She was a noted landscape architect, pacifist, and inveterate traveler. She was also the niece of the sculptor Augustus Saint-Gaudens (1848–1907), whose Robert Gould Shaw and the 54th Regiment Memorial (see p. 94) is nearby on Beacon Street. She died in 1960, and the museum is her legacy. It is well worth a visit: Nowhere else do you get such an intimate insight into the life of the Boston aristocracy.
🅜 Map p. 87 ✉ 55 Mount Vernon St. ☎ 617/227-6993 🕐 Closed Sun.–Mon., Sun.–Wed. Nov.–April & all Jan. 💲 $$ 🚇 T: Park St., Charles/MGH ∎

The open spaces of Boston Common and the Public Garden provide the city's lungs, while Back Bay is busy with stores, galleries, restaurants, and houses. Towering above them is the John Hancock Tower, New England's tallest building.

Boston Common & Back Bay

**A popular resident of
Boston's Public Garden**

Boston Common & Back Bay

BOSTON COMMON IS THE ONLY PART OF THE CITY THAT THE ORIGINAL settlers would recognize. In their time, Back Bay was water. Today, Back Bay refers to the finest 19th-century development in the United States. On the south side is Copley Square, with its triumvirate of eye-catching buildings: the soaring John Hancock Tower, the ponderous Trinity Church, and the massive Boston Public Library.

Boston Common has been public land for nearly 300 years. Nowadays, it provides a place for picnics and a space for Frisbee throwers. Statues and plaques have been added, along with water fountains and paving stones. There are memorials to the city's founders and to those who fell in the Boston Massacre, including Crispus Attucks (1723–1770), the first African American to die in the colonists' fight for freedom. Purists argue, with much justification, that Boston Common should remain unspoiled, even unkempt, in contrast to the busy urban life that hems it in from all sides.

With its neat lawns, geometric flower beds, and small lake, Boston's Public Garden is the antithesis of the Common. It was origi-nally a marsh, like the rest of Back Bay, and records show that British soldiers ice-skated here while confined to Boston during the winter siege of 1775. When the great landfill operations began in the 1830s, 25 acres (10 ha) were set aside for a botanical garden. From here, the new development of Back Bay stretched westward, laid out in a tidy grid pattern that contrasts with the maze of lanes in the old part of Boston. The planners looked to France for inspiration, and made Commonwealth Avenue (usually abbreviated

Above: Newbury Street in Back Bay, famous for shops Below: Frescoes in the interior of Trinity Church

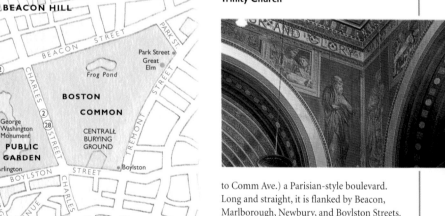

to Comm Ave.) a Parisian-style boulevard. Long and straight, it is flanked by Beacon, Marlborough, Newbury, and Boylston Streets. Commonweath Avenue's cross streets progress in alphabetical order, from Arlington and Berkeley through to Hereford.

Copley Square was the final piece in the jigsaw puzzle of man-made land that is Back Bay. There are concerts in the summer and street entertainers year-round, but the plaza remains a bleak open space. Three of Boston's best-known buildings are on the square: Trinity Church, the Public Library, and the John Hancock Tower. It also boasts one of the city's most delightful sculptures: a tortoise striding ahead of a resting hare. ■

The swan boats in Boston's Public Garden have been popular with children since 1877.

Boston Common & the Public Garden

BOSTON COMMON AND THE PUBLIC GARDEN TOTAL NEARLY 70 acres (28 ha) of open space at the heart of the city. Locals jog and walk their dogs, children play, and office workers eat lunch. To the north the State House stands on Beacon Hill; to the west is the blue glass of the John Hancock Tower. It is impossible to get lost, and it is fun to wander, looking at the statues and monuments.

Boston Common

Map pp. 106–107

T: Arlington, Boylston St., Park St.

Not only are the Common and the Public Garden separated by Charles Street, they look and feel quite different. The wide-open Boston Common, crisscrossed by paths and broken up by clusters of trees, still resembles the rolling pasture it was back in the 1630s. Designated as common land for "the feeding of Cattell," it also provided a "trayning field" for the colony's militia. From 1768 to 1776, it served as a camp for British soldiers. Nearly a century later, the men of Massachusetts gathered here before heading off to fight in the Civil War. Over the years, the 44 acres (17.8 ha) have attracted crowds for major events.

Four Quakers were hanged at the **Great Elm** between 1659 and 1661. One of them, Mary Dyer (died 1660), is commemorated with a statue in front of the State House. The repeal of the Stamp Act was celebrated here in 1766 and, almost two centuries later, Rev. Martin Luther King, Jr. (1929–1968), advocated civil rights. In October 1979, some 100,000 watched Pope John Paul II celebrate an open-air mass.

From the **Park Street Visitor Center,** walk parallel to Beacon Street through the north part of the Common. You can't miss **Frog Pond,** once the haunt of tadpoles but now a concrete wading pool, which transforms into a skating rink in winter. Nearby is a monument to the Oneida Football Club of Boston, the first organized football group in the United States. Today, the sporty play tennis on the courts and softball at the sports field at the Boylston Street end, where the 18th-century **Central Burying Ground** includes the grave of portrait painter Gilbert Stuart (1755–1828). The common's cows were banished in 1830 by mayor Harrison Gray Otis. He and his fellow owners of the expensive houses on Beacon Hill decided that a cattle pasture was not a suitable place for a promenade.

PUBLIC GARDEN

The Public Garden dates from 1837. In colonial days, Charles Street was the water-lapped edge of the peninsula on which Boston stood. The filling in of Back Bay created land for development, but in 1837 Mayor Josiah Quincy decided that 25 acres (10 ha), should remain a public space, designated as the first botanical garden in the country. The landscaping, with ornamental bridges and paths, formal beds, and a lake, dates from 1860. Only 17 years later, the swan boats were launched. They are still a favorite with children, who insist on a ride in the open-sided boats, run by the Paget family for more than a century. Youngsters want to see the ducks: the bronzes of Mrs. Mallard and her eight children by Nancy Schon, from the much-loved book, *Make Way for Ducklings.* Find them on the north side.

Horticulturists spot flowers and trees, labeled so that everyone can tell their elms from their beeches. Medical types search out the **Ether Monument** in the northwest corner. A florid Victorian concoction of granite and red marble, it commemorates the discovery "that the inhaling of ether causes insensibility to pain" (see p. 50). The first administration during an operation was on October 16, 1846, in the Ether Dome of Massachusetts General Hospital. The most impressive monument is the statue of **George Washington,** astride a horse. It was modeled on an animal called Black Prince, which carried the real Prince of Wales, later Edward VII (*R.*1901–1910), while he reviewed the Boston militia on an official visit in 1860. ∎

Boston Common provides a refreshing swath of green in the midst of the city.

Trinity Church

ON THE EAST SIDE OF COPLEY SQUARE STANDS TRINITY
Church, consecrated in 1877. See it in the late afternoon, when
the sun shines directly on the highly decorated west facade. The
church epitomizes Richardson Romanesque—named for architect
Henry Hobson Richardson (1838–1886; see pp. 37–38). He solved the
problem of building on landfill by driving wooden piles into the earth.

**Trinity Church,
reflected in the
glass panels of the
John Hancock
Tower, exemplifies
the mix of past
and present found
everywhere in
Boston today.**

Trinity Church
- Map pp. 106–107
- Copley Sq.
- 617/536-0944
- $
- T: Copley, Back Bay

Since the John Hancock Tower
went up in 1975, blocking natural
light from the south, the maroon
and brown colors inside have
looked even more somber than
before. There are no tours, but you
can look around by yourself. The
interior was planned by John La-
Farge (1835–1910), whose frescoes
include the intricacies of the central
tower ceiling, 103 feet (31 m) high.
Some of the stained-glass windows
are his work, others are by Sir
Edward Burne-Jones (1833– 1898)
and William Morris (1834– 1896),
leaders of the 19th-century English
Arts and Crafts Movement. Their
windows are high in the north
transept, and in the baptistery. Here
"David's Charge to Solomon"

depicts the tale of David and
Goliath and shows Goliath's head
with a hole in his forehead. Other
designs include "Adoration of the
Shepherds, the Worship of the
Magi" and "Flight into Egypt."
Here, too, is the Augustus Saint-
Gaudens's (1848–1907) bust of
Phillips Brooks. Rector of the
parish from 1869 to 1893, Brooks is
best known outside Boston for his
Christmas carol, "O Little Town of
Bethlehem." In 1885, Trinity
Church topped an American
Institute of Architects survey of the
ten best buildings in the United
States. When the poll was repeated
a century later, Trinity Church
came sixth, the only building to
appear in both ratings. ■

Boston Public Library

FACING TRINITY CHURCH IS A RESOLUTELY SECULAR building, the Boston Public Library. "The Commonwealth requires the education of the people as the safeguard of order and liberty," declares the carved frieze on the first large, free, municipal library in the United States. Founded in 1848, it was also the first to allow books to be taken out and the first with a special room for children.

Designed by McKim, Mead & White, the Renaissance Revival design was as influential on American architecture as the Richardson Romanesque. These doors opened in 1895; today some 2.5 million people visit the library every year to use the research facilities here and take books out of the starkly functional, 1972 Johnson building (entrance on Boylston Street). If you enjoy controversial pictures and sculptures, look for the collection of works by Augustus Saint-Gaudens, Daniel Chester French (1850–1931), John Singer Sargent (1856–1925), and John Singleton Copley (1738–1815).

Start with the huge mural that adorns the grand double staircase in the McKim building, painted by French artist, Pierre Puvis de Chavannes (1824–98). Unveiled in 1895, its theme of muses and enlightenment was approved by the citizens of Boston. They were shocked a year later when they saw a much smaller artwork in the courtyard: the "Bacchante with Infant Faun" by Frederic MacMonnies (1863–1937). The lecherous look of the young dancing woman caused such a scandal that the bronze was removed from public view. Modern locals are a tad less easily embarrassed: In 2000, the bronze was restored to its rightful position in the renovated courtyard, a delightfully peaceful spot.

In 1919 heated debate centered on Sargent's "The Triumph of Religion" on the third floor. Here, the

panels "Synagogue" and "Church" appear to portray the collapse of Judaism and ascendancy of Christianity. Sargent claimed his allegory was misunderstood, and left it unfinished. The third controversial work is at the entrance to the **Rare Books and Manuscripts department** on the third floor. This is only the plaster version of the memorial made by Gutzon Borglum (1867–1941) to the Italian immigrants Sacco and Vanzetti. Convicted of murder, they were executed in 1927, though supporters claim the evidence was flawed and the men were innocent. This *cause célèbre* remains contentious, and the real sculpture has never seen the light of day. ■

The Boston Public Library's impressive staircase features 19th-century murals and handsome carved lions.

Boston Public Library

🅰 Map pp. 106–107

✉ Copley Sq.

☎ 617/536-5400

🕐 Closed Sun. a.m. Oct.–May

🚇 T: Copley, Back Bay

More places to visit in Boston Common & Back Bay

GIBSON HOUSE

No props would be needed for filming a 19th-century costume drama in this house, which was built by Catherine Gibson in 1860 and is still filled with her family's furniture and mementos. With limited hours, you have to plan a visit here, but the guided tour makes it well worth your while. As well as the Gibson family's social and literary aspirations, you learn about their daily life, and how they spent their money. Compare the gloomy downstairs rooms with the **Ladies' Parlor,** redecorated by Catherine's daughter-in-law in 1890. Out went the dark colors; in came Chinese porcelain and rugs and a white marble fireplace, in line with the latest fashion in interior decorating. Most fascinating are the bathroom, state of the art for 1902, and the basement kitchen and laundry room, with its 1909 washing machine. Like the Nichols House Museum

Installation and photographic art at the Institute of Contemporary Art

(see p. 104), this is a small attraction that deserves to be better known. The house is locked while tours take place, so you may have to wait outside.

🅰 Map pp. 106–107 ✉ 137 Beacon St.
☎ 617/267-6338 🕐 Closed Mon.–Tues., Mon.–Fri. Nov.–April. Tours: 1 p.m., 2 p.m., & 3 p.m. 💲 $$ 🚇 T: Berkeley

INSTITUTE OF CONTEMPORARY ART (ICA)

The clever reuse of an old fire station (next to a handsome one that is still in working order) makes this an attractive space that showcases the works of local, national, and international artists in regular exhibitions. Open since 1936, it has no permanent collection. In the early years, Paul Gauguin, Edvard Munch, and Oskar Kokoschka were shown here, followed by exhibitions of Andy Warhol, Robert Rauschenberg, and Roy Lichtenstein, all before they became world-famous.

🅰 Map pp. 106–107 ✉ 955 Boylston St.
☎ 617/266-5152 🕐 Closed Mon.–Tues.
💲 $$ 🚇 T: Hynes/ICA

JOHN HANCOCK TOWER

Vying for the title of "best view of Boston" are the John Hancock Tower and the Prudential Tower. Taller and closer to Downtown is the Hancock Tower. Just inside the door on the 60th floor you can discover more about Hancock the man, the company, and the building, before moving on to the "Boston 1775" multimedia show, one of the best explanations of the growth of the city from little more than an island to a modern metropolis. In the viewing gallery, try using the touch-screen computers to identify buildings, and listen to air-traffic controllers at Logan International Airport communicating with pilots. The famously shiny skin of the tower is made of a special reflective glass.

🅰 Map pp. 106–107 ✉ Copley Sq. (entrance to direct elevator on St. James Ave.)
☎ 617/572-6429 💲 $$ 🚇 T: Copley, Back Bay

PRUDENTIAL TOWER

The Hancock may be taller, but the Prudential's Skywalk boasts a 360-degree panorama, with a better view of the Fens and baseball's Fenway Park. Its other appeal is the Top of the Hub, a bar and restaurant that is particularly romantic at sunset. At the foot of the tower is a large indoor complex of stores and places to eat.

🅰 Map pp. 106–107 ✉ 800 Boylston St.
☎ 617/236-3318 💲 $$ 🚇 T: Prudential ∎

The Fenway is where you will find the jewels in Boston's cultural crown, with two great art galleries and a concert hall, as well as Fenway Park, the home of the Boston Red Sox.

The Fenway & Brookline

Baseball: a Boston passion

The Fenway & Brookline

THE FENWAY IS THE CULTURAL CENTER OF BOSTON, WITH MUSEUMS, concert halls, and music schools. Most of these stand on or near Huntington Avenue, which was given the title Avenue of the Arts in 1998. The linchpin is the Museum of Fine Arts, known as the MFA, an enormous complex with one of the best collections in the United States. A total contrast is the Isabella Stewart Gardner Museum, just around the corner. This Italianate mansion is a delightful place at any time, but the regular Sunday concerts are a special treat and well worth making an effort to attend. The grandees of the music scene, however, are the Boston Symphony Orchestra, whose Symphony Hall home is just a few steps away from the prestigious New England Conservatory. This is one of the oldest music schools in the country, where pupils play in Jordan Hall.

"The Appeal to the Great Spirit" (1909) by Cyrus Dallin stands outside the MFA.

All of these are within easy walking distance of the parks, ponds, and greenery—known as the "Emerald Necklace"—that are the pride of Boston and neighboring Brookline. Say the word "Fenway" to a sports fan, and "Red Sox" will be the reply. The baseball team's home, Fenway Park, is a short walk from Kenmore Square, where the enormous CITGO sign (behind Fenway's legendary "Green Monster" left-field wall) has been a landmark since the 1960s. Fenway Park, built in 1912, is the smallest park in the major leagues. Just how long it can survive in the world of super-stadiums is a subject of debate.

Between Fenway Park and the MFA are the Back Bay Fens, a swath of greenery that is one of the jewels in Frederick Law Olmsted's (1822–1903) Emerald Necklace. In the second half of the 19th century, he was commissioned to tidy up the edges of landfill projects, clean up streams and rivers, and convert marshland into a recreational resource. He saw Commonwealth Avenue as the link between Boston Common and Fenway's Back Bay Fens, with the greenery continuing south to Franklin Park. Anyone interested in this landscape architect, who also created Central Park in New York, should visit his home and office, the Frederick Law Olmsted National Historic Site (see p. 123). The Arnold Arboretum has a broader appeal. As well as its acres of trees and flowering shrubs, it has one of the highest hills

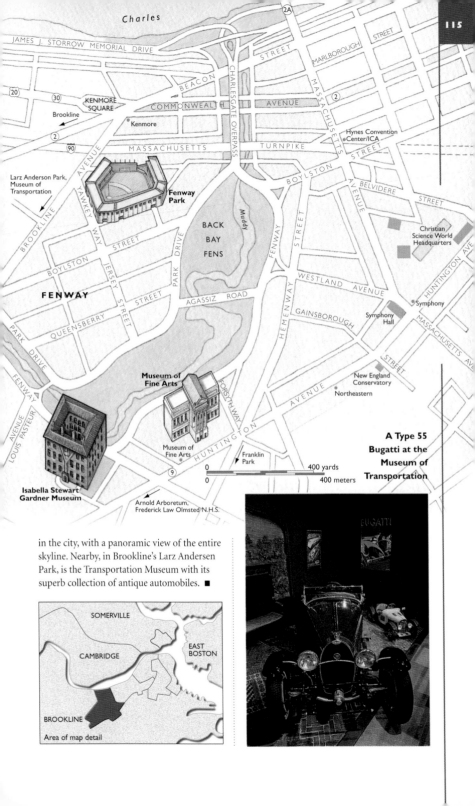

Charles

JAMES J. STORROW MEMORIAL DRIVE

BEACON STREET

CHARLESGATE OVERPASS

MARLBOROUGH STREET

20

30

KENMORE SQUARE

Brookline

2

90

Kenmore

COMMONWEALTH AVENUE

MASSACHUSETTS

TURNPIKE

2

Hynes Convention Center/ICA

STREET

Larz Anderson Park, Museum of Transportation

YAWKEY WAY

Fenway Park

BOYLSTON

STREET

BELVIDERE STREET

BOYLSTON STREET

BACK BAY FENS

Muddy

FENWAY STREET

Christian Science World Headquarters

HUNTINGTON AVE

JERSEY STREET

PARK DRIVE

MASSACHUSETTS AVE

BROOKLINE

FENWAY

QUEENSBERRY STREET

AGASSIZ ROAD

HEMENWAY STREET

WESTLAND AVENUE

GAINSBOROUGH

Symphony

Symphony Hall

PARK DRIVE

FENWAY

Museum of Fine Arts

FORSYTH WAY

New England Conservatory

STREET

Northeastern

LOUIS PASTEUR AVENUE

Museum of Fine Arts

HUNTINGTON AVENUE

Franklin Park

9

0 400 yards
0 400 meters

A Type 55 Bugatti at the Museum of Transportation

Isabella Stewart Gardner Museum

Arnold Arboretum, Frederick Law Olmsted N.H.S.

in the city, with a panoramic view of the entire skyline. Nearby, in Brookline's Larz Andersen Park, is the Transportation Museum with its superb collection of antique automobiles. ■

SOMERVILLE

CAMBRIDGE

EAST BOSTON

BROOKLINE

Area of map detail

The Museum of Fine Arts attracts enthusiastic crowds to both its permanent galleries and its blockbuster exhibitions.

Museum of Fine Arts

THE MUSEUM OF FINE ARTS, ALWAYS KNOWN LOCALLY AS the MFA, is the grande dame of New England art institutions, and has dominated Huntington Avenue since 1909. Must-sees include the Impressionist paintings, American art of the 18th and 19th centuries, plus art and artifacts from Japan and ancient Egypt. With over one million visitors each year, it appeals both to art specialist and to the wider public.

Museum of Fine Arts

www.mfa.org

Ⓜ Map p. 115

✉ 465 Huntington Ave.

☎ 617/267-9300

Ⓢ $$$. Thurs.–Fri. free after 4 p.m.; outside school hours free for those under the age of 17

🏛 Museum of Fine Arts

The columns and porticos of the original building were typical of civic architecture in the early 20th century. Behind is the starkly dramatic **West Wing,** opened 20 years ago. Designed by I.M. Pei (born 1917), it includes the Gund Gallery, used for recent blockbuster exhibitions such as "Monet in the 20th Century" and "John Singer Sargent." Although these special shows attract hundreds of thousands of visitors, it is the permanent collection that makes the MFA one of the great treasure houses in the United States. But in a museum of this size and age, there is much more. You can go back to the beginnings of Western art in the Greek, Etruscan, and Roman galleries, or trace the development of a specifically American style in furniture, ceramics, glass, and silver. There are costume and textile galleries, and a fine collection of 19th-century French silver. Don't forget to admire the recently restored **Rotunda** and **Grand Staircase,** decorated by John Singer Sargent (1856–1925).

HOW TO VISIT

With one entrance on Huntington Avenue and another in the West Wing, the MFA can be confusing for first-time visitors. Its sheer size, with miles of galleries, can easily produce visual indigestion. To make sense of it all, pick up a color-coded map and plot a route. Even better, take one of the free tours. You can opt for the general overview or one with a specific focus. An audio guide, called "Director's Choice," is also available. Rent the headphones and CD-player, then take as long as you like to enjoy the selection of 50 works throughout the museum.

It takes time to absorb all that the MFA has to offer, so take a break in one of the four restaurants. Children are made welcome, with reduced price admission and special programs. There is a program of concerts and films, and don't forget the store, with its extensive array of art books and lovely gifts.

EGYPTIAN ART

If you enter through the Huntington Avenue entrance, the **Nubian Gallery** is on the right. The museum's collection of Nubian art and artifacts is the most significant outside of Africa. Nearby, the **Egyptian Funerary Arts Gallery** is a most dramatic example of new installations. Step through the entrance, with its pillars and portico, and you will feel as if you have entered a tomb where the lighting is low and the atmosphere is hushed. Here you discover how the Egyptians prepared for the afterlife during the period between 1570 B.C. and A.D. 395. Artifacts range from an 8-foot-tall (2.4 m) sarcophagus of General Kheper-Re to gold covers for tongues and fingernails, and even a mummified cat.

Most fascinating of all are the highly decorated coffins of Nes-mut-aat-neru, a Theban aristocrat (767–656 B.C.). The three coffins would have been placed one inside the other before the mummy, which was wrapped in linen decorated with intricate blue beadwork, was laid to rest. Upstairs are more artifacts from the Harvard-led excavations of the Giza pyramids that were conducted from 1905 to 1945.

EUROPEAN ART

On the second floor, the **Koch Gallery** and **Evans Wing** are walk-through encyclopedias of European art. Start in the Koch Gallery, where the two-story-high, coffered ceiling recreates the look of a European palace. Hung with religious works and portraits of princes from France, Italy, Spain, and Flanders, it shows the

This 2,600-year-old Greek vessel is one of many fine antiquities in the collections of classical art.

development of art from 1550 to 1700. The portrait of "Fray Hortensio Felix Paravicino" (1609) by El Greco (1548–1614), a study in stark black and white, was purchased on the recommendation of John Singer Sargent. Move into the Evans Wing to see the 17th-century Dutch paintings, where the six Rembrandt (1606–1669) portraits include the seated Reverend Johannes Elison and his wife. When these were painted in 1634, such full-length depictions were highly expensive and therefore unusual; this pair is one of only three painted by the artist in his entire career. Continue to the next century in the next room, which reflects the era of the Grand Tour through Europe by English aristocrats, who purchased art as souvenirs.

As well as a typical postcard view of Venice by Canaletto (1697–1768), you can see portraits of those high society figures in all their silken finery by English artists of the 18th and 19th centuries: Sir Thomas Lawrence (1769–1830), Sir George Romney (1734–1802), Sir Thomas Gainsborough (1727–88), and Sir Joshua Reynolds (1723–92).

Once you get to the barrel-vaulted gallery of 19th-century paintings, slow down. Here, each of

Right: "Where Do We Come From? What Are We? Where Are We Going?" (1897) by Paul Gauguin

Evans Wing

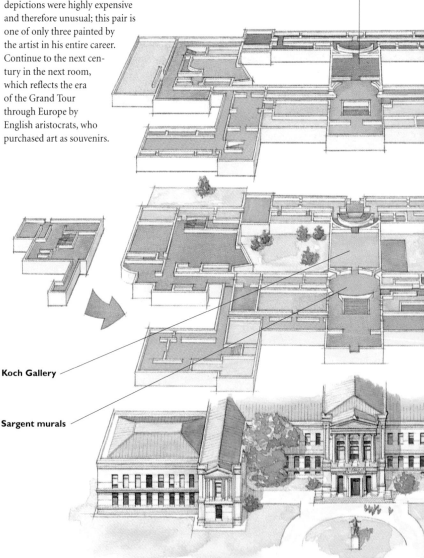

Koch Gallery

Sargent murals

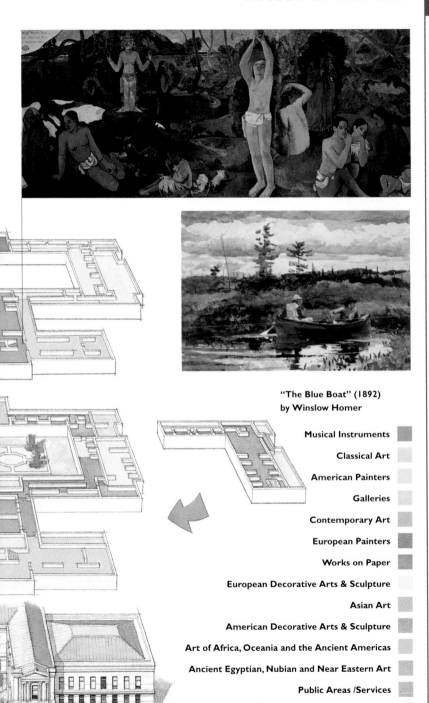

"The Blue Boat" (1892)
by Winslow Homer

Musical Instruments

Classical Art

American Painters

Galleries

Contemporary Art

European Painters

Works on Paper

European Decorative Arts & Sculpture

Asian Art

American Decorative Arts & Sculpture

Art of Africa, Oceania and the Ancient Americas

Ancient Egyptian, Nubian and Near Eastern Art

Public Areas /Services

Other Areas

"Watson and the Shark" (1778), by John Singleton Copley, depicts the heroic rescue of a young English merchant.

the works by Jean-Baptiste Corot (1796–1875), Gustave Courbet (1819–1877), Eugene Delacroix (1798–1863), Édouard Manet (1832–1883), and Jean-François Millet (1814–1875) is a classic. "Slave Ship" (1840) by J.M.W. Turner (1775–1851) shows why he is often called the Father of Impressionism. You can hardly see the boat, with the bodies of slaves being thrown overboard, against the raging red and yellow sky. "If I were reduced to rest Turner's immortality upon any single work, I should choose this," so said the painting's first owner, the influential 19th-century English critic, John Ruskin (1819–1900).

The **Impressionism** gallery is similarly comprehensive. The five works by Vincent van Gogh (1853–1890) illustrate his sense of color and belief in the dignity of the working man, while the enormous "Where Do We Come From? What Are We? Where Are We Going?" (1897) was the work Paul Gauguin (1848–1903) considered his master-

piece. The 36 paintings by Claude Monet (1840–1926) comprise the largest group outside of France and include several from his Rouen Cathedral and the Haystacks series. There are fine examples of Paul Cézanne (1839–1906) and Edgar Degas (1834–1917), but one of the signature paintings of the collection is the "Dance at Bougival" (1883) by Auguste Renoir (1841–1919). His feathery brush strokes depict a timeless moment: A couple are dancing on a warm evening and you can almost hear the sweet nothings whispered by the suitor to the pretty young girl.

AMERICAN PAINTING

Directly below on the first floor of the Evans Wing are the American paintings, from colonial portraits to the later 19th century. Most come from Boston or points nearby.

With a total of 110 works by the two great painters of the early United States, John Singleton Copley (1738–1815) and Gilbert

Stuart (1755–1828), this gallery must not be missed. Compare Copley's "Watson and the Shark" (1778), his first large-scale historical painting and one that is full of action, with Stuart's "Washington at Dorchester Heights" (1806), a surprisingly static scene that focuses more on the general than on the battle raging behind him. Copley's famous portrait of Paul Revere (1768) is here, alongside Revere's own silver Liberty Bowl, made in the same year. Artists of the 19th century include Winslow Homer (1836-1910), James McNeill Whistler (1834–1903), and, of course, Sargent, each represented by a famous portrait they painted of a society family.

You can spend hours in these galleries, coming into the later 20th century with George Bellows (1882–1925), Edward Hopper (1882–1967), then Stuart Davis (1894–1964), Georgia O'Keeffe (1887–1986), and Jackson Pollock (1912-1956).

ASIAN ART

For a total contrast, visit the Asian Art galleries on the first and second floors. Here is the Japanese collection, which includes some exquisite 19th-century costumes from the Noh theater, armor, and examples of the woodblock prints that influenced Western artists in the late 19th century.

Upstairs you can see the highly rated Japanese Buddhist art displayed in specially designed rooms. Particularly effective is the great hall, where the shadowy light emphasizes the contemplative nature of the huge statue, an early 12th-century Dainichi, Buddha of Infinite Light.

NEW DIRECTIONS

Malcolm Rogers has initiated many changes since taking over as direc-

tor in 1994. The original entrance on Huntington Avenue has reopened and new galleries have been added to the overall display space. The Egyptian and Japanese collections, too, have benefited from dramatic new installations. There are more programs for children, special discount tickets for admission, and extended hours of opening. Not only is the MFA open after office hours on three nights a week, but the museum stayed open throughout one Saturday night on the final weekend of the "John Singer Sargent" exhibition in 1999. That headline-making decision brought some 5,000 extra visitors through the doors.

Looking to the future, the MFA has commissioned Sir Norman Foster, the renowned British architect, to design a master plan for expansion and renovation. Some of the changes initiated by Rogers have been controversial, but the Museum of Fine Arts has certainly shed its image of being a fusty, old-fashioned institution. ∎

John Singer Sargent captured the individual poise and grace of his friend's girls in "The Daughters of Edward Darley Boit" (1882).

Emerald Necklace

A pioneer in the field of town planning, Frederick Law Olmsted (1822–1903) is best remembered for creating Central Park in New York. This landscape architect, who had no formal training, also left an indelible legacy in Boston: the Emerald Necklace. The jewels are a 9-mile (14 km) string of parks, stretching from Boston Common to Franklin Park on the south side of the city.

In 1878, after his successful urban projects in New York and Chicago, Olmsted was hired by the Boston Park Commission to beautify the city. Much-traveled in both Europe and the United States, Olmsted believed that the squalor and drudgery of city life could be ameliorated by the beauty of nature. Indeed, his influence helped in the drive to create the National Park Service.

**Frederick Law
Olmsted National
Historic Site**

✉ 99 Warren St.,
  Brookline

☎ 617/566-1689

🕐 Closed Mon.–Thurs.

Arnold Arboretum

✉ 125 Arborway,
  Jamaica Plain

☎ 617/524-1718

Franklin Park

✉ 1 Franklin Park Rd.

☎ 617/541-5466

💲 Zoo: $$

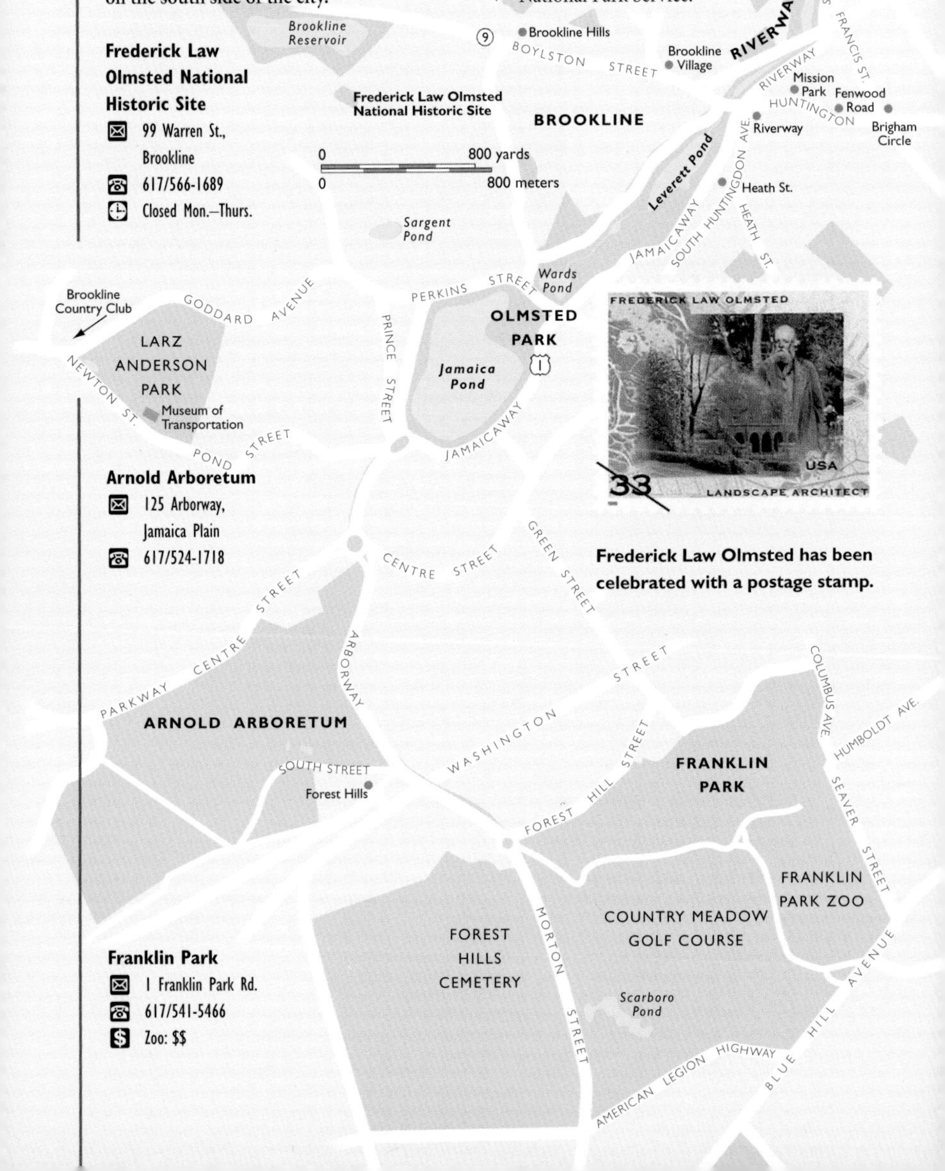

Frederick Law Olmsted
National Historic Site

0   800 yards
0   800 meters

**Frederick Law Olmsted has been
celebrated with a postage stamp.**

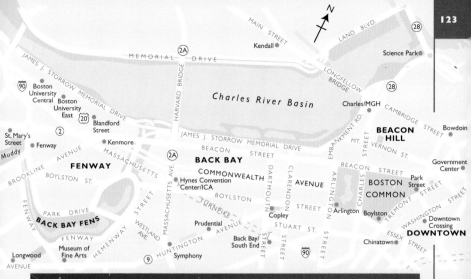

Flying kites in Franklin Park is a popular pastime for residents and visitors of all ages.

He moved his home and office from New York to Brookline in 1883. Now called the Frederick Law Olmsted National Historic Site, it is a memorial to this forward-thinking designer. Around the rust-red clapboard house are 200 varieties of shrubs and trees. Inside are nearly one million original drawings, constituting an invaluable reference for his renovation projects across the United States.

Olmsted's philosophy rested on six alliterative principles: scenery, suitability, sanitation, subordination, separation, and spaciousness. His aim in Boston was flood control and beautification. He succeeded on both counts, reclaiming and transforming five areas of swamp and marshland in the suburbs. Connected by parkways, they were linked via Commonwealth Avenue to the Public Garden

and the Common, creating a total of some 1,300 acres (520 ha) of parks and gardens.

The Arnold Arboretum covers 265 acres (107 ha) and is one of the United States' finest botanical gardens. Here, Olmsted worked in collaboration with Charles Sprague Sargent, the arboretum's first director. The arboretum is at its most spectacular on Lilac Sunday in mid-May, when the 250 varieties of lilacs are usually at their peak. Landscape gardeners and horticulturists visit year-round to study some 15,000 trees and shrubs. For locals, it is a quiet spot for jogging, walking, and cycling.

Franklin Park in Dorchester stretches over 527 acres (213 ha) and is juxtaposed with one of the city's tougher neighborhoods. The Zoo is a pleasant, old-fashioned attraction, more popular with locals than with visitors. ■

Isabella Stewart Gardner Museum

JUST AROUND THE CORNER FROM THE MUSEUM OF FINE Arts is the Isabella Stewart Gardner Museum, fondly known as The Gardner. Once through the front door of her mansion, Fenway Court, everything you see reflects the taste of Mrs. Gardner, who not only chose the art but even arranged the individual items herself before opening it to the public in 1903. Her taste has been described as eclectic and eccentric—here's your chance to decide for yourself.

**Isabella Stewart
Gardner Museum**
www.boston.com/gardner
- Map p. 115
- 280 The Fenway
- 617/566-1401
- Closed Mon. Talks
  Tues.–Fri. 11:30
  a.m. & 1 p.m. Tours
  Fri. 2:30 p.m.
- $$$
- T: Museum of Fine
  Arts

Built along the lines of a 15th-century Venetian palazzo, the three floors overlook a central courtyard, full of plants and flowers that are protected from the Boston weather by an enormous skylight.

Turning a private collection into a museum was unheard of at the turn of the century, but Mrs. Gardner was a strong-minded individual (see p. 126). Not for her the rarefied atmosphere of the museums of her day, with windowless galleries. She wanted a more welcoming setting that would appeal to ordinary people. Her aim was to create an overall aesthetic experience, so you won't find the

artworks in chronological order, nor in strict schools of art. Quite simply, she placed them where they looked best, and nothing has been changed since she died in 1924. Her motto, *C'est mon Plaisir,* means "It is my Pleasure," and it neatly sums up the intensely personal nature of The Gardner.

As for the collection, it includes works by Rembrandt (1606–1669), Titian (1477–1576), Piero della Francesca, (1420–1492), Edgar Degas (1834–1917), and Henri Matisse (1869–1954). As a patron of the arts, Isabella Gardner became friends with American painters of her time, such as James McNeill

Whistler (1834–1903) and John Singer Sargent (1856–1925), and purchased many of their works. Furniture, sculpture, manuscripts, drawings, personal letters, and more are spread over three floors, but not all the objects are labeled. This can be frustrating, but there are docents ready to answer questions, as well as free weekly tours, and audio guides to rent.

FIRST FLOOR

Once through the main entrance, the first thing you see is the huge "El Jaleo" (1882) at the far end of the **Spanish Cloister.** Sargent was only 26 when he painted this perpetual performance; the viewer provides the audience for the flamenco dancer as she struts and swishes her skirts. So dramatic is the moment that you hardly notice the 12th-century doorway imported from France or the 17th-century Mexican wall tiles that are part of the cloister's decoration. Walk through to the **Courtyard,** flooded with light from the glass roof. A keen horticulturist, Mrs. Gardner designed this space as a

Mediterranean garden. Among her favorite plants were the South American nasturtiums, which cascade 20 to 30 feet (9 m) from the balconies in the spring.

Looking up, each story has a different style of window. All are Venetian, although they were removed from various buildings dating from the 14th to the 16th centuries. Many visitors assume that this is a real palace that Mrs. Gardner bought, dismantled, and shipped to the United States. In fact, it was designed specifically to accommodate not just the art, but also the architectural pieces from France, Italy, and Spain. Before you go to the upper floors, take a look at the **Blue Room,** near the entrance. Here Mrs. Gardner used five different 18th-century fabrics as a decorating theme, stretching and draping them across the walls. Thanks to recent restoration, the room looks almost as it did in 1903.

SECOND FLOOR

You never know what to expect in this museum. Take the **Early Italian Room** on the second

The dramatic "El Jaleo" (1882) by John Singer Sargent is the focal point of the Spanish Cloister.

A self-portrait (1629) by Rembrandt was the museum's first important purchase.

"She is the one and only real potentate I have ever known. She lives at a rate and intensity and with a reality that makes other lives seem pale, thin and shadowy."
—Bernard Berenson, art critic and friend of Isabella Gardner (1865–1959) ■

floor. Although named for the 14th- to 16th-century Italian works, such as the "Hercules" (circa 1475) fresco by Piero della Francesca, it also has an 18th-century lacquered table from Japan and a pair of growling bronze bears from China (Han dynasty, first century B.C.). Next door is the **Raphael Room,** which exemplifies the difference between the private atmosphere of The Gardner and that of traditional museums. The walls are lined with

red-silk damask, as you might see in a European palace. In one corner hangs the "Portrait of Tommaso Inghirami" (1516) by Raphael (1483–1520). Below, propped up on a desk, is his "Pieta," painted 12 years earlier as part of a large altarpiece in Perugia. Nearby is another work by a notable painter of the Italian Renaissance, Sandro Botticelli (circa 1444–1510). "The Tragedy of Lucretia" (circa 1500) depicts a tale of ancient Rome: the rape of a maiden by the son of a despot, her suicide, and the revolt that led to the founding of the Roman Republic.

Even the small rooms have treasures, such as the portrait of Mrs. Gardner in the **Short Gallery.** Painted by the family friend, Swedish artist Anders Zorn (1860–1920), it shows her in Venice, as if she has just stepped in from the balcony. The long string of pearls, her signature jewelry, glisten against her white dress. In this room, the cabinets hold prints and drawings, including one by Michelangelo (1475–1564). You can go ahead and open the doors, as it is allowed in this unusual museum.

Pass through the Little Salon to the next large gallery, the

Isabella Stewart Gardner

Stories abound of Mrs. Gardner's eccentric behavior; most are false. She did not, for example, keep pet lions, let alone take them for walks on a leash. However, she was a strong individual with definite tastes, and after inheriting 1.6 million dollars from her father in 1891, she could indulge them. Many charities benefited from her generosity. Mrs. Gardner (1840–1924) had wide-ranging personal interests. She was intrigued by Asian philosophy, she supported the

Boston Red Sox, but the arts were her passion. Friends included actors, musicians, painters, and sculptors. Although her husband, John Lowell Gardner, backed the museum idea, he died in 1898, a year before building work began. Thus Fenway Court was truly her own creation. When her architect, Willard T. Sears, was honored by the Philadelphia Society of Architects, he declared that the medal really deserved to go to Isabella Stewart Gardner. ■

Tapestry Room. The largest room of all, it was designed for concerts and is still used for musical events. While listening to the music, audiences of 300 can work out the story of the two sets of tapestries hanging on the walls; they are not in narrative order. Around the corner is the **Dutch Room,** where the light is always changing, thanks to windows on two sides. This is the room you cannot miss, since it has some of the best-known works in the entire museum. Take time to appreciate the German artists Albrecht Durer (1471–1528) and Hans Holbein the Younger (circa 1497–1523), who was court painter to Henry VIII of England. Then look at the portraits by Flemish painters Peter Paul Rubens (1577–1640) and Sir Anthony Van Dyck (1599–1641). A signature work of the museum is Rembrandt's "Portrait of the Artist as a Young Man." The work dates from 1629, when he was just 23; the expensive clothes show that the young painter was already successful. Purchased in 1896, it was the first work bought by Mrs. Gardner

specifically for her museum project. Originally, three more Rembrandt portraits hung on these walls. These were stolen in March 1990, along with "The Concert" (circa 1658–1660), a famous painting by Jan Vermeer (1632–1675). Sadly, the frames remain empty.

THIRD FLOOR

Up on the third floor, pass through the **Veronese Room** to reach another gallery decorated in red, the **Titian Room.** Here, the two most famous paintings are the large "Europa" by Titian and the portrait of a haughty Philip IV of Spain by Velazquez (1599–1660). Across the courtyard in the **Gothic Room,** you come face to face with your hostess, Isabella Stewart Gardner, as painted by Sargent when she was 47. The portrait was controversial in its time, probably because of the figure-hugging dress she was wearing, and its décolletage.

FOURTH FLOOR

The fourth floor was the apartment of Mrs. Gardner, who lived here for the last 20 years of her life. ■

Mrs. Gardner's house-museum remains exactly as she left it; it can never be rearranged.

Crazy about sports

Sports are as much a part of Boston's history as the American Revolution. Boston clubs provided the building blocks of professional sports in the United States, and several have reigned as world champions.

For half a century, the city boasted two major league baseball teams. The Boston Red Stockings (later the Boston Braves) were one of the nine founding franchises, with pitcher Al Spalding and the fabled Wright brothers

Babe Ruth began his career as a Red Sox.

helping them to four of the first five titles, between 1872 and 1875. The first game in the newly founded National League was played in Boston on April 22, 1876. Later, Cy Young (1867–1955), for whom the annual pitching award is named, was lured to the Pilgrims (soon the Red Sox) in a rival American League in 1901. Their home, Fenway Park, opened in 1912 (see pp. 130–31) and is now one of the oldest baseball grounds still in use in the major leagues.

Until replaced by the FleetCenter in 1995, the Boston Garden was another venue of sporting legends, famous as the home of the Boston Celtics and Boston Bruins. In the glory days, the Celtics set standards in basketball that remained unmatched in the 20th century. Founder members of the Basketball Association of America, later the NBA, they became a dynasty under coach Red Auerbach (born 1917). After his arrival in 1950, he built great teams around point guard Bob Cousy (played 1950–1963), center Bill Russell (played 1956–1969), and forward Larry Bird (1980–1992). As coach, Auerbach won nine titles, followed by another seven as general manager. Thanks to a galaxy of Hall of Famers such as Sam Jones, K.C. Jones, John Havlicek,

and Dave Cowens, the Celtics took eight titles in a row between 1958 and 1966—a record unlikely to be beaten. As for the Bruins (ice hockey), they have appeared in 17 of the NHL's Stanley Cup finals. Two names are forever on fans' lips: Bobby Orr (played 1966–1976), a great defenseman, and free-scoring center Phil Esposito (played 1967–1976). Founded in 1924, the Bruins are the oldest ice-hockey franchise in the United States.

More sporting legends were produced in boxing. The Boston Strong Boy, John L. Sullivan (1858–1918), was the last bareknuckle world champion. Rocky Marciano (1923–1969) was the only professional boxer to win every bout in his career. He retired with a 49 fights, 49 wins record. In the more genteel world of golf, Francis Ouimet stunned the establishment by winning the U.S. Open in 1913. The 20-year-old amateur triggered the golf boom in the United States by defeating Britain's established stars on his home course, the Brookline Country Club.

But Boston's contribution to sports is not limited to professionals. Harvard introduced football goalposts in 1874, and the Davis Cup tennis tournament was the brainchild of Dwight Davis (1879–1945), a Harvard student. The Boston Marathon, held on Patriots' Day (April 19), is not only the world's oldest annual marathon (1897), but also a major fixture on the international calendar, attracting approximately 16,000 runners. ∎

On Patriot's Day, the streets of Boston are filled with runners and lined with crowds of supportive onlookers for the Boston Marathon.

Fenway Park and the Green Monster, the legendary wall in left field

Fenway Park

THE MESSAGE IS SIMPLE: GET HERE SOON. AFTER SOME 90 years, one of the greatest sporting venues in the country is threatened with the wrecker's ball. With a capacity of 33,871, Fenway Park, home of the American League Boston Red Sox, is the smallest stadium in professional baseball. It makes no economic sense in the 21st century.

Fenway Park

- 🅰 Map p. 115
- ✉ 4 Yawkey Way
- ☎ 617/267-1700. Tickets: 617/482-4SOX. Tours: 617/236-6666
- 🕐 Baseball season: April—Sept. Tours: May—Sept. Mon.—Fri.
- 💲 $$$
- 🚇 T: Kenmore Square

Fenway Park's appeal, however, has nothing to do with money. If ever a ballpark was a "Field of Dreams," this is it. Players still get to play on grass, real people still work the scoreboard, the shape of the field is irregular, and fans get closer to the action than anywhere else in the major leagues. That is what makes Fenway Park (built in 1912) so special, and it attracts fanatics ranging from Senator Ted Kennedy to author Stephen King. If you cannot

get to a game, take one of the tours of this living museum of baseball.

Most fans ask the guides about The Wall. Also known as the Green Monster, the 37-foot-high (11 m) barrier in left field has an almost mystical presence. According to the numbers painted on it, The Wall is 315 feet (96 m) from home plate, but it looks and looms much closer. It replaced an earthen bank, nicknamed Duffy's Cliff after a Red Sox outfielder, that had marked the

Curse of the Bambino

"If only…" is the familiar cry of sports fans everywhere. In Boston, it goes, "If only Red Sox owner Harry Frazee hadn't sold Babe Ruth (1895–1948) to the New York Yankees in 1920." The greatest player in baseball history made his major league debut in Boston, helping them to three World Series wins. Over the decades, fans have blamed the Red Sox's lack of success on the "Curse of the Bambino."

Some say that witches put a curse on the club, others that Fenway Park is haunted by the spirits of Indians buried beneath it, even that Babe Ruth himself had condemned them to eternal frustration. A left-hander, with 94 career wins and a 2.28 ERA, Ruth was a top-class pitcher in Boston. He is best remembered, however, as the Sultan of Swat, a prodigious hitter with 714 career home runs to his credit. ■

boundary of left field until 1934. A huge billboard of sheet metal was then put up and covered with advertisements for soap and razor blades; when this was painted green in 1947, the Green Monster was born.

Stories abound in Fenway Park. Guides point out the numbers **9-4-1-8** on the right-field grandstand. These are the retired numbers of four Red Sox greats: Ted Williams (9), Joe Cronin (4), Bobby Doerr (1), and Carl Yastrzemski (8). To the superstitious, however, they represent a significant date, the eve of the World Series that began on September 4, 1918. The Red Sox won it, but they have not won another since. Then there is the eye-catching, lone red seat in the green bleachers in right field. This is a memorial to spectator Joseph Boucher, who was sitting here in 1946 when hometown hero Ted Williams hammered a 502-foot (152 m) home run, the longest ever seen in the park. Boucher was blinded by the sun for a split second, and the ball bounced off his straw hat. Ted Williams, known as the Splendid Splinter, also hit a huge home run in his last at bat in the major leagues, back in 1960.

Fenway Park stages the only

morning baseball game in the country. This is on the Patriots' Day holiday in April, and starts at 11:05. Some fans high above home plate can even spot the lead runners in the day's other big sports event, the Boston Marathon, as they pass through Kenmore Square at about 2 p.m. It was also here that Franklin D. Roosevelt made his last speech in his successful presidential campaign of 1944. ■

Right: Red Sox fans claim they are the country's most loyal followers.

More places to visit in the Fenway & Brookline

CHRISTIAN SCIENCE WORLD HEADQUARTERS

This huge space between Huntington and Massachusetts Avenues is devoted to the Christian Scientist Movement, founded in Boston by Mary Baker Eddy (1821–1910) at the end of the 19th century. The original Romanesque Mother Church (1894) was soon overshadowed by the 5,000-seat First Church of Christ Scientist, with its massive organ. In 1973 architect I.M. Pei's slablike office block appeared at the far end of a 670-foot-long (203 m) reflecting pool. The headquarters house the editorial offices of the *Christian Science Monitor* newspaper, and the curious Mapparium, a stained-glass globe of the world, marked up with the names of countries as they were when it was crafted in the 1930s.
🅼 Map p. 115 ✉ 75 Huntington Ave.
☎ 617/450-2000 🚇 T: Prudential

The Boston Symphony orchestra performs in Symphony Hall.

MUSEUM OF TRANSPORTATION

If you trek out to Brookline to visit the Larz Anderson Park, you can enjoy a visit to the oldest collection of cars in the United States, together with a fine view of Boston. A century ago, Larz Anderson and his wife, Isabel, shared a passion for the new-fangled motorcar. After their original purchase of a single cylinder

Winton in 1899, they bought a new automobile every year for some 30 years. They kept every single one, and first displayed them to the public in 1927. Highlights include the 1908 Bailey Electric that could travel 80–100 miles (130–160 km) per charge, at speeds of up to 30 mph (48 kph). Note the footman's seat, added because ladies of Mrs. Anderson's high social standing did not drive alone in those days. You don't have to be a car enthusiast to enjoy this museum. The stories of the Andersons are entertaining, while the Carriage House itself, where the exhibition is held, is a stunning building. Then there is the spectacular view from the top of the hill, over the greenery of the Arnold Arboretum to the Boston skyline.
🅼 Map p. 115 ✉ Larz Anderson Park, 15 Newton St., Brookline ☎ 617/522-6547
🕐 Closed Mon. 💲 $$ 🚇 T: Reservoir Station, Cleveland Circle, then No. 51 bus to Newton St. Go left and walk 400 yards (366 m) to park entrance.

SYMPHONY HALL

Like a woman whose plain wool coat hides an elegant ball gown, Symphony Hall's dark red-brick and limestone exterior belies the glorious, gilt-trimmed auditorium within. Designed by McKim, Mead & White, the hall celebrated its Centennial in October 2000 with a gala that re-created the opening program. Some 2,600 concert-goers sat in the leather seats, where they had a fabulous view of the statues of Greek gods and satyrs in the niches above and enjoyed the perfect acoustics. They have Wallace Sabine to thank for the quality of the sound. The Harvard professor founded the science of acoustics, and it was Symphony Hall that proved his theories. Today, as well as the main concerts, there are open rehearsals at discounted prices and programs of chamber music. In 2002, Seiji Ozawa (born 1935) will leave the Boston Symphony Orchestra after nearly 30 years as its music director. The Boston Pops, founded in 1885, also perform here.
🅼 Map p. 115 ✉ 301 Massachusetts Ave.
☎ Information: 617/266-1492. Bookings: 617/266-1200 🚇 T: Symphony ∎

On the north bank of the Charles River lies Charlestown, which was established even before Boston. It has a proud tradition of shipbuilding, centered on the U.S.S. *Constitution*. Bunker Hill is its most prominent landmark.

Charlestown

Reliving the Battle of Bunker Hill

Charlestown

JUST AS BOSTON'S WATERFRONT HAS UNDERGONE A RENAISSANCE, SO TOO, have parts of Charlestown. With its easy access to Cambridge and the downtown business district, the old houses down by the river have attracted young professionals, while City Square is the home of some of Boston's trendiest restaurants.

For centuries, Charlestown was synonymous with shipbuilding. Today, following the Freedom Trail, most visitors head straight for the old Navy Yard, a 30-acre (12 ha) site administered by the National Park Service. The original shipyards were seven times the size and stretched for over a mile (2 km) along the waterfront. Here, the star attractions are the U.S.S. *Constitution* and the excellent free museum, which gives both the nautical and political background to the battleship. Bunker Hill, with its key role in the Revolution, should also be a major draw, but fewer Freedom Trail followers hike up to the top. Most will stop at the visitor center, the Bunker Hill Pavilion, which is down by the entrance to the shipyard.

Take time to explore the old heart of Charlestown. Although founded by ten Puritan families in 1628, two years before Boston, most of it was burned by the British in 1775. You can, however, see some handsome wood and brick federal houses built after the fire. Find them on Main Street and Warren Street. Typical of the period is the John Larkin House *(55–61 Main St.),* named for Deacon John Larkin, the patriot who lent Paul Revere his horse for his famous midnight ride. Farther along is the 200-year-old Warren Tavern *(105 Main St.),* which is still dispensing hospitality. Walk up Monument Street, past renovated row houses that sport polished brass door knockers and tidy window boxes.

Don't be confused if you see the name Harvard Square. The one in Cambridge may be more famous, but Charlestown's Harvard Square has some attractive early 18th-century houses. It is named for minister and Cambridge University graduate John Harvard (1607–1638), who lived nearby for 14 months. In his will, he left his books and £800 ($1,400) to a new college in nearby Newtowne (now Cambridge). The grateful community named the college for him. Running between City Square and Harvard Square is another tribute to the benefactor, the leafy Harvard Mall.

In summer you can take a water taxi from Long Wharf, near the Aquarium, to Pier 4, a short walk from Charlestown Navy Yard. ■

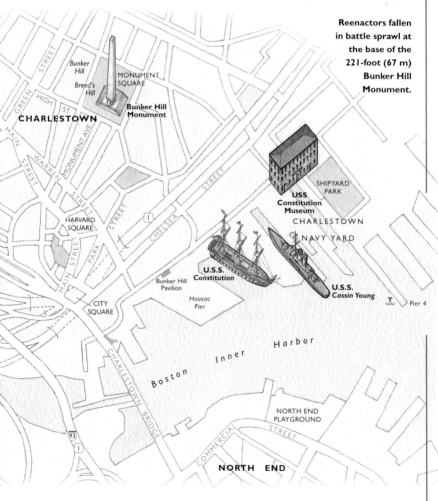

Reenactors fallen in battle sprawl at the base of the 221-foot (67 m) Bunker Hill Monument.

Bunker Hill

Breed's Hill

MONUMENT SQUARE

Bunker Hill Monument

CHARLESTOWN

GREEN STREET

HIGH ST.

MAIN STREET

WARREN STREET

MONUMENT AVE.

HARVARD SQUARE

PARK STREET

CITY SQUARE

CHELSEA STREET

STREET

Bunker Hill Pavilion

Hoosac Pier

U.S.S. Constitution

USS **Constitution** Museum

SHIPYARD PARK

CHARLESTOWN NAVY YARD

U.S.S. Cassin Young

Pier 4

CHARLESTOWN BRIDGE

93

I

Boston Inner Harbor

NORTH END PLAYGROUND

COMMERCIAL STREET

NORTH END

Bunker Hill

THE BUNKER HILL MONUMENT IS A MAJOR BOSTON landmark. You see it flying into Logan Airport and from I-93 as you head north from the city. An obelisk made of Quincy granite, it thrusts 221 feet (67 m) into the air. Today, it looks a mere stripling compared to the skyscrapers Downtown, but on completion in 1843, the monument was the highest structure in the city. It was also the first memorial on such a scale anywhere in the United States.

Bunker Hill Monument

Map pp. 134–35

✉ Monument Sq., Charlestown

☎ 617/242-5641

🕐 Closed in winter if conditions are icy

🚇 T: Community College

⛴ Pier 4, Charlestown Navy Yard

A ten-minute walk from the U.S.S. *Constitution* is the **Bunker Hill Monument,** standing in a spacious square at the top of a steep hill. A statue of Col. William Prescott (1726–1795), ready for action, looks toward the Charles River. With sword in hand and farming tools underfoot, he epitomizes the romantic image of the colonial soldier-farmer. It was Prescott who commanded the patriots on June 17, 1775, in the battle won by the British but which proved to be a moral victory for the Americans. It was not, however, fought on Bunker Hill. History got it wrong: The main hostilities took place on Breed's Hill, and that is where this monument was built. Bunker Hill is the larger slope to the north.

At the foot of the monument is a small museum explaining the buildup to the battle, with dioramas depicting the layout of the land, the British troop movements, and the battle itself. A ranger gives regular talks about the battle and warns that there is no elevator inside the monument. The only way to appreciate the view over Boston is to climb up the 294 steps. At the top, even though the windows are small, you can easily pick out the modern FleetCenter, the Old North Church, and Custom House Tower. ■

Right: Col.
William Prescott
takes a defiant
stance atop the
Bunker Hill
Monument.

Battle of Bunker Hill

When you look at today's skyline across the harbor, it is hard to imagine the events of early summer, 1775. Remember that British-held Boston was under siege by men from Massachusetts and neighboring Colonies. Gen. Thomas Gage (1721–1787) declared martial law on June 12. Any Colonist bearing arms, or aiding those who did, was deemed to be a traitor. On the other hand, he offered to pardon anyone who swore allegiance to the Crown. Two exceptions to the amnesty were Samuel Adams (1722–1803) and John Hancock (1737–1793).

Tensions rose, with rumors of British plans to take Charlestown, whose hills overlooking the city and harbor were strategically important. Under cover of darkness on June 16, Col. William Prescott and some 1,600 patriots set off to dig a fortification on Breed's Hill. At dawn, 2,400 British troops launched an assault, but only on the third attempt did they capture the hill. Prescott retreated, chased by the redcoats as far as neighboring Bunker Hill. The British had won the day, but suffered 1,054 casualties, including many officers. American losses numbered in the hundreds; more importantly, in what was the first battle of the Revolution, the Colonists showed that they were opponents to be reckoned with. Two weeks later, George Washington arrived in Cambridge to take over as commander-in-chief of the colonial forces and turn them into a trained army. In the Bunker Hill Pavilion visitor center, a multimedia show called "The Whites of their Eyes" tells the story of the battle (closed Jan.– March). Every year, on the Sunday nearest June 17, locals parade through the streets of Charlestown. On Bunker Hill Day itself, there is a remembrance service at a nearby church and speeches at the monument. ■

U.S.S. *Constitution*

"HUZZAH! HER SIDES ARE MADE OF IRON!" THE CHEERS OF American sailors as British cannonballs bounced off the sides of the United States' most famous warship have echoed down through history. When the U.S.S. *Constitution* pounded H.M.S. *Guerriere* to defeat on August 19, 1812, it was the first time a United States naval frigate had bettered a frigate from the mighty British navy that ruled the ocean. Her nickname, Old Ironsides, was born.

The most honored ship in the United States Navy, the U.S.S. *Constitution* was launched in Boston in 1797, and is still alive and well in the city of her birth. It is a wonderful story and another must for any visitor to the city. Still a commissioned warship, she is the oldest in the world still afloat (Britain's H.M.S. *Victory* is older but sits in dry dock). She is manned by serving sailors, who also act as guides for the regular tours. They explain that her nickname was justified. Made of three layers of wood, the extra-strong walls held a secret ingredient: live oak. Neither France nor Britain had access to these trees, native to the southeastern United States. Not only is the wood tough, it doesn't rot in water.

The statistics on the tour continue thick and fast. The main mast is 198 feet tall (60 m), from top to bottom, or "keel to truck." The sail area measures over 42,000 square feet (3,902 sq m). Children are fascinated by the 54 cannon on board, even though firing them was a dangerous business. Each recoiled violently, hurtling back at 65 mph (100 kph). Not all the facts are pleasant. Among the crew of 450 to 500 were 30 boys aged 12 to 16 whose dangerous duties included supplying powder to the guns during battle. The sailor-guides love to explain slang, especially expressions like "letting the cat out of the bag," which refers to the cat o' nine tails, a whip kept by the bosun in a bag

on his belt. Three or four times a year, the U.S.S. *Constitution* leaves the dock for a stately tour of Boston Harbor. It's one of the highlights of July 4th to see the 200-year-old naval war hero out on the water.

After touring the ship, make for the nearby **USS Constitution Museum,** where you learn more about the construction of the warship, as well as the political climate in the early 1800s. Alongside the history are hands-on exhibitions. "Ready, Aim, Fire!" gives an idea of how complex it was to load and fire a 24-pound gun. Sponging, loading, and ramming home the cartridge were just three of the 17 steps required before you could aim the cannon and fire it at the enemy. You can climb into a sailor's hammock and even try to refight the battles of 1812 on computers. Beware: They are programmed to allow the British to win if you choose the wrong tactics.

The core exhibition, "Old Ironsides in War & Peace," spans 200 years of the ship's history. You are reminded that the U.S.S. *Constitution* and the new State House were built within two years of each other, with several of the city's best craftsmen working on both. Paul Revere's foundry provided 15 tons of copper bolts, as well as the ship's brass bell, made "as cheap as anyone and as well" for a price of $3,820.33.

Take a good look at the 13-foot-long (4 m) model of Old Ironsides.

U.S.S. *Constitution*
- Map pp. 134–35
- Charlestown Navy Yard
- 617/242-5601
- T: North Station
- Pier 4: ferry to Long Wharf

USS Constitution Museum
www.ussconstitutionmuseum.org
- Map pp. 134–35
- Charlestown Navy Yard
- 617/426-1812
- North Station, Community College
- Pier 4: ferry to Long Wharf

Right: The U.S.S. *Constitution*, with her spiderweb of rigging, rests at a permanent berth in Boston Harbor.

Her 36 sails were cut from nearly an acre (0.5 ha) of canvas, making her the high-tech ship of her day, sailing at speeds of 13 knots (15 mph/24 kph), which allowed her to chase and capture smaller vessels, or to escape from danger. A timeline follows her 18-year front-line career. In her glory days, she won one of the shortest naval battles on record (30 minutes in the American version, an hour and 30 minutes in the British). By 1830, she was consigned to the scrap heap. Only a poetic plea by Oliver Wendell Holmes (1809–1894) rallied public opinion, helping to ensure that she was saved and restored for posterity. Upstairs, an exhibit covers the most recent restoration (1992–1996), and modelers are usually working away, happy to answer questions.

Main mast

Mizzen mast

Spar deck

Gun port

Below: A detail of the intricate decorations on the U.S.S. *Constitution*

Berth deck

Diagonal rider

Fore mast

In the **USS Constitution Museum**, you can watch volunteers build model ships.

"**Commodore William Bainbridge**," Commander of the **U.S.S.** *Constitution*, by **Gilbert Stuart**

Bowsprit

Copper plating

Gun deck

U.S.S. *Cassin Young*

ONLY A FEW STEPS AWAY FROM THE U.S.S. *CONSTITUTION* IS the 20th-century warship, the U.S.S. *Cassin Young*. She may play second fiddle to her more famous neighbor, but this World War II destroyer has a proud naval record of her own.

U.S.S. *Cassin Young*, 150 years younger than the neighboring U.S.S. *Constitution*

Anywhere else, she might well be the star of the show. But situated as she is in the shadow of "Old Ironsides" (see pp. 138–141), the first question most visitors pose to rangers when they clamber aboard is, "Who was Cassin Young?"

Ted Cassin Young was a hero of Pearl Harbor, and he was awarded the Medal of Honor for his heroic work rescuing survivors from the conflagration of the battleship *Arizona*. He was promoted to captain, and soon took command of the heavy cruiser *San Francisco*, but within a year he was dead, killed in action at the Battle of Guadalcanal. Posthumously awarded the Navy Cross, he was recognized for his bravery when a new destroyer, commissioned on September 12, 1943, was named the U.S.S. *Cassin Young*. She saw action in the Pacific Theater and, later, the Korean War.

With a crew of 325, she was almost as claustrophobic as the U.S.S. *Constitution*. The ranger-led tours (4–5 daily) are limited to a dozen visitors at a time, but there are plenty of plaques on the main deck to answer most questions. Children want to know about the guns; Navy men are more interested in the engines. She is now stripped back to look as she did in the 1950s, so you have to watch your head going through the hatches: This is no playground for youngsters. Even though the 2,050-ton, Fletcher-Class destroyer was not built in the Charlestown Yard, 14 sister ships were. In service all over the world until 1960, the *Cassin Young* was overhauled six times in Charlestown, and, after decommissioning, has become a permanent memorial both to destroyers and the men who served aboard her. ■

U.S.S. *Cassin Young*

🗺 Map pp. 134–35
✉ Charlestown Navy Yard
☎ 617/242-5601
🚇 T: North Station, Community College, Haymarket Square. Bus: 93
⛴ Pier 4: ferry to Long Wharf

Cambridge may seem like a suburb of Boston to outsiders, yet this home of two of the world's most prestigious universities is an exciting and inspiring city in its own right.

Cambridge

Cambridge is home to Harvard University.

Cambridge

JUST ACROSS THE CHARLES RIVER FROM BOSTON, CAMBRIDGE IS A CITY APART, one that offers a different atmosphere from its big sister. Much of the difference can be credited to the student population of two world-famous universities: Harvard and the Massachusetts Institute of Technology, known far and wide as MIT. But Cambridge also has its own history, to say nothing of its noteworthy museums, grand houses, chic boutiques, and fashionable restaurants. No wonder an old saying goes, "Boston could disappear tomorrow and Cambridge would still go on."

The community radiates from three squares: Kendall in East Cambridge (next to MIT), Central, and Harvard itself. A useful information booth stands by the exit from the T (subway) stop. Here, the Out of Town News kiosk caters to an international readership, with newspapers in many languages. Turn through a 360-degree circle and you will see professors, students, mothers with small children, street entertainers, and folk with pierced bodies and weird hair. Bicycles are a favorite mode of transportation; you see them everywhere, zooming along the streets and locked to parking meters and street signs.

It seems as if the whole world is reflected in Cambridge. As well as the stories of the two universities, explained on student-led tours, both campuses have fine buildings, outdoor sculptures, and many treasures indoors in overlooked museums. Bookstores specializing in the erudite and the

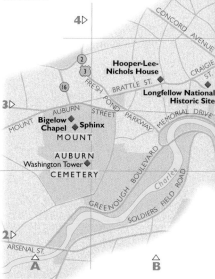

Harvard Square is at the heart of both Cambridge and Harvard University.

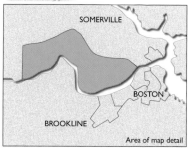

ancient, as well as the latest novels, are often open late. Jazz and folk clubs have an enthusiastic following, as do specialty food stores. Then there is historical Cambridge. The home of Henry Wadsworth Longfellow (1807–1882), for example, also served as the headquarters for George Washington in his role as general of the Continental Army during the Siege of Boston in 1775–1776.

Even back then, Cambridge was a well-established town. Only ten years after the *Mayflower* landed, a group of Puritans had founded Newtowne (1630). For four years, this was the capital of the Commonwealth of Massachusetts. Although the settlers lost the seat of government, they gained a new college. Naming it for its benefactor, John Harvard (1607–1638), they also changed the name Newtowne

Harvard's "Statue of Three Lies" commemorates benefactor John Harvard.

to Cambridge, in honor of Harvard's alma mater, Cambridge University in England. Echoes of those early days remain, with some street signs subtitled with their original names. Mason Street, for example, was Watertown Path back in 1630. ∎

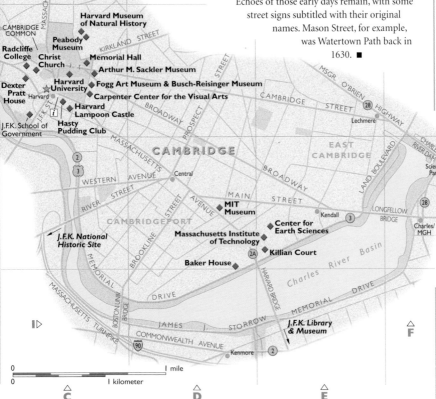

Harvard University

ONE OF THE MOST GLORIOUS SIGHTS IN GREATER BOSTON is of the Charles River and the white towers of Eliot, Dunster, and Lowell Houses standing out against a blue sky. These residence halls are just a few of the buildings on the large campus that dominates the center of Cambridge. The oldest university in the United States includes Harvard and Radcliffe Colleges, as well as ten graduate and professional schools.

Founded in 1636, Harvard is old even by European standards, but the school is respected not just for its age. The roll call of famous alumni includes six presidents of the United States, plus writers such as Henry Wadsworth Longfellow (1807–1882), Henry James (1843–1916), T.S. Eliot (1888–1965), John Updike (born 1932), and Michael Crichton (born 1942), who went on to the Harvard Medical School before penning *Jurassic Park*. Leonard Bernstein (1918–1990), composer and conductor, went to Harvard, as did actors Jack Lemmon (born 1925) and Tommy Lee Jones (born 1946); the latter roomed with former Vice President Al Gore. Over the years, faculty members have amassed some 30 Pulitzer Prizes and 30 Nobel Prizes.

The students, some 18,000 in the undergraduate and graduate schools, come from around the world. Nowadays, the annual tuition plus room and board is about $35,000. Back in the 17th century, fees might be paid with cloth, tools, crops, or even a cow. Although many students did become ministers, Harvard has always been a secular school, unaligned to any particular religious group. The early years saw the founding of principles that have remained at the forefront of the university. In 1650, the Charter set out its goals as "The advancement of all good literature, artes, and Sciences." More surprising was the stated aim to educate not just the English but also "the Indian youth of this country." In 1665, Caleb Cheeshahteaumuck, from the Wampanoag tribe, was the first Native American to graduate.

It is easy to meet a current Harvard student; just sign up for one of the free tours that start at the **Harvard Events & Information Center** in Holyoke Center. But you can also stroll through the quadrangles by yourself. Follow the walking tour (see pp. 148–49) to see the old heart of

Left: Harvard's Memorial Church is typical of the elegant architecture at the campus's core.

the university, but there is much to see elsewhere on this expansive campus. Don't miss **Memorial Hall** on Cambridge Street, a High Gothic building dating from 1874 that looks like a cathedral. Its sober brick walls rise to an explosion of color and pattern on the roof. Built to commemorate the Harvard graduates killed in the Civil War, this was where the British prime minister, Winston Churchill (1874–1965), received an honorary degree in 1943. To the north, on Oxford Street, are the **Peabody Museum** and the **Harvard Museum of Natural History** (see pp. 15657). To the south, on Quincy Street, are the **Harvard University art museums** (see pp. 150–51) and the glass and concrete **Carpenter Center for the Visual Arts** (1963). It is the only work in the United States designed by the Swiss-born French architect, Le Corbusier (1887–1965).

Not surprisingly, Harvard boasts a litany of firsts and oldest in the country. The oldest theatrical association in the country is the **Hasty Pudding Club** on Holyoke Street. Established as an exclusive social club in 1795, it has produced shows since 1844. Six presidents of the United States were members during their Harvard student days, ranging from John Adams in the 18th century to John F. Kennedy in the 20th. Not far away on Mount Auburn Street is the **Harvard Lampoon Castle,** the headquarters of the nation's oldest humor magazine, the *Harvard Lampoon*. Established in 1876, the magazine is published five times each year. One of the earliest schools of higher education for women (see p. 149) was **Radcliffe College.** ■

Graduating Harvard students celebrate on the university's leafy grounds.

Harvard Events & Information Center
www.harvard.edu
🅰 145 C3
✉ Holyoke Center, 1350 Massachusetts Ave.
☎ 617/495-1573
🕐 Closed Sun. Free tours: Mon.–Fri. 10 a.m., 2 p.m., Sat. 2 p.m.
🚇 T: Harvard Square

Old Cambridge walk

Like Boston, Cambridge is best appreciated on foot. In addition to Harvard University, there are reminders of the Revolution and the wealthy Royalists who once lived there. But history here is not confined just to one area. The past coexists happily with the 21st century throughout the city.

Start at the information booth by the MBTA entrance in Harvard Square. Turn and walk along Massachusetts Avenue, past the Cambridge Savings Bank. In front of Au Bon Pain, tables are marked with chessboards. You can watch, or even play, for free. Cross what is always called Mass. Ave. at Holyoke Street, and go through the McKean gate to **Harvard Yard** *(private)*, the original 22-acre (8.9 ha) campus. On your left is the yellow **Wadsworth House;** built in 1727 as the official residence of the heads of the university, when Harvard was already into its eighth president. In July 1775, the house served as General Washington's headquarters for a short time. The path leads to the **Old Yard** ❶, transformed into a park in the 1820s after Harvard President Kirkland cleared out an accumulation of breweries and privies.

Follow the path to **University Hall** ❷, designed by Charles Bulfinch (see pp. 92–93). In front stands the statue titled "John Harvard, Founder, 1638." Its nickname is the Statue of Three Lies, because the college was established in 1636, it was named for, not founded by, John Harvard, and this is not his likeness. As no portrait existed of the 17th-century cleric, 19th-century sculptor Daniel Chester French (1850–1931) used a student as a model.

Walk around University Hall and into **New Yard,** used for graduation ceremonies since 1911 and given the grandiose title Tercentenary Theater on the university's 300th birthday in 1936. The enormous temple on one side is **Widener Library** ❸. Printed in Latin in 1723, the first catalog of Harvard's library listed some 3,500 books. Today, with a million volumes on some 50 miles (80 km) of shelves, only the Library of Congress is bigger. Built in 1914, it commemorates Harry Elkins Widener (class of 1907), a collector of rare books who drowned in the *Titanic* disaster. Opposite the library is **Memorial Church,** or Mem. Church. Built in 1932 to honor the

Memorial Church rises high above the heart of the university.

Harvard men who served in World War I, it also commemorates those who fought in subsequent conflicts in the 20th century. On the west side, note the stone to the right of the front doors. It is from the church in London where John Harvard was baptized in 1607.

Return to the Old Yard and walk west, toward Johnston Gate. The wrought ironwork is only a century old, but the gate was the original entrance to the university. On the left is **Massachusetts Hall.** Dating from 1720, this is the oldest building on campus. In 1775, it housed Washington's troops. Today freshmen still live on the upper floors, above the offices of the president of the university.

Exit through the gate and cross Peabody Street, then Massachusetts Avenue. The **First Church in Cambridge (Unitarian Universalist)** ❹ *(3 Church St., tel 617/876-7772)* is on the left. Although the building dates from 1833, the long list of ministers

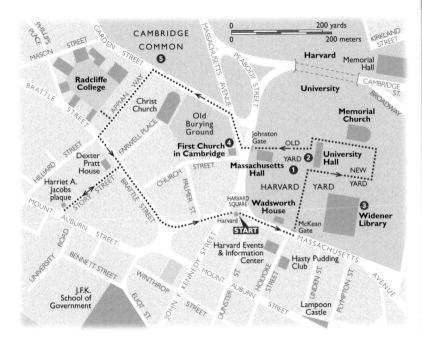

dates back to the 1630s. It was here, at the Harvard graduation of 1837, that Ralph Waldo Emerson (1803–1882) delivered his famous "American Scholar" speech, dubbed by Oliver Wendell Holmes (1809–1894) as "America's Intellectual Declaration of Independence."

Walk along Massachusetts Avenue, veering left onto Garden Street. Now a quarter of its original size, **Cambridge Common** ⑤ was used, like all town greens, for grazing livestock, public meetings, and training militia. On the south side, at the intersection of Garden Street and Appian Way, is a bronze plaque recalling the Washington Elm, the tree where, in 1775, George Washington formally took command of the Continental Army.

Turn left on Appian Way. The entrance to Radcliffe Yard is on the right. Founded in 1879, **Radcliffe College** catered to women students, who were taught separately by Harvard professors until classes were merged in 1943. However, it took another 20 years before "Cliffies" became official members of Harvard University.

Follow Appian Way to **Brattle Street,** turn left, and walk to Story Street. Walk down Story Street, and at the far end, on the corner of Mount Auburn Street, you will find a

🅜	Map p. 145
►	Harvard Square
🅒	1.16 miles (1.85 km)
🅒	1 hour
►	Harvard Square

NOT TO BE MISSED
- Harvard Yard
- Massachusetts Hall
- Cambridge Common

plaque honoring Harriet A. Jacobs (circa 1813–1897), "abolitionist, author and women's rights advocate." Born into slavery in North Carolina, she escaped in 1835, fled to New York, and was freed in 1852. She lived in a house on this site, and her book, *Incidents in the Life of a Slave, Written by Herself,* was published in 1861. Return to Brattle Street, and follow it back to Harvard Square. At the intersection of Brattle and John F. Kennedy Streets the lettering in an upstairs window advertises the law firm of Dewey, Cheetham & Howe. It's a joke! Pronounced "Do we cheat 'em—and how!", it signposts the offices of Tom and Ray Magliozzi, hosts of NPR's *Car Talk* program. ∎

Harvard University Art Museums

Harvard University Art Museums
www.artmuseums.harvard.edu

145 C3

Fogg & Busch-Reisinger: 32 Quincy St., Sackler: 485 Broadway

617/495-9400

Closed Sun. a.m.

$$. Free to those under the age of 18. Sat. 10–noon & Wed.

T: Harvard

TAKEN TOGETHER, HARVARD'S THREE ART MUSEUMS ARE world-class. Forget about the university connection: Any city would be proud to claim these collections. Between them, the museums offer students—and visitors—a detailed examination of the art of Western Europe and Asia.

The oldest and most popular of these three museums is the **Fogg Art Museum,** which specializes in the art of Italy, Great Britain, and France from medieval times to the present day. The nearby **Busch-Reisinger Museum** focuses on German and Northern European art, whereas the galleries at the **Arthur M. Sackler Museum** showcase ancient Asian, Islamic, and Later Indian art. Luckily these so-called study collections are also open to the public. One ticket is good for all three museums, if it is used within a single day. As there are informative guided one-hour tours of all three museums, starting at 11 a.m. (Fogg), 1 p.m. (Busch-Reisinger), and 2 p.m. (Sackler), it is possible to have a swift, but informed, overview of each. There should also be time for a short break for lunch.

Claude Monet's "Red Boats, Argenteuil" (1875) hangs in the Fogg Art Museum.

Left: Galleries surround the Fogg's Italian Renaissance courtyard, based on a 16th-century facade in Montepulciano, Italy.

FOGG ART MUSEUM

Early benefactors dubbed the Fogg a "laboratory for the Fine Arts." The mock 15th-century, Italian palazzo courtyard sets the mood. In the **Warburg Hall,** with its high, beamed ceilings, the theme is "Investigating the Renaissance." Every docent has his or her specialty, so no tour is the same. In an age when few could read, painters used symbols. A skull represented the temporality of life; the Tree of Life, salvation; and the pelican with its bleeding breast, Christ's sacrifice. All three appear in "Christ on the Cross between the Virgin and Cardinal Torquemada and Saint John the Evangelist," a work completed in 1451 by Fra Angelico (1387–1455).

Of course, there is no need to wait for a tour. Many visitors head straight for the **Maurice Wertheim collection,** boasting works by many famous names from both the Impressionist and Postimpressionist periods. Here, paintings by Dufy, Gauguin, Matisse, Monet, Seurat, and van Gogh are juxtaposed to demonstrate how much they influenced one another. Classics include two Monets: "Gare Saint-Lazare, Arrival of a Train" (1877), with its clouds of sooty smoke, and "Red Boats, Argenteuil" (1875), deep in the country, with the smoke of Paris in the distance. All the great names of the art world are represented here, from Europeans such as Picasso in 1901 to giants of American art, such as Jackson Pollock.

An exciting bonus is available, 2–4:45 p.m., Monday to Thursday, in the study rooms at the **Agnes Mongan Center.** You can ask to see examples from the fabulous collection of works on paper, such as sketches, drawings, and photographs. The curators will bring out whatever you request. Just ask for their "greatest hits"; they'll understand what you mean. Out

will come sketches by Ingres and John Singer Sargent, or perhaps watercolors by Winslow Homer, set up on an easel for you. You might see "Key West" (1903) or "Sailboat and Fourth of July Fireworks" (1880), painted when Homer was living in the lighthouse on Ten Pound Island in Gloucester Harbor.

BUSCH-REISINGER MUSEUM

The Busch-Reisinger claims to be the "only museum of its kind in the Western Hemisphere." The collection has an unusual focus: Central and Northern European art, particularly German expressionism, Vienna secession art, and design examples from the Bauhaus school. Much smaller than the adjacent Fogg Museum, the Busch-Reisinger has white walls and a plain wood floor. You start at the "Turn of the (20th) Century," move on to "Early Expressionism" and the Bauhaus, then go on to "Realist Art," and the 1930s and 1940s.

If you have just walked in from the Fogg and its Impressionist paintings, the contrasts are stark. Max Beckmann (1884–1950) painted quite savagely. His "Self-Portrait in Tuxedo" (1927) once hung in the National Gallery in Berlin, but was deemed degenerate and removed. In 1941 it was the first modern work purchased for the collection that was to become the Busch-Reisinger Museum. Beckmann fled Germany in 1937 and spent the war hiding in the Netherlands from the Nazis. The gallery devoted to the Bauhaus is small, but features the archives of the movement's director (and later Harvard professor) Walter Gropius (see p. 180). The movement aimed to bridge the gap between fine and applied arts, while embracing new technology and celebrating craftsmanship. A steel-and-canvas chair by Marcel Breuer (also at Harvard) is now a classic. As at the Fogg, works on paper can be viewed Tuesday to Friday afternoons.

Paul Klee painted "Hot Pursuit" in 1939; you'll find it in the Fogg Art Museum.

This T'ang dynasty prancing horse, now in the Sackler Museum, once decorated a Chinese tomb.

SACKLER MUSEUM

The contrast between the exterior and interior of the Arthur M. Sackler Museum could not be greater. The building was designed by contemporary British architect James Stirling, and the collection ranges from ancient Chinese, Korean, and Islamic treasures to Roman and Greek classics. A tour is recommended, particularly if you are not familiar with Asian art. If you are viewing the museum on your own, start at the top of the building, where you will find ancient Chinese jades, bronzes, and ceramics. Experts rate the collection of jades as second only to that in Beijing in quality and importance. Among the bronze *guangs* (or pouring vessels) from the Shang Dynasty in China is one decorated with the face of a tiger that is thought to be 3,300 years old. The highlight of the collection of Buddhist stone sculptures is the delicately decorated "Kneeling Attendant Bodhisattva." It was found in the Caves of the Thousand Buddhas in Gansu Province in China, and dates back to the seventh century.

Continue down through Japanese, Thai, and Cambodian art, with their stunning ceramics and religious figures, and into the ancient Greek and Roman galleries. As well as a selection of familiar-looking vessels, decorated with terra-cotta figures (340–500 B.C.), you can see a Roman copy of a fourth-century-B.C. Greek statue. A fine example of a classical Greek hero, the figure is lit up at night and is clearly visible to passersby on Broadway, the street outside.

In the **Egyptian gallery,** look for the "Portrait of a Woman with Earrings," a mummy painting dating from about A.D. 130–150. If you saw her in an Egyptian bazaar tomorrow, wearing those clothes and earrings, you would recognize her immediately. It is as realistic as any photograph of a modern Egyptian woman. ■

The Kennedy connection

Forever associated with Boston is John Fitzgerald Kennedy, the 35th President of the United States (President 1961–1963). The Kennedy clan is a political dynasty stretching back to Boston mayor John F. Fitzgerald, nicknamed Honey Fitz. His daughter, Rose, married the son of an Irish immigrant and gave birth to John F. Kennedy on May 29, 1917. Echoes of J.F.K are everywhere in Boston and Cambridge: J.F.K. Street, J.F.K. Park, J.F.K. School of Government, and even a J.F.K. stop on the T.

He lived the first four years of his life in a house in Brookline, now the John F. Kennedy National Historic Site *(83 Beals St., tel 617/566-7937, closed Mon.–Tues. & all winter, $).* Shown by guided tour only, the house holds some furniture that the Kennedys owned between 1914 and 1921, such as the piano, Oriental rug and a gate leg table in the living room. One of J.F.K.'s favorite books, *King Arthur's Knights,* lies on a chair upstairs—prescient, perhaps, of his so-called Camelot administration.

Kennedy attended Harvard University, graduating *cum laude* in 1940. In his senior honors thesis he constructed an analysis of the political situation in Great Britain and Europe in the years leading up to World War II; this was the basis for his popular book *Why England Slept.* He commanded a PT boat during World War II, and won the Purple Heart for bravery. In politics, he progressed from democratic congressman for Massachusetts to senator (1952), running for president in 1960. He was the first Roman Catholic and the youngest man ever to hold the post. He was assassinated on November 22, 1963.

For anyone under 50 who cannot comprehend the sense of hope that J.F.K. aroused, both at home and abroad, a visit to the John F.

John F. Kennedy, member of the Boston-bred political dynasty

Kennedy Library and Museum *(Columbia Point, tel 617/929-4500, $$),* south of the city on Columbia Point, is illuminating. Overlooking the water, the building, designed by I.M. Pei (born 1917), is arresting in itself.

Inside, the museum examines the President's three years in office. Before you set off on the tour, which is chronologically arranged, stop to watch the short film recording of his early life. The sights and sounds of the Los Angeles Convention Hall, where he won the Democratic nomination for President in 1960, put you back in that era. Every step of the campaign, including the first-ever television debate (with Richard Nixon), is covered. Once the President is in office, you are "in" the White House, walking along a corridor, sitting in on a press conference, and looking at a re-creation of his oval office desk. There is a selection of video clips highlighting some of the major moments in Kennedy's brief administration, including his famous speech in Berlin, the founding of the Peace Corps, the Cuban Missile Crisis, the Space Race, and civil rights legislation.

The role of the First Lady is not forgotten. Not only do you see Jacqueline Bouvier Kennedy's 1962 television tour of the White House, even the red dress that she was wearing at the time is on display. The lasting memory is of contrast: the chill of a near-forgotten Cold War rivaling the optimism of those swinging sixties.

Admission to both attractions is included in "J.F.K.'s Boston," a 3.5-hour themed trolley tour, with a guide on board. *(Old Town Trolley Tours, tel 617/269-7150, $$$).* ■

I. M. Pei's spectacular design for the John F. Kennedy Library and Museum is on the south side of the museum.

Harvard Museum of Natural History

Harvard Museum of Natural History

www.hmnh.harvard.edu

145 C3

26 Oxford St.

617/495-3045

$$. Free Sat. a.m.

T: Harvard

A THREE-IN-ONE MUSEUM, WITH GALLERIES DEDICATED to botany, zoology, and mineralogy, this still looks like the research facility it sets out to be. Don't expect computer screens and high-tech gadgetry. This is the way museums used to be, with carefully labeled specimens in glass cases. You can almost hear a professor exhorting you to compare and contrast. In fact, the displays are so old-fashioned, they should have a preservation order on them!

Thousands come to see just one exhibit: the famous blown-glass flowers in the **Botanical Galleries.** Officially called the **Ware Collection of Blaschka Glass Models of Plants,** what you see is a far cry from the glass trinkets sold in gift stores. These are life-size, botanically correct copies of flowers, designed to replace the drawings, prints, and dried cuttings previously studied by botanists. A strawberry plant, for example, has perfectly formed stems, leaves, and roots, plus healthy as well as moldy fruit. It is hard to believe they are made of glass. An exhibition, "Modeling Nature," explains how these surprisingly realistic specimens were made by craftsmen Leopold Blaschka and his son, Rudolph, between 1886 and 1937. In all, the Blaschkas created some 3,000 models in 830 species. Look at the display of simple tools from their workshop near Dresden, Germany, then go back to the flowers: from the minute hairs, "much magnified," on the stem of a lady's-slipper to a banana leaf nearly two

The Harvard Museum of Natural History is a resource for local schoolchildren as well as college students.

feet long (0.75 m), the precision of their work is astonishing.

From the glass flowers, move into the **Zoological Galleries,** with their mounted specimens. The **Thayer Hall of North American Birds** is like a three-dimensional *Fielding's Guide,* with everything from a tiny hummingbird to a California condor. In a lineup of skeletons, contrast the bones of a gibbon, an orangutan, and a man. Look for the head of the Triceratops, which is called a "type specimen," since it was the first documented, and the one against which all others are compared. And, for the trivia fans, there are the (mounted) golden pheasants given to George Washington by the French General Lafayette back in 1786. Despite recent renovation and improved lighting, the **Mineralogical Galleries** are really for the specialist. But it is fun to learn about your birthstone and touch a meteorite.

The **Peabody Museum** has two entrances: on floor 3 of the Museum of Natural History, through the Mineralogical Galleries, or directly from Divinity Avenue. Founded in 1866, with a bequest from George Peabody (who also funded the Peabody Essex Museum in Salem, see p. 186), this museum was one of the world's first devoted to anthropology and ethnology. Again, most rooms lack popular appeal, although the revamped galleries on Floor 1 are more user-friendly. Here, a color coding system, which corresponds with the map of the museum, helps you find your way around the **Hall of the North American Indian.** The displays deal with culture shock, showing how the Native Americans reacted to the arrival of Europeans, absorbing design and fashion ideas, then translating them into clothes, blankets, and baskets.

A glass iris from the Ware Collection of Blaschka Glass Models of Plants

One example is a deerskin coat. The style may be 1780s European, but the decoration is Native American. Each tribe had a specialty: A dress from the Oglala Teton Sioux is decorated with shells.

Spend some time in the **Portrait Gallery of Southeast Indian Chiefs,** a roll call of Seminole, Cherokee, and Creek leaders whose proud faces and Western clothes belie the Hollywood stereotypes. The most dramatic exhibits are the grand totem poles from the Northwest, showing the transition from tree to finished pole. Both the Pacific Islands Hall and the Encounters with the Americas Hall reflect further interaction between European colonists and native tribes. Undeniably interesting, both demand more time and background knowledge than many visitors have. ∎

Brattle Street

WITH ITS LARGE, OLD HOUSES, BRATTLE STREET HAS LONG been an expensive place to live. Back in the 1700s, it was an enclave of seven mansions owned by wealthy families, all related by marriage. Their loyalist sympathies sparked the nickname Tory Row.

The Longfellow National Historic Site memorializes this beloved 19th-century author.

Longfellow National Historic Site

www.nps.gov/long

- 144 B3
- 105 Brattle St.
- 617/876-4491
- Call for hours
- Call for details
- T: Harvard

The pathway between Christ Church and the cemetery brings you to Farwell Place, which leads to Brattle Street. Directly opposite, at No. 54, is the **Dexter Pratt House,** home of the "Village Blacksmith" of Longfellow's poem. The "spreading chestnut tree" is long gone, but beside the house the sculpture of a wrought-iron tree, plus hammer and tools, recalls Pratt, smithy and friend of the poet.

The most famous is No. 105, the handsome, yellow **Longfellow National Historic Site.** Few houses in the United States can claim a history to match this one. First, it was Washington's command headquarters in 1775; here he and his senior officers met to plan the early campaigns of the Revolution. In the 19th century, it was the home of Henry Wadsworth Longfellow (1807–1882), the best-loved American poet of his age. He lived here for 45 years, but even after his death, the house remained in the family, and is still furnished with Longfellow paintings, books, and memorabilia. On the ranger-led tours, you get a real sense of the man behind the poet: a devoted husband, father, and friend to some of the greatest literary and philosophical minds of the day. Charles Dickens (1812–1870) breakfasted with him in the dining room.

Currently closed for extensive renovations, the house should reopen in 2002. Highlights of the tour include the dining room, with its portraits of Longfellow's wife, Fanny, and their daughters. You see them as they were described in the poem, "The Children's Hour:" "grave Alice and laughing Allegra and Edith with golden hair." The study, however, is where you feel

Longfellow's presence most. If you look at the photograph of him in this room you will see that nothing much has changed. He wrote his most famous poems at the folding desk, and the wood for the big, ornately carved chair that he sat in came from the chestnut tree by the Dexter Pratt house, which was felled to widen the road. Some 70 years earlier, this room served as the office of George Washington. ■

Henry Wadsworth Longfellow and his wife, Frances Appleton Longfellow, with their sons, Charles and Ernest (circa 1849)

Henry Wadsworth Longfellow

The author of *The Courtship of Miles Standish* and *Paul Revere's Ride* was a megastar whose most popular works celebrated American themes. The royalties from *The Song of Hiawatha* alone paid for newfangled indoor plumbing. Much-read in Britain, Longfellow (1807–1882) was a favorite of Queen Victoria and was the first American to be commemorated at Poets' Corner in Westminster Abbey.

Longfellow grew up in Portland, Maine, and graduated from Bowdoin College. In 1835 he became professor of modern languages at Harvard. A frequent traveler to Europe, he spoke eight languages and read 12. Little is known of his first wife, May, who died in Rotterdam after a miscarriage. Longfellow and his second wife, Fanny, were a devoted couple. Tragically, in 1861, her dress caught fire and she died the next day. Longfellow was burned when he tried to smother the flames, so he grew a beard to cover the scars. ■

Christ Church

JUST OPPOSITE CAMBRIDGE COMMON, CHRIST CHURCH dates from 1759. Like King's Chapel in Boston (see pp. 60–61), it was designed by Peter Harrison of Newport. Both were Anglican churches, and therefore the focus of patriot anger in the 1770s. In the vestibule you can see a bullet hole to the right of the door.

One of the oldest churches in the Boston area, Christ Church still holds services.

Christ Church
- 145 C3
- Zero Garden St.
- 617/876-0200
- Closed Sat. p.m.
- T: Harvard

Legend has it that the British were responsible; in fact, it was probably the Colonists, who stormed the church during the funeral of a British soldier in 1778. This was one of only two services held here between 1774 and 1790. The other was on New Year's Eve, 1775, during the Siege of Boston. Find pew 93, on the left; Gen. George Washington sat here with his wife, Martha. Adjacent to Christ Church is the **Old Burying Ground.** Despite being on Massachusetts Avenue, this is a peaceful spot, with the graves of educators, ministers, merchants, and farmers. Here lies the first president of Harvard, John Dunster (1610–1659), as well as some of his successors, such as John Leverett (died 1724), Benjamin Wadsworth (died 1737), and Edward Holyoke (died 1769). All have university buildings named after them. Also buried here is Stephen Day (died 1668), whose printing business in Cambridge, opened in 1639, was the first in the English-speaking colonies. Graves in this cemetery are hard to find. Relatively easy to spot is that of Washington Allston (1779–1843), a poet and painter well known for his romantic landscapes. ∎

Hooper/Lee/Nichols House

IF YOUR APPETITE FOR LOCAL HISTORY HAS BEEN WHETTED, walk on from Longfellow's house. Fifteen minutes down Brattle Street is the Hooper/Lee/Nichols House, the second oldest house in Cambridge (it dates from the late 17th century) and the current headquarters of the Cambridge Historical Society.

Although almost a century older than Longfellow's home, the Hooper/Lee/Nichols House is something of a time capsule. Since each owner left a mark on this building, you can see the evolution of tastes and styles in architecture and interior decoration over some 300 years.

Knowledgeable guides show visitors through the house. First, you see the series of wooden models that show how the house developed over the centuries, from the plain 1688 home to the fashionable, remodeled Georgian style in the 1740s. An extra floor and large new windows were added. A century later, scenic wallpapers were the latest fashion, with dramatic mural-like scenes: the Straits of Bosphorus for the west parlor, the Bay of Naples upstairs. What brings the house to life, however, is the diary of 11-year-old John Nichols. Ask the guide to read some of his entries describing everyday life in the 1860s. He recorded the weather, the activities of the family, even noting how many eggs he collected. Suddenly, you can see Cambridge as it was back then: a small, rural community on the banks of the Charles River. ∎

The composite of styles in the Hooper/Lee/Nichols House records Boston's architectural evolution.

Hooper/Lee/Nichols House

- 144 B3
- 159 Brattle St.
- 617/547-4252
- Open Tues. & Thurs. p.m.
- $$
- T: Harvard

Mount Auburn Cemetery

BOSTON AND ITS CITIZENS HAVE BEEN INNOVATIVE IN MANY
fields, from politics and science to literature and even cemeteries. A
deliberate break with the tradition of cramped burying grounds, with
headstones carved with skulls, is Mount Auburn Cemetery, right on
the Cambridge–Watertown border. Just as the Granary Burying
Ground (see p. 90) has graves of heroes from the Revolutionary era,
so Mount Auburn Cemetery is full of memorials to the famous names
of the 19th century.

Founded in 1831 by the amateur
enthusiast members of the fledgling
Massachusetts Horticultural
Society, it was the first "garden" or
"rural" cemetery designed as a place
of beauty, comfort, and peace. The
idea caught on and was copied
across the nation.

The 174-acre (70 ha) site was
chosen for its scenic hills and dales.
The highest rises some 125 feet (38
m) above the Charles River and is
topped by the **Washington
Tower** (1850s). From here, the
river basin spreads out below, with
easy-to-spot landmarks ranging
from the Bunker Hill Monument
and glistening dome of the State
House to the John Hancock and
Prudential towers. Among the best-
known monuments is the **Sphinx,**
near the main entrance, the Mount
Auburn Street gate. A classical symbol, this statue was a post-Civil War
commemoration of the fight to end
slavery and to preserve the Union.
A few steps away from this sculpture stands the **Bigelow Chapel**
(1850s), with stained-glass windows from Scotland.

The first burial was of a stillborn
child, back in 1832. Since then,
influential Bostonians, such as
Henry Wadsworth Longfellow (see
p. 159) and his friend, writer Oliver
Wendell Holmes (1809–1894), have
been interred here. Art collector
Isabella Stewart Gardner (see pp.
124–27) and architect Charles
Bulfinch (see pp. 92–93), freed slave

Harriet A. Jacobs (see p. 149), and
"Battle Hymn of the Republic"
author, Julia Ward Howe (1819–
1910), are names to recognize.
Then there is Charles Dana Gibson
(1867–1944), of "Gibson Girl"
fame, and Fannie Merritt Farmer
(1857–1915), author of the 1896
Boston Cooking-School Cook Book.

Among the 5,000 trees are some
20 "champions," the largest of their
kind either in Massachusetts or
New England. In spring, look for
the 38-foot-tall (11.5 m) flowering
dogwood, spectacular when in full
bloom. In the fall, the branches of
the threadleaf Japanese maple are a
feathery cascade of yellow and red.
Birds thrive. A chalkboard near the
Mount Auburn Street gate lists the
daily wildlife sightings and locations. During the migratory season,
you may be lucky enough to see
red-tail hawks, dark-eyed juncos,
and yellow-bellied sapsuckers.

Stop at the office for an array of
leaflets on the birdlife, trees, flowering plants, and the best-known
graves and memorials. You can join
a guided walk given by the Friends
of Mount Auburn. They host 35
walks a year, each one honoring a
different personality, on whose
birthday a pilgrimage walk leaves
the Entrance Gate at 2 p.m.; other
walks focus on birds, horticulture,
or history. The friends also sell an
audiotape (*$$*), an hour-long guide
to the 10 miles (16 km) of roads
that wind around three lakes. ∎

**Mount Auburn
Cemetery**

🗺 144 A3

✉ 580 Mount Auburn
St.

☎ 617/547-7105

🚇 T: Harvard, then bus
71 or 73

**At Mount Auburn
Cemetery, his-
toric memorials
and headstones
are set among
spectacular
landscaping.**

Modern buildings and sculptures dominate the MIT campus.

Massachusetts Institute of Technology

THE "OTHER"—OR "PRINCIPAL," DEPENDING ON YOUR POINT of view—seat of higher learning in Cambridge is the Massachusetts Institute of Technology, always referred to as MIT. Unlike many college rivalries in the United States, the competition between MIT and its neighbor, Harvard, is not fought on the football field but in the laboratory. These two private schools are both world leaders in innovation. MIT's 1,000 professors are at the top of their fields; more than 4,000 MIT alumni are professors at universities and colleges around the world.

MIT
- 145 E2
- Information Center, Building 7–121, 77 Massachusetts Ave.
- 617/253-4795
- T: Kendall/MIT

Cambridge has more faces than you might expect. Contrasting with the leafy quadrangles of Harvard University and the old houses of historic Brattle Street are gritty commercial areas that are the legacy of industrialization that occurred in the second half of the 19th century. South of Central Square is Cambridgeport; East Cambridge is just across the Charles River from downtown. MIT lies between these two areas, and its campus rambles along the Charles River for about a mile (1.6 km), from the Longfellow Bridge to just short of the Boston University Bridge. Ironically, **Harvard Bridge** leads straight to the heart of this university. Whereas Harvard is all romantic old brick and ivy, MIT is modern, angular, glass, concrete, and steel. If you have time, take one of the 75-minute, student-led tours *(from the Information Center, weekdays 10 a.m., 2 p.m.)*. Otherwise you can collect a free pamphlet and set off on your own.

The heart of the campus is **Killian Court,** with its imposing Great Dome. The great names of the science world are carved on the walls: da Vinci, Faraday, Newton, and Darwin. Architecturally significant buildings on campus include **Baker House,** a dormitory designed by Finnish architect Alvar Aalto (1898–1976). Dedicated in 1949, each room was designed individually with a different view from each window. Another noted 20th-century architect and MIT graduate (1940), I.M. Pei, has designed three buildings, including the **Green Building,** which houses the Center for Earth Sciences.

Often perceived as a school for "techies," MIT also incorporates a lively visual arts faculty, and its campus boasts outstanding contemporary sculpture, including works by Henry Moore and Pablo Picasso. Alexander Calder's "La Grande Voile" (The Big Sail, 1965), which has become an emblem of the school, stands between the Green Building and the Charles River. But above all, it is MIT's advances in science that impress, from computer science and astronautics to brain and cognitive sciences, and even ocean engineering. The courses are a far cry from the straightforward civil engineering, architecture, and pre-med classes offered when the school was founded in Back Bay in 1861. ■

The Memorial Wall at MIT's Roger's Hall

Cambridge, the mother of inventions

Cambridge has a long association with technology and invention. Famously, a 1970s undergraduate named Bill Gates took time off from Harvard and set up a company called Microsoft. In 1972, Ray Tomlinson, a computer engineer at BB&N (Bolt, Beranek and Newman) devised the simple e-mail address system we all use today: john@mycompany.com. But the annals of computer development show that MIT was working on a computer back in 1928, and that the "Harvard Mark I," using a clock for synchronization and a register to store information, was the world's first fully automated calculator (1944). World War II also saw scientists at MIT's Rad Lab (Radiation Laboratory) working on microwaves, later applied to ovens and police speed guns. In 1948 the first Polaroid cameras went on sale for $89.75. The inspiration for inventor Dr. Edwin Land (born 1909) of MIT was his three-year-old daughter's demand to see a photograph as soon it was taken. Then there is U.S. patent no. 638,920, awarded to Boston's George Grant in 1899. It is for the smallest but most important part of a golfer's gear: the tee. ■

MIT Museum

NOT FAR FROM CENTRAL SQUARE, THE MIT MUSEUM IS small, fun, and a must for parents of scientifically oriented youngsters. But technologically challenged adults will also find much here that is intriguing. In 2001, a bright new facade gave a much-needed facelift to the old, industrial-looking building.

MIT Museum

- 145 D2
- 2nd Floor, 265 Massachusetts Ave.
- 617/253-5927
- Closed Sat. & Sun. a.m. & all Sun.
- $$
- T: Central

The first of the permanent exhibitions is devoted to holography. Used in everything from credit cards to architectural models, holography has even enabled archaeologists to create an image of Lindow Man, buried in a peat bog in England for some 23 centuries. What most visitors remember, however, is *Kiss I* (1973). As you pass by, one Pamela Brazier winks and blows you a kiss. Then there are kinetic sculptures by Arthur

"Milkdrop Coronet" (1957), by Harold E. Edgerton

Ganson. Push a button and his "Machine with Oil" (1990) weaves its hypnotic spell. In an example of continuous movement, a bucket scoops into a tray of black oil, rises, tips it out, and scoops again....

Harold Edgerton's strobe-light photographs capture a millisecond of time, from a crown of splashing milk to a bullet tearing through an apple. These beautiful photos also illustrate principles of physics. His experiments with night photography were important in the Normandy landings of World War II.

Thinkapalooza is an interactive zone, full of high-tech fun. Ever played a game where you roll a marble through an obstacle course of holes? In the "Metafield Maze," you are the marble, finding your way through a virtual maze. You can create music and learn to think like an inventor. "Robots and Beyond: Exploring Artificial Intelligence at MIT," examines the possibilities and the limitations of developments in robot technology.

The most fun exhibit of all is the **Hall of Hacks.** A hack is slang for prank, and MIT's students have produced some of the best. Secrecy and surprise are the hallmarks of their elaborate, clever, and technologically based feats. Here you learn about various pranks: Over the years, the Great Dome, 150 feet (45 m) high and 108 feet (33 m) across, has been turned into a Halloween pumpkin, and topped by a snowman in the middle of summer. In 1982 a telephone booth appeared up there. When police climbed up to investigate, the phone began to ring. During the 1982 Harvard–Yale football game, a weather balloon suddenly emerged from under the ground. As it inflated in front of the fans, the letters MIT appeared on the balloon before it burst in a shower of talcum powder. The following day, the headline in a local paper said it all: "MIT Wins the Harvard-Yale Football Game." ∎

Just outside Boston, Concord was the scene of both political and literary revolution. Neighboring Lexington played a famous role in the birth of the nation in 1775, while Lowell and Lincoln featured in the industrial revolution.

West & northwest of Boston

Revolutionary reenactor in Lexington on Patriots' Day

West & northwest of Boston

LEXINGTON AND CONCORD: FOR OVER TWO CENTURIES, THE NAMES HAVE been linked inextricably, thanks to the events of April 18–19, 1775. Few crucial moments in history have been better chronicled than the start of the American Revolution. Although contemporary eyewitnesses from both sides recorded every incident, it is the account related in *Paul Revere's Ride,* Henry Wadsworth Longfellow's romanticized version, that is most often quoted. To discover what really happened, drive west from Boston, first to Lexington and then on to Concord.

Both towns have museums and historic houses open to the public. Lexington is the closer to Boston and has the more suburban flavor; Concord still has the look of a traditional New England community. Linking the two is Minute Man National Historical Park, with its excellent Battle Road Visitor Center. The two towns come into their own on Patriots' Day (April 19) each year, when their residents dress up in colonial uniforms, pick up their (unloaded) muskets, and reenact the deeds of their forefathers.

Concord has a second claim to fame, as an influential literary and philosophical colony. In the middle of the 19th century, significant names in American literature, such as Ralph Waldo Emerson, Henry David Thoreau, Nathaniel Hawthorne, and Louisa May Alcott, lived, met, and talked in Concord. Their legacy also demands to be explored.

The contrast between genteel Concord and gritty Lowell, to the north, could not be more extreme. Standing on the Merrimack River, Lowell was part of another revolution, the American industrial revolution, with massive mills producing endless rolls of cloth. Lowell National Historical Park pays tribute to this heritage. Be sure to see the Boott Cotton Mills Museum, with its working looms, and also the American Textile

The textile industry was vital in the development of the Boston area economy.

History Museum just a few blocks away. Art and architecture fans head south from Concord to Lincoln to see the DeCordova Museum and the home of Bauhaus founder Walter Gropius, who was one of the most influential architects of the 20th century. ■

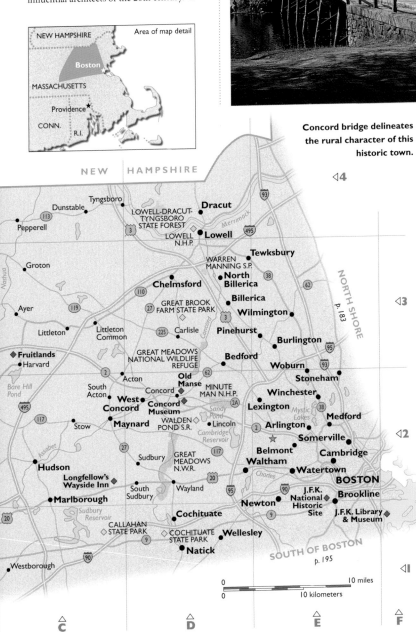

Concord bridge delineates the rural character of this historic town.

The best place to be on Patriots' Day is at the North Bridge in Concord.

Lexington & Minute Man National Historical Park

VISITORS FROM AROUND THE WORLD TROOP TO Lexington to see where it all began. Their destination has evolved into a prosperous commuting suburb of Boston, but a number of well-preserved sites evoke the events of 1775. Minute Man National Historical Park, stretching from Lexington to Concord along the route of the fighting, provides insight into that turbulent period.

Minute Man National Historical Park

www.nps.gov.mima

169 D2

Lexington

✉ Battle Road Visitor Center, Mass. 2A, W of Lexington

☎ 781/862-7753

Concord

✉ North Bridge Visitor Center, 174 Liberty St., Concord

☎ 978/369-6993

The most important sight in Lexington is the triangular **Battle Green,** where the first encounter between British troops and the Colonists took place. Here, the much-photographed statue of Capt. John Parker, leader of the local militia, stares down Massachusetts Avenue, waiting for the redcoats. When the 700 troops arrived, Parker and his 77 men were lined up on the green. No one knows who fired the first shot, but when the smoke lifted, eight Colonists lay dead. They are buried behind the Revolutionary War Monument, on the Massachusetts Avenue side of the green.

Many visitors go straight on from here to Concord, but if you want to immerse yourself fully in the events of April 19, there are a number of other small sites to visit in Lexington before you move on. Just off Battle Green is the **Buckman Tavern** *(Bedford Rd., tel 781/862-5598, closed Dec.–Feb.),* where some of the Minutemen waited for the British troops. Nearby is the Hancock-Clarke House (see p. 172); 2 miles (3 km) east, on Massachusetts Avenue toward Cambridge, are the Munroe Tavern (see p. 172) and the **Museum of Our National Heritage** (see p. 172).

MINUTE MAN NATIONAL HISTORICAL PARK

Minute Man National Historical Park covers the majority of the route between Battle Green in Lexington and the North Bridge in Concord. The long park encompasses stone-walled meadows that look much as they did 200 years ago and sites such as the Paul Revere Capture Site and Meriam's Corner (see p. 173 for both).

Do not miss the **Battle Road Visitor Center.** In this modern lodge, the main attraction is the multimedia show *The Road to Revolution,* shown every half hour throughout the day. This transports you back to 1775 and makes you feel part of the momentous events. Both British and Colonial viewpoints are presented fairly, and you learn what happened where, when, and why on April 19. There is also an exhibition, "Prelude to Battle," with a diorama of the Siege of Boston, which started in June 1775.

Take time to walk or cycle the **Battle Road Interpretive Trail,** a path connecting many sites in the park. It starts east of the visitor center and ends at Meriam's Corner. It can be accessed from several parking lots along its 5.5-mile (9 km) length.

Right: Capt. John Parker, leader of the local militia, inspired the familiar "Minute Man" statue on Lexington Green.

"Whoever dares to look upon them as an irregular mob, will find himself very much mistaken. They have men among them who know very well what they are about."
—Hugh, Earl Percy, British general, 1775 ■

The National Park sites in Concord include the Wayside (see p. 175) and **North Bridge.** Rangers are stationed here from May to the end of October, and are ready to explain that the wooden span you see is only 45 years old and that the "Minute Man" statue by Daniel Chester French dates from 1875, the centennial of the day when "the embattled farmers stood / And fired the shot heard round the world." ■

Revere was not alone

Henry Wadsworth Longfellow (1807–1882) has a lot to answer for. His poem, *Paul Revere's Ride,* has a driving rhythm, but takes considerable poetic license. To begin with, Revere was not in Charlestown waiting for the "signal light." He knew that the British were going "by sea"; the lantern was to alert others, in case he was captured. There was also a second messenger, William Dawes, who set out from Boston on the longer land route along Boston Neck. Both reached Lexington and then continued to Concord together. Stopped by a British patrol, Revere was captured; Dawes escaped, but did not reach Concord. The man who did was Dr. Samuel Prescott, who had joined the duo in Lexington. So why did Revere get all the credit? Some say Longfellow was friendly with his descendants; others reckon that Revere is just easier to rhyme than Dawes or Prescott. ■

Driving the Revolutionary trail

Follow this route from Lexington to Concord and you follow in the footsteps of the British soldiers, who marched to Lexington, continued on to Concord, and then retreated to Boston on the first day of the American Revolution, April 19, 1775.

Driving west from Boston on Mass. 2, take the exit for Mass. 4/225 (Pleasant Street), which dead-ends into Massachusetts Avenue. Turn left for **Lexington.** About a mile farther, on a hill to your left, is the **Museum of Our National Heritage** ❶ *(33 Marrett Rd./Mass. 2A, tel 781/861-6559).* Here a display entitled "Lexington Alarm'd!" reflects life in the town in 1775, as well as the events leading up to April 19. Massachusetts Avenue is the route taken by Paul Revere as he rode to Lexington, where he warned John Hancock and Samuel Adams (both wanted by the British) that the British were approaching. Farther along on the left is **Munroe Tavern** ❷ *(1332 Massachusetts Ave., tel 781/674-9238, closed Nov.–mid-April).* On the morning of April 19, this tavern was empty because the innkeeper, William Munroe, had left to join the colonial militia. By afternoon, it was a field hospital for wounded British.

Massachusetts Avenue leads straight through the center of Lexington to the triangular **Battle Green** ❸, with its statue of Col. John Parker (see p. 170). Keep to the right of the Green, on Bedford Street, then turn right onto Hancock Street. Number 36 is the **Hancock-Clarke House** ❹ *(Tel 781/862-1703, closed Nov.–mid-April),* once the home of the Reverend Jonas Clarke (1730–1805).

This vicarage was the first destination of messengers Paul Revere and William Dawes. Clarke was a cousin of John Hancock, who was his guest that night, along with Samuel Adams. The prized displays in the small museum are the silver pistols of English Maj. John Pitcairn (1722–1775) and the drum of William Diamond (1758–1828), the boy who summoned the Minutemen to Battle Green.

Return to the green, rejoin Massachusetts Avenue, and follow it out of Lexington and over 8I–95/Mass. 12. Turn right on Wood Street, then right onto Mass. 2A. This follows the route that the British took to Concord, now preserved within **Minute Man National Historical Park** ❺ (see p. 171). On the right is the **Battle Road Visitor**

⛰ See area map pp. 168–69
▶ Lexington
🔁 11.5 miles (18.5 km)
🕐 Half a day, with stops
▶ Concord

NOT TO BE MISSED

- Battle Green
- Minute Man National Historical Park
- North Bridge

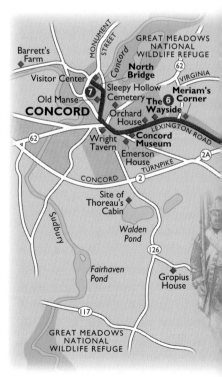

Center. Leave your car in the parking area and take a short walk along Nelson Road, a half-mile (800 m) length of the Battle Road. In 1775 the whole of Battle Road looked like this, with a crushed stone surface.

Back in your car, continue on Mass. 2A westward; a memorial on the right marks the **Paul Revere Capture Site.** Although Revere was held, Dr. Samuel Prescott escaped (see p. 171).

When Mass. 2A forks left, veer right on Lexington Road, leading toward the center of Concord. At **Meriam's Corner,** the Colonists sniped at the British as they retreated to Boston. Farther on is **The Wayside 6** (see pp. 175–76), which has both Revolutionary and literary history, and the **Concord Museum** (see pp. 174–75), well worth a visit if you have the time.

When the British reached Concord, they began searching for the arms and ammunition. One of the known hiding places was Barrett's Farm, north of town. To get there, the redcoats had to cross the **North Bridge 7**

over the Concord River. When you reach the green in Concord, turn right on Mass. 62 (*Bedford St.*), then immediately left, and right again on Monument Street. This leads to the North Bridge, the site of the first battle of the American Revolution in which the Colonists were successful. Walk up the hill to the visitor center at North Bridge or return to Concord, where there is much to see. ■

Lexington Church on Lexington Green

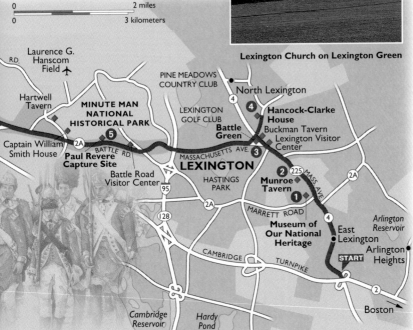

Concord

WITH A WHITE CHURCH, HISTORIC HOUSES, AND PLEASANT stores, Concord is a charming example of an old-fashioned New England community, only 22 miles (35 km) west of Boston. Concord figures in the annals of the United States for two reasons: the battle at the North Bridge in 1775, and the group of writers who made it the intellectual capital of the young country in the 19th century.

Concord has national historical park sites, four authors' homes, a fine museum, and even a historic cemetery, so there is much to see.

The **Concord Museum** provides visitors with an overall view of the Revolutionary and literary eras. Extended and revamped, this museum is now much more than a collection of local memorabilia. The "Why Concord" exhibit begins with "Establishing" and "Defending" Concord, from the era of the native Algonkian—who called this spot Musketaquid—to the buildup to the Revolution.

Concord was the obvious choice for a depot for military supplies; the hub of several roads, it was a six-hour march for soldiers from Boston, but a rider and mount could gallop that distance in a fraction of the time. A prized exhibit is the lantern hung in the Old North Church—the "signal light" of Longfellow's poem.

After the politics of the 18th century, you move on to the intellectual revolution of the 19th century and the movement known as Transcendentalism (see pp. 178–79). A re-creation of Ralph Waldo Emerson's study looks as if the great man has just stepped out. You can see his books, sofa, table, and chairs, then listen through headphones to the reminiscences of friends such as the young Louisa May Alcott. The museum also displays the bed, desk, and chair from Thoreau's cottage on Walden Pond (see p. 176).

A little way up the street from the Concord Museum stands the **Emerson House** (*28 Cambridge Turnpike, Lexington Rd., tel 978/ 369-2236, closed Oct.–mid-April*). A reconstruction of the 1829 original (damaged by fire in 1872), it has all the clutter of a family home. Tour guides tell of the influential author, who believed that American writers should break free of Old-World literary tradition. Yet Emerson loved visiting Europe, and the parlor is full of souvenirs from his trips.

Nearby are two more historic houses: **Orchard House** and The Wayside. Between 1858 and 1877

Concord
🔺   169 D2
Visitor information
www.concordchamber.org
✉   Concord Chamber
     of Commerce,
     2 Lexington Rd.
☎   978/369-3120

Left: Louisa May Alcott was living with her family at Orchard House when she wrote *Little Women* in 1868.

"A View of the Town of Concord," painted between 1775 and 1825, shows British troops stationed in the village.

Concord Museum

- ✉ Cambridge Turnpike
- ☎ 978/369-9763
- 🕐 Closed Sun. a.m.
- 💲 $$
- 🗺 Concord

Orchard House

- ✉ 399 Lexington Rd.
- ☎ 978/369-4118
- 🕐 Closed Sun. a.m.
- 💲 $
- 🗺 Concord

the two-story, brown clapboard Orchard House was the home of the Alcotts. On the tour, guides relate stories of family life and compare them with *Little Women*. You can see the melodeon, or pump organ, played by Louisa's sister Beth. Readers of *Little Women* will recall that she died young. The youngest sister was called May, however (not Amy, as in the book). An accomplished artist, May taught the young Daniel Chester French (later a famous sculptor); you can see her works throughout the house.

"It looks different from the movie" is a common reaction by visitors to Louisa's bedroom, with its sleigh bed and sloping floor, where she spent two months writing *Little Women*. Published in 1868, it has never been out of print since. Learn about the girls' father,

A. Bronson (see p. 182), whose views on areas including education, temperance, women's suffrage, and abolition were ahead of their time.

Down the street is **The Wayside** (*455 Lexington Rd., tel 978/369-6975, closed Wed. & Oct.–May, tours 10 a.m., 11 a.m., noon, 1.30 p.m., 3 p.m., 3.45 p.m., $*) Before embarking on the guided tour, look at the exhibition on the authors who lived here: Louisa May Alcott, Nathaniel Hawthorne, and Harriet Lothrop, who wrote *The Five Little Peppers* series under the name of Margaret Sydney. When compared to the lively atmosphere of Orchard House, The Wayside is more of a museum. Nevertheless, there is plenty of interest. Overall, the decor reflects the 1920s and the Lothrops' taste, but there are literary reminders throughout. In the

bay-window room, the Alcott girls played "Pilgrim's Progress," and Nathaniel Hawthorne's wife later taught Sunday school. Best of all is Hawthorne's sky parlor. Up a steep flight of stairs is the tower he added on to the house; this was his retreat, where, at the stand-up desk, he wrote *Tanglewood Tales* (1853).

Over by the North Bridge is the **Old Manse** (*Monument St., tel 978/369-3909, Closed Oct.–April, $$*). Built in 1770 for William Emerson (grandfather of Ralph), it was in the family until 1939. Unusual for a house of this age, all the furnishings are original. That would be reason enough to take the tour. But the people who lived and visited here were special, too. William Emerson was the local pastor and a confirmed patriot. His

family had a grandstand view of the confrontation at the North Bridge, and he wrote an eyewitness account. In the early 19th century, Ralph stayed in the Old Manse and wrote his first book, *Nature*. Novelist Nathaniel Hawthorne lived here with his bride, Sophia, in the 1840s. Like Emerson, he used the upstairs study for writing, penning much of *Mosses from the Old Manse* in the small room. Guides point out the windows, with graffiti such as: "Nathaniel Hawthorne. This is his study 1831." The garden was planted as a wedding present for the Hawthornes by Thoreau. You also learn about everyday life in the 18th and 19th centuries. You see a "tin kitchen," the latest gadget of the 1780s, and learn how the phrase "upper crust" was coined.

Many people seek inspiration at atmospheric Walden Pond, as Henry David Thoreau once did.

Bedford St. Mass. 62) is one of the loveliest. Tall trees shade the hillsides and the maze of pathways. A map from the Chamber of Commerce (see p. 174) will help you to locate Authors' Ridge, where the graves of Emerson, Thoreau, Hawthorne, Louisa May Alcott, and Harriet Lothrop are found. On the opposite side of the cemetery lies sculptor Daniel Chester French, who—in addition to being responsible for Lexington's "Minute Man" statue (see p. 171)—was the creator of the statue of Abraham Lincoln that dominates the imposing Lincoln Memorial in Washington.

South of Concord is **Walden Pond,** a place of pilgrimage for fans of Henry David Thoreau's *Walden* (1854), a record of the Transcendentalist writer's two-year retreat here. A re-creation of his cabin stands by the parking area, but a better way to appreciate the beauty of the site is to follow one of the walking trails to the far side of the pond, where he actually lived. A cairn marks the spot where his cabin stood. Walden Pond is part of a 304-acre (123 ha) state reservation that still attracts local families for picnics *(915 Walden St. Mass. 126, tel 978/369-3254).* ■

BEYOND CONCORD
The Boston area has many graveyards, but **Sleepy Hollow Cemetery** *(just out of Concord on*

The Emerson family memorials can be found on Authors' Ridge in Sleepy Hollow Cemetery.

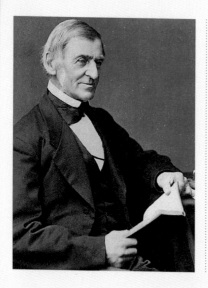

In the middle of the 19th century, Ralph Waldo Emerson (left) and Louisa May Alcott (right) were both influential members of Concord's literati.

Boston scribes

Boston and New England are often referred to as the cradle of American culture, thanks in the main to one group of writers. Early writing was limited to descriptions of life in the infant colony. Puritan theologians, such as Cotton Mather, were both prolific and conservative. Political pamphleteers included Boston lawyer James Otis, often credited for the rallying cry for the Revolution, "no taxation without representation." But it was not until the early 19th century that the "flowering of New England" burst into bloom in and around Boston.

During the early 19th century, half a dozen great names, and a host of minor authors, all contemporaries, often met in Cambridge, Concord, or at publishers Ticknor & Fields above the famous Old Corner Bookstore in Boston (see p. 66). What began with a spiritual revolt against the conservative church led to the New England Transcendental Movement, which trusted in the moral value of intuition. In a speech at Harvard University in 1837, Ralph Waldo Emerson (1803–1882) set out his optimistic belief in individualism, indepen-dence, and self-sufficiency. Disciple Henry David Thoreau (1817–1862) put theory into practice by "going back to nature," living in a cabin on Walden Pond (see p. 177), and writing about his two-year retreat. His lyrical essays were only recognized after his death.

By contrast, writers who focused on man's constant struggle with evil were Nathaniel Hawthorne (1804–1864) and Herman Melville (1819–1891). Hawthorne, from Salem, (see p. 186) was fascinated by the Puritan mind, with its legacy of guilt, sin, and remorse. Melville, a sailor aboard a New Bedford whaler as a youth, wrote *Moby Dick*, an allegorical giant of a book, run through with tragedy. A more down-to-earth contemporary, using wit to purvey his rationalist ideas, was medical professor Oliver Wendell Holmes (1809–1894). It was he that described the State House as "the hub of the solar system," which Bostonians cheerfully shortened to "the Hub" and applied to the whole of their home town. ("Hub" remains convenient shorthand for "Boston" in local newspaper headlines.) His phrase "Boston Brahmins" was also highjacked to describe the Beacon Hill aristocracy.

Ralph Waldo Emerson's study has been re-created at the Concord Museum, where modern visitors can absorb the atmosphere in which the great man worked.

The greatest poet of his day was Henry Wadsworth Longfellow (1807–1882, see p. 159), whose verse captured the imagination of the nation, creating overnight icons such as Paul Revere and Hiawatha. Equally popular was Louisa May Alcott, raised in Concord and influenced by the literary giants around her. *Little Women* was based on her own family life. After the Civil War, Boston's intellectual superiority faded, although the city was home to publishing companies such as Little, Brown (1847), Houghton, Mifflin (1852), and E.P. Dutton (1852). Recent literary successes include poet Robert Lowell (1917–1977), whose collection "For the Union Dead" won acclaim in the late 1960s, and Lowell-born Jack Kerouac (1922-1969), whose novel *On the Road* (1955) inspired the Beat generation. ■

Little Women by Louisa May Alcott has been a favorite with children for more than 130 years.

Lincoln & Lowell

LINCOLN AND LOWELL OFFER CONTRASTING IMAGES OF what constitutes a "typical" New England community. Located just south of Concord, Lincoln looks rural, with stone walls enclosing fields and woods where maples put on a fiery show in October. Lowell, however, has grown from its roots as a gritty mill town to become a showpiece of early American industrial history.

"Still life in autumn" by Scott Prior, one of the many regional artists represented at the DeCordova Museum

Lincoln

🅰 169 D2

DeCordova Museum & Sculpture Park

www.decordova.org

✉ 51 Sandy Pond Rd.

☎ 781/259-8355

🕐 Museum: closed Mon. Free tours Wed., Sun. Sculpture Park: closed Sat.–Sun. May–Oct.

💲 $$ (museum)

Gropius House

✉ 68 Baker Bridge Rd.

☎ 781/259-8098

🕐 Closed Mon.–Tues. June–Oct. 15, Mon.–Fri. Oct. 16–May

💲 $$ (includes tour)

LINCOLN

There are two reasons for visitors to make their way to Lincoln. The **DeCordova Museum and Sculpture Park,** which marked its 50th anniversary in 2000, is the only museum in New England to concentrate on regional artists. The highlight is the outdoor sculpture park, spread over some 35 acres (14.2 ha). Whether you set out with the museum map to find specific works, or trust to serendipity, this is a delightful place on a fine day. Alexander Liberman's *Cardinal Points* (1965) is one of the few works here produced before 1980.

Not far from the DeCordova is the **Gropius House.** Walter Gropius (1883–1969) founded the famous Bauhaus school of design in Germany before fleeing Germany for Harvard (see Busch-Reisinger

Museum, p. 150). In this small, boxlike house, built in 1938, you can see his theories put into practice. Step through the front door and it looks as if he and his wife, Ise, have just left. In the study, letters and a pair of glasses are on the desk, the latter designed by Marcel Breuer (1902–1981), a Bauhaus colleague, who also designed the tubular steel furniture. During the tour, the guide tells you about Gropius, his life and ideas. Revolutionary in its day, the house still looks contemporary. One of his students, architect I. M. Pei, also stayed here.

LOWELL

New England is dotted with 19th-century mill towns, but Lowell was where the integrated factory system was first introduced. This meant that a bale of cotton came in and a bolt of cloth went out. By 1876, some 70 percent of the city was taken up by 11 enormous factories, with housing close by for their workers. From 1823 to 1924, Lowell prospered. The boom ended abruptly. After decades of decay, the rundown city has been startlingly renovated. There are now open-air

89 looms are working at any one time. Workers had to endure the cotton dust, noise, and high humidity (to keep the yarn from breaking) for long hours at a time. Upstairs is the Dawn of an Era exhibition, which tells the story of Lowell's industrialization. Models demonstrate the ten stages of production,

The looms are in working order at the Boott Cotton Mills, part of the Lowell National Historic Park.

Lowell
🏚 169 D4

Boott Cotton Mills Museum
www.nps.gov/lowe
✉ John St.
☎ 978/970-5000
💲 $
🚆 Train: Gallagher Terminal, Lowell Line

New England Quilt Museum
✉ 18 Shattuck St.
☎ 978/452-4207
💲 $
🚆 Train: Lowell

Lowell National Historical Park
🏚 169 D4
✉ Visitor center, 246 Market St.
☎ 978/970-5006

American Textile History Museum
✉ 491 Dutton St
☎ 978/441-0400
🕐 Closed Mon.
💲 $$
🚆 Train: Gallagher Terminal, Lowell Line

concerts and boat rides along the canals. You can join a workshop at the **New England Quilt Museum** or pay your respects to Lowell author Jack Kerouac (1922–1969). Memorable lines by the Beat generation's spokesman are carved into granite columns on an unusual plaza at the intersection of Bridge and French Streets.

The linchpin of the industrial legacy is the **Boott Cotton Mills Museum,** part of **Lowell National Historical Park.** Thundering looms re-create the noise and dust of the past, so park rangers give you an introductory overview at the entrance. The rest of the visit, through the museum's two floors, is unaccompanied. The Weave Room is noisy enough outside; step inside it and the din is deafening. Yet only 15 or 20 of the

from raw material to finished fabric. Try your hand at weaving, listen to audio archives of former mill workers, hear workers and bosses debate the strike of 1912.

Across the old downtown is the **American Textile History Museum,** relocated here from North Andover. The 100 exhibits show how textiles were made, from the days of cottage industry to early factory machinery. Even more interesting are the textiles themselves, from period costumes to bed coverlets. Don't miss the housekeeping manual from the 1840s, with its three pages of detailed instructions on how to make a bed! One area is set up to look like an 1870s woolen mill, with a roomful of spinning frames. In the gift shop, you can buy coverlets and placemats woven on the museum's own looms. ■

More places to visit west & northwest of Boston

FRUITLANDS, HARVARD

In the days of the Transcendental Movement (see p. 178), Fruitlands was an idealistic experiment in self-sufficiency. Amos Bronson Alcott (1799–1888), father of writer Louisa May, set up this vegetarian and celibate commune in 1843, some 15 miles (24 km) northwest of Concord. While he and his men friends philosophized, the women were expected to farm. The experiment lasted seven months. Deep in the country, Fruitlands is a "museum of the New England landscape," with tributes to the commune in the former farmhouse, to Shakers (in an original Shaker building), and to local Native Americans. Another gallery displays Hudson River School paintings. It is a quiet place to walk, picnic, and relax.

🅰 169 C3 ✉ 102 Prospect Hill Rd.
☎ 978/456-3924 🕐 Closed Nov.–mid-May
💲 $$

"Farewell to Lincoln Square," by Ralph Sayer

LONGFELLOW'S WAYSIDE INN, SUDBURY

Although travelers have been stopping by this country pub ever since 1716, you have to blame Longfellow if find yourself crushed in the rush to be served at the Old Bar. The poet immortalized the plain rooms of this inn, and the hearth with its spitting logs, in his poetic book, *The Tales of a Wayside Inn* (1863). Of course, the most famous tale of all of these was *Paul Revere's Ride*. A change of name by the inn from the original "Red Horse Inn" was a virtual guarantee of regular custom. After he bought the inn in 1923, benefactor Henry Ford built a reproduction grist mill on the grounds and later added an authentic 1798 schoolhouse.

🅰 169 D2 ✉ Wayside Inn Rd. (off Mass. 20)
☎ 978/443-1776

LYMAN ESTATE, WALTHAM

The Lyman Estate, dating back to 1793, is one of those horticultural jewels that gardeners love to visit. The greenhouses, which are among some of the oldest in the United States, are lovingly maintained by S.P.N.E.A. (Society for the Preservation of New England Antiquities). Although the main house is open only by appointment, you can drop by and visit the estate and its greenhouses at any time of the year. As well as the regular flower shows that are held here, the collection of 100-year-old camellias and grapevines are both popular attractions with visitors.

🅰 169 D2 ✉ 185 Lyman St. ☎ 781/893-7232 💲 Donation

WORCESTER ART MUSEUM, WORCESTER

Less than an hour west of Boston, this underpublicized museum claims to be the second largest in New England. It also claims to be the first art gallery in the United States to purchase works by Monet (of his water lilies) and by Gauguin (of his brooding Tahitian women). They were bought back in 1910, a decade after the gallery opened. Since then, the collection has grown spectacularly. As well as conventional works of art by Dutch and Flemish masters, there is a collection of fine mosaics from Roman times. One of the best has been carefully laid on the floor of the neo-Renaissance courtyard. To get the most out of this huge collection, take an audio tour, or a public tour with a docent on Sundays.

🅰 168 B1 ✉ 55 Salisbury St. ☎ 508/799-4406 🕐 Closed Mon.– Tues. 💲 $$. Free Sat. a.m. ∎

The North Shore extends north of Boston, toward New Hampshire. Along the coastline are historic towns such as Salem and Marblehead, Rockport and Essex, plus swimming beaches and a wide range of small museums.

North Shore

Buoys at Rockport

North Shore

THE COASTLINES NORTH AND SOUTH OF BOSTON ARE DIFFERENT FROM EACH other. By and large the south is flat, while the north can be quite rugged, with craggy head-lands guarding pretty coves and broad bays. Look at a map, and names such as Gloucester, Essex, Ipswich, Salisbury, Amesbury, and Newbury are reminders of the first settlers' homes back in England.

The swathe of coast runs from Lynn north-ward, past the Merrimack River to the New Hampshire border. Add in a few inland com-munities, and you have the diverse region known as the North Shore. Today's North Shore has much to tempt the visitor. There are fine museums and historic buildings, plus delightful seaside towns such as Rockport, Marblehead, and the smaller Manchester-by-the-Sea. There are the outdoor attractions: beaches, hiking trails, and the Parker River Wildlife Refuge, a haven for birdlife.

In the early days, farming and fishing were the mainstays of life here. First and foremost, the North Shore bred some of the world's finest seamen and shipbuilders. They fished for cod and whales, they manned the mer-chant vessels that roamed the globe, and, when needed, built battleships and cruisers. Their home ports record their deeds and the wealth that their skippers accrued. Visit Salem to explore the Peabody Essex Museum, which

opened in 1799 and can reasonably claim to be the oldest museum in the United States. With its treasures from the China trade, it is certainly one of the finest of its kind. Gritty Gloucester greets visitors with the statue of "The Man at the Wheel"; it, too, has nautical treasures, at the excellent Cape Ann Historical Museum. In Essex, you can hunt for antiques or visit the Shipbuilding Museum, while New-buryport has handsome houses as well as the Custom House Maritime Museum. Marble-head was known as "the greatest Towne for fishing in New England" as early as 1629 and still boasts one of the finest mansions of the colonial era.

But the North Shore has grisly memories, too. In Salem, the victims of the witch trials are sadly exploited today, although the city also has more serious reminders of that brief but terrible period. The Puritan legacy also affected local novelist Nathaniel Hawthorne (1804–1864), who altered his name to rid

Picturesque Rockport harbor

himself of the connection with an ancestor, one of the notorious judges during the trials. Down near Manchester is Hammond Castle, the extraordinary mansion of one of the greatest, yet least recognized, scientific inventors in U.S. history. Stubby Cape Ann has long been an artists' colony, with its rocky landscapes, tall lighthouses, and clear, shimmering light providing inspiration for great painters such as Winslow Homer (1836–1910) and Edward Hopper (1882–1967). ∎

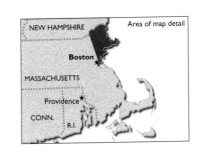

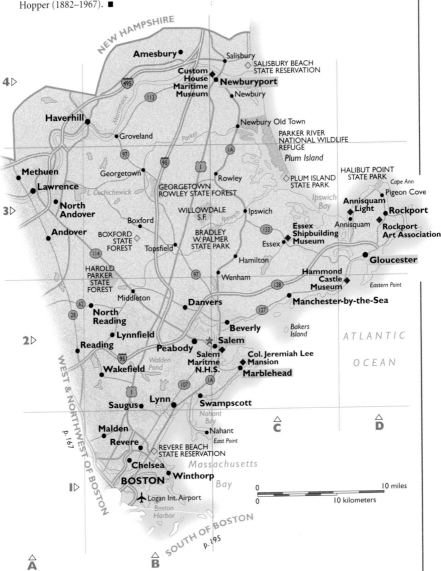

Salem

THE NAME SALEM IS SYNONYMOUS WITH WITCHES.
Waxworks, cafés, souvenir stores, and a museum all trade on the fascination for the witch trials of 1692. But this was no more than a sad chapter in the town's rich history. At its mid-eighteenth-century peak, Salem was one of the richest ports on the East Coast, home to sea captains and merchants who traded around the world.

The East India Marine Hall at the Peabody Essex Museum in Salem

Salem

🅰 185 C2

Visitor information

www.easternnational.org

✉ National Park Service Regional Visitor Center, 2 New Liberty St.

☎ 978/740-1650

Peabody Essex Museum

www.pem.org

✉ East India Sq.

☎ 978/745-9500

🕒 Closed Mon. Nov.–May

💲 $$$, includes historic house tours

🚆 Train & bus: Salem Depot

⛴ Salem ferry to & from Boston

For an insight into this historic legacy, pick up a brochure for the Heritage Trail at the **National Park Service Regional Visitor Center** and follow the 1.7-mile (2.75 km) red line on the sidewalk.

The **Peabody Essex Museum** is the jewel in the crown of this historic city. A cornucopia overflowing with art and artifacts from around the world, it also houses valuable archives, including documents from the Salem witchcraft trials and novelist Nathaniel Hawthorne's manuscripts.

The museum started out as a club, the East India Marine Society, founded in 1799. To become a member you had to have sailed around either Cape Horn or the Cape of Good Hope. The club's aims were to support widows, to improve knowledge of navigation, and to show off souvenirs. In 1825 the East India Marine Hall was

built to house their "cabinet of curiosities." Restored for the U.S. Bicentennial celebrations in 1976, the upstairs gallery showcases nine ship's figureheads and a portrait of founder member Benjamin Carpenter. By 1840, the collection had grown to 4,300 objects; today, there are about two million.

Although exhibitions change regularly, "Maritime New England," near the entrance, is a permanent display telling the story of seafaring in New England. It includes artworks such as "The Ship *Southern Cross* leaving Boston Harbor" (1851), by local painter Fitz Hugh Lane (1804–1865).

The China trade included India, Japan, the east coast of Africa, and the Pacific Islands. The 5-foot (1.5 m) statue of Kuka'ilimoku from Hawaii is one of only three remaining in the world. The collection of 19th-century Chinese photographs provides a record of China before the Communist regime.

Asian export art consists of objects made specifically for sale to Westerners. Pride of place goes to the Moon Bed, with its exquisite carving and inlay. Made for the 1876 Centennial Exposition in Philadelphia, the bed consists of 83 individual pieces held together by three wooden wedges. There are also renowned collections of 19th-century Japanese folk art and Korean art, together with significant holdings of Native American art, particularly from the Pacific Northwest. Like the original China trade collections, these were a direct result of profits from the sealskin business.

During Salem's heyday (1780–1820), the wharves on Derby Street bulged with imported goods. In one year alone, 12 million pounds (5.5 million kg) of pepper passed through this port. The handsome Custom House was the hub of the harbor, now part of the **Salem Maritime National Historic Site.** Here, too, are several fine houses and the West India Dry Goods Store, where you can still see, smell, and buy coffee, tea, and spices. On Central Wharf you can watch craftsmen work on a full-size reproduction of the 1797 merchant ship, *Friendship.*

Also down by the water is the **House of the Seven Gables,** which still matches the description in Nathaniel Hawthorne's 1851 novel of the same name. During the tour, guides separate fact from fiction, explaining that while Hawthorne worked at the Custom House, he often visited his cousin, Susannah Ingersoll, who lived in the rambling home. Don't miss the secret staircase leading up to an attic bedroom. Some think this may have been used to hide slaves escaping on the underground railroad. On the same site is Hawthorne's birthplace, a house moved here from Union Street, Salem.

A forbidding statue of Roger Conant, who founded Salem in 1626, stands next to the **Salem Witch Museum** on Salem Common. Inside the museum, a 25-minute presentation combines audiovisuals and tableaus. Although the narrator's sepulchral tones are more suited to horror films than factual presentations, the facts are well researched. The names of those executed for witchcraft included John Proctor and Giles Cory, familiar from Arthur Miller's play *The Crucible,* on which the 1996 movie was based.

Take time to explore the **McIntire Historic District.** The area is named after the self-taught Salem architect Samuel McIntire (1757–1811). Handsome Chestnut Street features several of his houses. ∎

The House of the Seven Gables was the inspiration for Nathaniel Hawthorne's popular 1851 novel of the same name.

Witches

In the 17th century, witchcraft was a crime, yet witchcraft delusions were not uncommon. When hysteria gripped a group of young girls in Salem in 1692, 19 innocent men and women were convicted and hanged between June 10 and September 22. Others died in jail. Even two dogs were executed. Fear fed on superstition and the courts gave no protection to the accused. At the end of October, Governor William Phipps installed a replacement court to pardon the condemned and release those in jail. The shame lingered on. One trial judge was John Hathorne. His descendant, writer Nathaniel Hawthorne, added a "w" to his birth name. Salem Village, once part of Salem Town, changed its name to Danvers in 1752. ∎

Salem Maritime NHS
www.nps.gov/sama
✉ 174 Derby St.
☎ 978/740-1650
💲 $ for tour

House of the Seven Gables
✉ 54 Turner St.
☎ 978/744-0991
💲 $$
🚆 Train & bus: Salem Depot
⛴ To & from Boston

Salem Witch Museum
✉ Washington Sq.
☎ 978/744-1692 or 800/544-1692
💲 $$
🚆 Train & bus: Salem Depot
⛴ To & from Boston

North Shore drive

This drive starts in Salem, then follows the rocky shoreline of Cape Ann. You'll pass impressive mansions, broad seascapes, and protected coves. Do take time to see the art galleries and museums, or take a walk around one of the old towns.

From Salem, take Bridge Street (Mass. 1A) north across the Danvers River, then follow Mass. 127 north for Manchester-by-the-Sea. One moment you are on a country lane, the next, you enjoy spectacular water views. At the railroad station in **Pride's Crossing,** waiting for a train is a political statement. The bench on the left is marked Democrats; the Republicans' bench is, of course, to the right.

Mass. 127 passes through the hamlet of **Beverly Farms** and into **Manchester-by-the-Sea ❶**. This old seafaring community has stayed small, hemmed in by the hilly, rocky coastline. There are Georgian, federal, Victorian, and Greek Revival houses, but the most photographed building is Seaside No. 1, an 1885 firehouse on the harbor.

Continue along the coast, where you can make a detour to see Hammond Castle (see p. 191) before stopping in Gloucester (see p. 191). Then take Mass. 127A, the scenic route to **Rockport ❷**. The setting for Stephen Spielberg's 1999 movie *The Love Letter* with Tom Selleck, this artists' colony (see p. 192) was famous for its granite. Stone quarried here was used to rebuild Chicago after its fire and San Francisco after its earthquake, and was even used in the construction of the Panama Canal. Pick up a walking map from the Chamber of Commerce *(3 Main St., tel 978/546-6575)* and head for the famous red fishing shack, which is nicknamed **Motif No. 1** (see p. 192). Overlooking the harbor, with its lobster boats, the wooden building is still painted and photographed (see p. 192). Up the hill is **First Congregational Church,** nicknamed the "Old Sloop" by fishermen, since its steeple could be seen miles out to sea. As the cannonball kept in a glass case shows, the steeple was also an obvious target for the British in the war of 1812. In July 1856, temperance activist Hannah Jumper and her "Hatchet Gang" of 150 women broke every bottle and barrel of rum in town. Rockport is still dry to this day, although you are allowed to bring your own bottle to restaurants.

Continue north on Mass. 127 to Pigeon Cove, past colorful, granite-built walls. They look like a pattern book, and were just that: a showcase of granite for sale to builders. In 1922 the Stenman family decided to build a house from old newspapers. **The Paper House ❸** *(52 Pigeon Hill St., tel 978/546-2629, closed Nov.–March)* took 20 years and 100,000 copies to build. The walls alone are 215 sheets thick. Inside you can see the paper furniture, including tables, chairs, and even a paper grandfather clock.

Head back toward Gloucester, but at the traffic circle take Mass. 128, then turn right onto Mass. 133 for **Essex.** Here every other building seems to be an antique store. Shipbuilding is the real name of the game, however, with more than 4,000 two-masted boats launched over the centuries. Find out more at the small **Essex Shipbuilding Museum ❹** *(66 Main St., tel 978/768-7541, closed Mon.–Fri. Labor Day–Mem. Day),* where you can also watch boats being built and repaired.

Stay on Mass. 133 for **Ipswich.** Detour out to the shore via Argilla Road for a walk or swim on Crane Beach, or tour the 59-room Great House on the **Castle Hill** estate *(290 Argilla Rd., tel 978/356-4351, tours in summer Wed.–Thurs.).* Take Mass. 1A south to return to Salem. ■

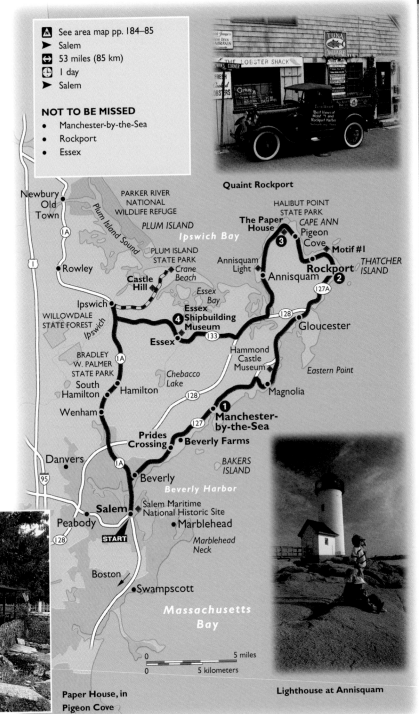

See area map pp. 184–85
► Salem
↔ 53 miles (85 km)
🕐 1 day
► Salem

NOT TO BE MISSED
- Manchester-by-the-Sea
- Rockport
- Essex

Quaint Rockport

Newbury
Old Town
Rowley
Ipswich
Castle Hill
PLUM ISLAND SOUND
Plum Island Sound
PARKER RIVER NATIONAL WILDLIFE REFUGE
PLUM ISLAND
PLUM ISLAND STATE PARK
Crane Beach
Ipswich Bay
WILLOWDALE STATE FOREST
Ipswich
Essex Bay
Essex ④ **Essex Shipbuilding Museum**
BRADLEY W. PALMER STATE PARK
South Hamilton
Hamilton
Wenham
Chebacco Lake
Annisquam Light
Annisquam
HALIBUT POINT STATE PARK
The Paper House ③
CAPE ANN
Pigeon Cove
Rockport ● Motif #1
THATCHER ISLAND ②
Gloucester
Hammond Castle Museum
Eastern Point
Magnolia
① **Manchester-by-the-Sea**
Prides Crossing ● **Beverly Farms**
Danvers
Beverly
BAKERS ISLAND
Beverly Harbor
Salem
Peabody
Salem Maritime National Historic Site
● Marblehead
Marblehead Neck
START
Boston
● Swampscott
Massachusetts Bay

0   5 miles
0   5 kilometers

Paper House, in Pigeon Cove

Lighthouse at Annisquam

Marblehead

When tourist season subsides, Marblehead can be an idyllic seaside town.

THE MARBLEHEAD PENINSULA PROTRUDES FROM THE North Shore into the Atlantic Ocean. The town itself is almost too picturesque to be true. The small curve of harbor, with some 900 boats moored in summer, is much photographed, as are the grand homes of sea captains and merchants, who made this the sixth largest town in the American Colonies in 1760. Streets are narrow, so park your car and walk through this delightful town.

Marblehead
🗺 185 C2

Marblehead Historical Society
✉ 170 Washington St.
☎ 781/631-1768
🕐 Closed Mon.–Fri. & mid-Oct.–June

Colonel Jeremiah Lee Mansion
✉ 161 Washington St.
☎ 781/631-1768
🕐 Closed Sun. a.m. & mid-Oct.–June
💲 $$

Right on the main street you will find the **Marblehead Historical Society,** which celebrated its centennial in 1998 by moving into new premises. The gallery upstairs is devoted to John Orne Johnson Frost, a local who began painting in 1922 when he was 70 years old. His colorful works record Marblehead life in the 19th century. "Bird's Eye View" (1867), for example, shows the entire harbor, including Marblehead Neck, where they held their fish fries.

Across the street is the **Colonel Jeremiah Lee Mansion.** A major restoration has returned this 1768 house to its full grandeur. One of the ten most impressive homes in the Colonies, it had the best ingredients that money could buy—Palladian design, fine china, carved woodwork, and expensive textiles. Note that the wood exterior has been carefully worked to look

like stone, to imitate the mansions of the English aristocracy. The star attraction is the scenic wallpaper, which depicts Roman vistas and is a rare example of a hand-painted, rather than hand-printed, English design. All of this is explained in the tours, which guide visitors through the 16 rooms.

A short walk up Washington Street leads to the 19th-century **Abbot Hall** (188 Washington St., tel 781/631-0528). Ask to see Archibald M. Willard's original painting of "The Spirit of '76" (1876), one of the best-known images of Americana, which hangs in the board of selectmen's boardroom. You can almost hear the drums and fifes of these Patriots, heading off to fight the British. Set off in the other direction from the Historical Society to reach the **Old Town House** on Market Square, which dates from 1727. ∎

Gloucester

GLOUCESTER IS THE GATEWAY TO CAPE ANN. FOUNDED IN 1623, it is the oldest working port in the country. Today it is well known thanks to Sebastian Junger's 1997 best-seller *The Perfect Storm*, which described the real-life sinking of the *Andrea Gail*, a Gloucester swordfishing boat caught in a fatal tempest in the early 1990s. Do not miss Hammond Castle, an extraordinary mock medieval fortress only a few miles away along the coast.

Gloucester
🗺 185 D3
Visitor information
✉ Stage Fort Park
☎ 978/281-8865

Near the grandiose City Hall on the top of the hill is the **Cape Ann Historical Museum.** Unlike many historical society museums, which are cramped for space and short of funding, this one spreads its well-chosen collection over three floors, with particularly good wall text explanations. Take time to study the paintings by Fitz Hugh Lane (1804–1865). Known for his seascapes, this local son of a sailor was as adept at portraying nature's calm side as he was the violent storms of the Atlantic Ocean. Other galleries celebrate the lure of the sea. In the Fish and Maritime Collection, find the tiny dory in which Capt. Alfred Johnson made the first single-handed crossing of the Atlantic in 1876.

The **"Man at the Wheel"** honors Gloucester's fishing fleet.

HAMMOND CASTLE

Between Manchester-by-the-Sea and Gloucester stands Hammond Castle, overlooking the sea. It was designed and furnished in the 1920s by John Hays Hammond, Jr., who stands second only to Thomas Edison as the most prolific inventor in United States history. Tucked away on the North Shore, this fascinating house-cum-museum remains almost undiscovered. On the self-guided tour, the most impressive room is the **Great Hall.** Modeled after St. Nazaire Cathedral in Carcassonne, in southern France, it is 100 feet (30 m) long, 65 feet (20 m) high, and was specially designed to hold the four-keyboard organ, with its 8,200 pipes. Hammond imported whole chunks of ancient European buildings: The interior **courtyard** upstairs is walled with facades taken from 15th-century French houses. His Renaissance-style **dining room** has a coffered ceiling from Spain and monastery walls from France. Hammond also had a quirky sense of humor. Legend has it that he would terrify guests by diving from an upstairs window into the seemingly shallow pool that was actually 8 feet (2.4 m) deep. He also invented an artificial environment system that produced "sunlight," "moonlight," and even "rain" from hidden sprinklers.

Hammond came from a wealthy family and rarely talked about his inventions, most of which were kept secret by the Pentagon. They are now revealed in the **Exhibit and Invention Rooms.** ∎

Cape Ann Historical Museum
✉ 27 Pleasant St.
☎ 978/283-0455
🕐 Closed Sun.–Mon. & all Feb.
💲 $

Hammond Castle Museum
www.hammondcastle.org/
🗺 185 D2
✉ 80 Hesperus Ave.
☎ 978/283-2080
🕐 Hours vary. Call or see website for details
💲 $$

Cape Ann artists' colonies

The rocky seaside landscape of Cape Ann has inspired painters for 150 years. Its vibrant, clear light and the ever-changing ocean drew artists such as Winslow Homer (1836–1910), Edward Hopper (1882–1967), and Maurice Prendergast (1859–1924). Because of their works, even those who have never visited Cape Ann feel they know Squam lighthouse, Gloucester Harbor, and the local fishing boats. Rocky Neck, a peninsula across from Gloucester Harbor, is recognized as the oldest artists' colony in the United States. Gloucester's own Fitz Hugh Lane (1804–1865), one of America's leading marine artists, is well represented in Salem's Peabody Essex Museum (see p. 186) and in the Cape Ann Historical Museum (see p. 191) with his memorable view of "Gloucester Harbor from Rocky Neck" (1844). The galleries lining Rocky Neck Avenue confirm that this is still a magnet for painters.

Wherever you go in Rockport, you're likely to encounter an artist working in pencil, pastels, or oil.

Summering on Cape Ann, Bostonian Winslow Homer (1836–1910) broke free from the restrictions of studio work and developed his lyrical watercolor technique. About 1900, more and more American artists arrived, many joining teacher Frank Duveneck (1848–1919). Perhaps the most famous of these "Duveneck boys" was Maurice Prendergast (1859–1924), the Boston-based artist whose lively watercolors stand out for their bold colors. He was influenced by the French painters Henri Matisse (1869–1954) and Paul Cézanne (1839–1906). Here, though, his cheerful views of Annisquam on the north shore of Cape Ann, Rockport, and Gloucester have all the exuberance of a fun vacation. Another influential visitor in the early 1900s was Childe Hassam (1859–1935). After seeing the Impressionists in Paris in 1886, the

Boston-born artist returned to lead the American impressionist movement.

Perhaps the best-known summer resident on Cape Ann was Edward Hopper (1882–1967). Although this New Yorker's haunting city scenes are the essence of urban life, he was equally inspired by the New England coast. His love of sailing is reflected in his depictions of sailboats, but another favorite subject was the lighthouse. One of the first of the many that he portrayed was Squam Light at Annisquam. Characteristically, he positioned his easel below the building, looking up, with bright sunshine gleaming on white paint. It was a technique he used often and successfully with other lighthouses. Equally powerful were the architectural studies of Gloucester's ordinary face: private houses and churches, tenements and shacks, railyards and factories. He was fascinated by the juxtaposition of light and shadow on roof lines, gaping windows, and shutters.

At the eastern tip of Cape Ann is Rockport, another artists' colony, where the 80-year-old Rockport Art Association (12 Main St., tel 978/546-6604) represents 250 local artists. By far the most popular subject for painters and photographers alike is a dark-red fishing shack on a wharf, overlooking the harbor. The unusual, weatherbeaten color is concocted by mixing used automobile crankcase oil with red paint. In the 1920s, when a student presented teacher Lester Hornby with yet another sketch of the shed, he exclaimed, "What? Motif No. 1 again?" Ever since, the building has been known as Motif No. 1. ■

Above right: Annisquam Lighthouse is another popular subject.
Below right: Motif No. 1, the fishing shack in Rockport, is still a favorite with painters.

Newburyport

Newburyport
🅰 185 C4

**Custom House
Maritime Museum**
✉ 25 Water St.
☎ 978/462-8681
🕐 Closed Jan.–March
💲 $

**Cushing House
Museum**
✉ 98 High St.
☎ 508/462-2681
🕐 Closed Sun.–Mon. &
Nov.–April
💲 $

Lowell's Boat Shop
✉ 459 Main St.
☎ 978/388-0162

SET AT THE MOUTH OF THE 177-MILE-LONG (285 KM) Merrimack River, Newburyport is a popular place for a day's outing. In the 1970s, the old waterfront was renovated, resulting in a Market Square area that bustles with stores, restaurants, fine sea captains' houses to admire along broad streets, and a riverside boardwalk.

Your first stop should be the **Custom House Maritime Museum** (1835). This granite box of a building was the hub of the port, where cargoes were registered and duties assessed. The galleries trace the town's proud history of trading and shipbuilding. In the 1770s, its shipyards launched two frigates for the infant United States Navy, followed by the fastest clipper ship of all, the *Dreadnought*, in the mid-19th century. The "wild boat

**Newbury's history
is on display
at the Custom
House Maritime
Museum.**

**Parker River
Wildlife Refuge**
✉ Northern Blvd., Plum
Island
☎ 978/465-5753

of the Atlantic" took just 13 days and 11 hours to sail from Liverpool, England, to New York City on the return leg of her maiden voyage, arriving at the same time as the steamship *Canada* that had left a day earlier.

Walking through the old heart of Newburyport is like flicking through an encyclopedia of architectural styles, from federal and

Queen Anne to Italianate and Greek Revival. The **Court House** (1805) on High Street was designed by Charles Bulfinch (see pp. 92–93). Farther on is the **Cushing House Museum,** another federal-style classic. Inside, you can see just how comfortably 19th-century merchants lived. Antique clocks reflect local skills, while tall teak-and-ivory Japanese cabinets were collected by Newburyport skippers from the far corners of the globe.

It is worth driving inland over to Amesbury, home of **Lowell's Boat Shop.** Founded in 1793, this is the oldest continuously working wooden boatbuilder in the United States, famed for two designs: the Amesbury skiff and the flat-bottomed dory, the small wooden boat lowered into the water from large vessels and whalers. You can rent a dory by the hour to row on the river.

The Society for the Preservation of New England Antiquities (S.P.N.E.A.) maintains four historic properties in the area. Two are open regularly: the **Spencer-Pierce-Little-Farm** (*5 Little's Lane, Newbury, tel 978/462-2634, closed mid-Oct.–end May*), an archaeological and conservation site, and the 1654 **Coffin House** (*14 High Rd., Newbury, tel 978/462-2634, closed mid-Oct.–end May*), an example of early New England architecture.

At the mouth of the Merrimack River is Plum Island. home to the **Parker River National Wildlife Refuge,** which is popular with birdwatchers, who can see migratory waterfowl, waders, and raptors. ■

You can retrace the steps of the Pilgrims by visiting Plymouth—and Plimoth Plantation—on the South Shore of Massachusetts. Farther south still, in neighboring Rhode Island, are stately Newport and historic Providence.

South of Boston

Detail of a pew, Old Ship Church

South of Boston

THE AREA TO THE SOUTH OF BOSTON HAS MUCH TO OFFER VISITORS. IN Massachusetts there are reminders of the Pilgrims, the home of two presidents, and a 19th-century whaling port. Moving into Rhode Island, Providence is a compact and walkable city, while Newport is second only to Boston in the range of attractions it offers.

The Pilgrims' first settlement was at Plymouth, less than an hour (though considerably longer than that in the 17th century) south of Boston, on Cape Cod Bay. The major draw today is a detailed reproduction of the *Mayflower,* the mythical Plymouth Rock, and the fascinating living history of Plimoth Plantation. Although Boston's Freedom Trail and its buildings are concrete reminders of the past, Plimoth Plantation offers a rare opportunity to get a sense (and a smell) of the early days of the original 13 Colonies. This is, however, no jolly replica of mid-17th-century life. By going about their daily lives, unhampered by any modern gadgetry, costumed participants at this Puritan village attempt to recreate the conditions experienced by the settlers in 1627. Corn struggles to grow in the poor soil, flies swarm in the heat of summer, and the Puritans sweat in hand-stitched clothes made of rough fabric. In a separate village in the Plimoth Plantation complex, Native Americans demonstrate their way of life from four centuries ago.

Currently experiencing a revival is New Bedford, farther south on Buzzards Bay. In this legendary whaling town, a young Herman Melville signed up as a deckhand.

Across the state line in Rhode Island are Newport and Providence. Newport is famous as a summer haven for the rich and famous of a century ago, whose breathtaking mansions demand a visit. The waters of Narragansett Bay, once a permanent home for the America's Cup yacht races, still attract thousands of sailors. A series of world-class summer concerts, especially the Jazz Festival, appeals to music lovers in the thousands. But Newport's long history goes back to colonial times. The oldest synagogue, as well as the oldest continuously used library in the United States, are in this most attractive of seaside towns.

State-of-the-art boats ensure the continuation of Newport's maritime heritage.

Founded by Roger Williams in 1636, Providence is a gem of a city, home to Brown University and handsome mansions along Benefit Street, which merits its ambitious nickname, the Mile of History. Compact and easy to walk, the state capital has transformed itself into a leisure destination. It boasts a rich past; the renovation of the downtown area, where major projects are still in progress, has ensured that it will have a healthy future. ■

NEW HAMPSHIRE   Area of map detail

Boston

MASSACHUSETTS

Providence

CONN.

R.I.

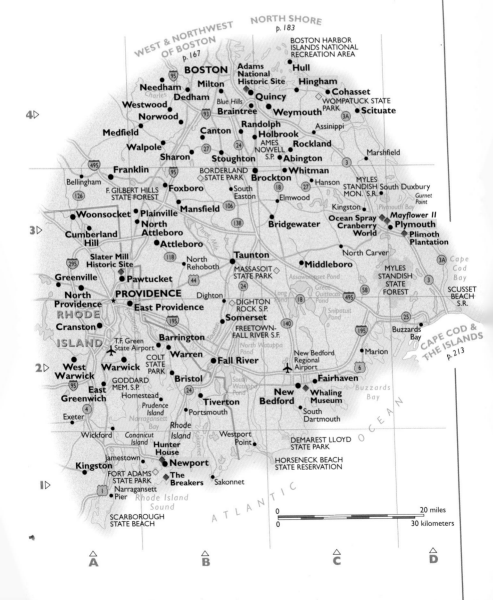

WEST & NORTHWEST OF BOSTON
p. 167

NORTH SHORE
p. 183

BOSTON HARBOR ISLANDS NATIONAL RECREATION AREA

BOSTON
Needham   Adams National Historic Site   Hull
Milton   Hingham
Westwood   Dedham   Quincy   Cohasset
Norwood   Braintree   Weymouth   WOMPATUCK STATE PARK   Scituate
Medfield   Canton   Randolph   Assinippi
Walpole   Holbrook
Sharon   AMES NOWELL   Rockland
Stoughton   S.P.   Abington   Marshfield
Franklin   BORDERLAND STATE PARK   Whitman
Bellingham   Brockton   Hanson   MYLES STANDISH   South Duxbury
F. GILBERT HILLS STATE FOREST   Foxboro   South Easton   Elmwood   MON. S.R.   Gurnet Point
Mansfield   Kingston   Plymouth Bay
Woonsocket   Plainville   Bridgewater   Ocean Spray Cranberry World   Mayflower II
North Attleboro   Plymouth
Cumberland Hill   Attleboro   Plimoth Plantation
Slater Mill Historic Site   North Rehoboth   Taunton   North Carver
Greenville   MASSASOIT STATE PARK   Middleboro   MYLES STANDISH STATE FOREST
North Providence   PROVIDENCE   Dighton   SCUSSET BEACH S.R.
RHODE   East Providence   DIGHTON ROCK S.P.   Cape Cod Bay
Cranston   Somerset
ISLAND   FREETOWN-FALL RIVER S.F.   Buzzards Bay
T.F. Green State Airport   Barrington   CAPE COD & THE ISLANDS p. 213
COLT STATE PARK   Warren   New Bedford Regional Airport   Marion
West Warwick   Warwick   Fall River
GODDARD MEM. S.P.   Bristol
East Greenwich   Homestead   New Bedford   Whaling Museum   Buzzards Bay
Exeter   Prudence Island   Tiverton   Fairhaven
Rhode   Portsmouth   South Dartmouth
Wickford   Conanicut Island   Rhode Island   Westport Point   DEMAREST LLOYD STATE PARK
Hunter House
Kingston   Jamestown   Newport   HORSENECK BEACH STATE RESERVATION
FORT ADAMS STATE PARK   The Breakers   Sakonnet
Narragansett Pier   Rhode Island Sound
SCARBOROUGH STATE BEACH   ATLANTIC OCEAN

0   20 miles
0   30 kilometers

A   B   C   D

Quincy

The Stone Library at the Adams National Historic Site, the birthplace of two U.S. presidents.

SEVEN MILES SOUTHEAST OF BOSTON IS QUINCY, PRO-nounced QUIN-zee. Today, young families and single people are adding a liveliness to a suburb that is easy to get to, either on the Red Line of the T (subway) or by ferry. Traditionally, this town was known for its shipbuilding and for its cluster of more than 50 granite quarries, whose stone was transported by sea to cities along the East Coast for use in harbors and official buildings.

Quincy
🅰 197 B4
Visitor information
✉ 1250 Hancock St.

Adams National Historic Site
✉ 135 Adams St.
☎ 617/773-1177
🕐 Closed Nov. 11–April 19
💲 $
🚆 Train & bus: Quincy Center

ADAMS NATIONAL HISTORIC SITE

In this suburb, nicknamed the "City of Presidents," stands a gray clapboard house that was home to four generations of the Adams family between 1787 and 1946. John Adams (1735–1826), the second President of the United States, and his son, the sixth President, John Quincy Adams (1767–1848), both lived here. The 13-acre (5.3 ha) site is now run by the National Park Service. In the **Old House,** you see the stand-up secretary brought home from Europe and used by John Adams in his later years for his long correspondences with Thomas Jefferson. In the garden is the barnlike **Stone Library,** a presidential library before the modern concept began. Rangers point out the Mendi Bible, given to John Adams by the Mendi people of West Africa, whom he defended successfully in the Supreme Court. This was the subject of the 1997 movie *Amistad.* The 11 buildings on the site include the plain 17th-century saltbox houses where the two men were born. Both presidents are buried at the **United First Parish Church** *(1306 Adams St., tel 617/773-0062, tours mid-April–mid-Nov. $).* ■

Plymouth

THE TOWN OF PLYMOUTH, WHICH LIES ABOUT 40 MILES (65 km) south of Boston, trades heavily on its place in history as the birthplace of modern America, and the United States. After a brief, and rather chilly stay on Cape Cod, the Pilgrims embarked on the *Mayflower* once more, and sailed across the bay. They eventually came ashore to settle on a site which is now on Leyden Street in present-day Plymouth.

According to tradition, Pilgrims came ashore at Plymouth Rock.

Plymouth

🅰 197 D3

Visitor information

✉ 130 Water St.

☎ 508/747-7525

Pilgrim Hall Museum

✉ 75 Court St.

☎ 508/746-1620

🕐 Closed Jan.

Mayflower II

www.plimoth.org

✉ State Pier

☎ 508/746-1622

🕐 Closed Dec.–April

💲 $$. $$$$ (including Plimoth Plantation)

Rising up on the bay side of Water Street is what looks like a Greek temple. This neoclassic structure covers a boulder, **Plymouth Rock.** In 1741, Elder Faunce, age 95 at the time, insisted that his "father had assured him that [the rock] had received the footsteps of our fathers on their first arrival." True or false, it is a symbolic site in the history of the United States.

Another mock Greek temple, built in 1824, houses the **Pilgrim Hall Museum.** Memorabilia include Governor Bradford's Bible, Myles Standish's swords, and the cradle of Peregrine White, born aboard the *Mayflower.* The two must-sees in Plymouth are **Mayflower II** and **Plimoth Plantation.**

Nothing prepares you for the fragility of *Mayflower II,* at State

Plimoth Plantation

www.plimoth.org

🅰 197 D3

✉ Bet. Mass. 3 & Mass. 3A (Main St.)

☎ 508/746-1622

🕐 Closed Jan.

💲 $$$$ (including *Mayflower II*)

The *Mayflower II* sailed across the Atlantic from England in 1957.

Pier, a few steps from Plymouth Rock. This reproduction of the ship that took 66 days to sail from England is only 106.5 feet (32 m) long and would float comfortably in an Olympic-size swimming pool. It is hard to imagine 102 men, women, and children crammed inside for such a long time. What you board today is a re-creation of a typical vessel of the 17th century, which was built over 40 years ago in England of Devon oak, rigged with hemp rope, and fitted with hand-sewn linen canvas sails. In 1957 she was sailed across the Atlantic. The costumed interpreters ensure that you receive a real insight into why the Colonists left England, what life was like in Holland (where they initially settled before immigrating to America), how they survived the transatlantic journey, and the hardships of landing in midwinter on an unfriendly shore. Each has learned an authentic English accent, and all are enthusiastic and knowledgeable, with plenty of references to whip-staffs (bars to extend the tiller), binnacles (compass housings), and beakheads (rostrums) to intrigue the nautically inclined.

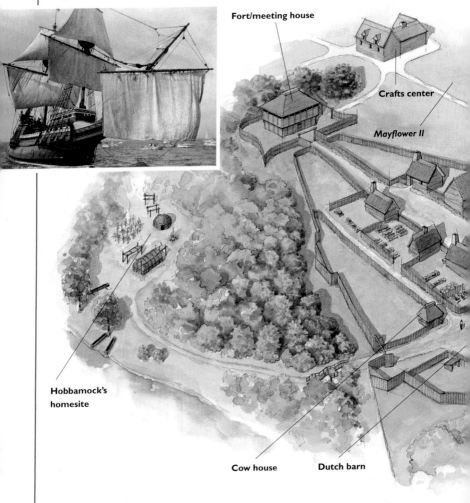

Fort/meeting house

Crafts center

Mayflower II

Hobbamock's homesite

Cow house

Dutch barn

PLIMOTH PLANTATION

Once you understand the background of the Pilgrims, you can see how they lived in their new land at Plimoth Plantation. Although living history experiences are common nowadays, this is the best in New England, and arguably in the country. The plantation is no theme park. What you see is scrupulously researched to ensure that it is the most accurate representation of Pilgrim life possible. Leaving the 21st century behind, you enter the 17th to watch Pilgrims going about their daily routines. Their clothes are coarse, crops look meager, and their simple homes are hot in summer, cold in winter. Nothing was easy. Their achievement becomes even more remarkable when you see just how hard it was to survive. You will also learn more about the Native Americans whom they met, and whose culture they affected. As fascinating for children as for adults, Plimoth Plantation is well worth a whole day's visit.

Start at the visitor center, where a short video provides useful orientation, debunking the myths and stereotypes both of the Pilgrims and the native Wampanoag. An exhibition, "Irreconcilable Differences," expands on how the

two cultures interacted. From here, you have a choice of four places to visit. To see what life was like before the Europeans arrived, walk down to Hobbamock's Homesite (see p. 202), a re-creation of a Wampanoag home. If you want to see artisans displaying their 17th-century skills, head for the Crafts Center (see p. 202). Animal lovers might like to check out the rare-breed livestock at the **Nye Barn.** Otherwise, join the majority and head for the **1627 Pilgrim Village.**

Re-creating a 17th-century community, Plimoth Plantation portrays the difficult life of early settlers.

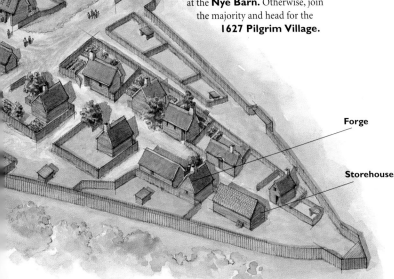

Governor's house

Forge

Storehouse

As you walk down the slope to the village, you see a two-story structure at the top of the hill. Protection and worship went hand in hand in this wooden fort, which doubled as a meeting house. Below, clinging to the hillside, is the settlement. Along the dusty track are pens with sheep and cows, and small cabins with thatched roofs. Use your free map to identify which family lived where, so you can find a particular character. Perhaps Capt. Myles Standish (1584–1656), in charge of the soldiers, or Deacon

At Plimoth Plantation, the inhabitants dress, work, and eat as the Pilgrims did.

Samuel Fuller (1580–1633), who acted as the physician. You can ask Elizabeth Hopkins about the birth of her son aboard the *Mayflower* or tune into the local gossip about Francis Billington (died 1684), a young man "not well-governed, who does not doff his hat and speaks out of turn." Throughout your visit, the residents stay strictly in character, answering your questions, but never wavering from their roles.

There is always work to be done, so they are always busy. In spring, you can watch them turning the ground and planting; in the fall, they gather the harvest. Every day, they turn out the sheep, prepare

meals, and air the sheets and blankets. Feel free to enter their homes and ask questions. If you stop at the Alden house, Priscilla explains that dinner, the main meal, consists of "pottage" made with cabbage, onion, and broth, seasoned with salt and peppercorns. No one in the village has a timepiece, so they rise, eat, and sleep according to the sun. With no honeybees, they have to buy expensive sugar and candles from England. She longs for proper apples, not the crab apples that grow wild, and hopes that the next ship will bring seeds to plant an orchard. Like the other houses, hers is one room, smoky and dark. Although all the interpreters speak in 17th-century dialect, nothing is scripted and you will hear different stories from different characters. It is all absolutely fascinating.

Down at **Hobbamock's Homesite,** you meet the Wampanoag, the "people of the dawn," or Eastern people. They lived in family groups, rather than villages. Instead of "living" a 17th-century life, the interpreters wear typical clothing and explain how life was lived. If you are lucky, they might be making a canoe, slowly burning out the center of a tree trunk. Or they might be cooking, building a *wetu* (house), or tanning hides. In the old days, they will tell you, deer, black bear, and even skunk were considered delicacies.

The **Crafts Center** is located in a modern building. Since the first colonists were not craftspeople, they had to import furniture, pottery, shoes, and baskets from England. Artisans demonstrate how these and other items, including the corsets worn by the women, were made. You learn how baskets were made for different purposes: one shape for eggs, a lidded design for holding the sewing, and a flat, open basket for carrying fruit. ■

New Bedford

AN HOUR'S DRIVE SOUTH FROM BOSTON IS NEW BEDFORD, which was once the whaling capital of the world. In the mid-19th century, New Bedford was the fourth largest seaport and one of the richest towns per capita in the United States. This was entirely due to the whaling industry, which also inspired the novel *Moby Dick*.

Scale model of a sailing ship in the New Bedford Whaling Museum

In 1841 a young Herman Melville wrote "nowhere in all America will you find more patrician-like houses, parks, and gardens more opulent, than in New Bedford." The establishment of a national historic park in 1996 helped to renew the rundown harborside, where the fishing fleet still brings home the second most valuable catch in the country. Fishermen also celebrate the Portuguese tradition of the Feast of the Blessed Sacrament each summer, while down on the waterfront, the state's official tall ship, the century-old schooner *Ernestina*, is a reminder of New Bedford's past.

On Johnny Cake Hill is a **Seamen's Bethel** *(Tel 508/992-3295)*, a church established in 1832 for the "moral and spiritual improvement of seamen." The walls are hung with memorials to those lost at sea, sobering reminders for young sailors such as Herman Melville. The prowlike pulpit is a 1959 addition, but Father Maple of the Whaleman's Chapel in *Moby Dick* could be based on the Reverend Enoch Mudge (1776–1850), chaplain here from 1832 to 1846.

Across the street is the **New Bedford Whaling Museum,** which contains one of the world's finest exhibits on the whaling industry and its practitioners. A particularly eye-catching display is the half-scale model of the *Lagoda*. Children are allowed to clamber aboard this 89-foot-long (27 m) reproduction of a whaling ship that sailed between 1841 and 1890. The atmosphere on the ship makes you

realize why, as they set out on voyages lasting from two to five years, New Bedford men would cry, "Around the world!" Pride of place in the new gallery goes to the vast skeleton of a blue whale, which is suspended from the ceiling. Display cases show over a hundred things to do with ivory and bone. There is also an exhibit devoted to *Moby Dick*, the book that Melville originally called *The Whale*, which was published in 1851. ■

New Bedford
🗺 197 C2

New Bedford N.H.P.
✉ 33 William St.
☎ 508/984-5964

New Bedford Whaling Museum
✉ 18 Johnny Cake Hill
☎ 508/997-0046
💲 $$

Historic Newport retains its charm.

Newport, R.I.

THERE ARE FEW MORE BEAUTIFUL APPROACHES TO A CITY than the drive over Newport Bridge. For a population of 27,000, the city has an embarrassment of riches: a colonial heritage, great yachting and tennis traditions, and renowned music festivals. At the top of everyone's list are the mansions, as grand as any European palace.

Newport, R.I.

 197 B1

Visitor information

✉ 23 America's Cup Ave.

☎ 401/845-9123

International Tennis Hall of Fame and Museum

✉ 194 Bellevue Ave.

☎ 401/849-3990

💲 $$. $$$$ (includes Beechwood & Belcourt)

Hunter House

✉ 54 Washington St.

☎ 401/847-7516

🕐 Closed Nov.–April

💲 $$

Start at the **visitor information center** for maps and details of tours and walks. The nearby **Museum of Newport History** *(127 Thames St., tel 401/841-8770, closed Tues., $$)*, explains how the city was settled in 1639 and developed by Quakers and Jews. The 17th- and 18th-century core of the city along with its fine 19th-century cultural institutions, are best explored on foot (see pp. 208–209). Past glories of the America's Cup tradition are preserved in the **Museum of Yachting** *(Fort Adams State Park, tel 401/847-1018, closed late Oct.–mid-May).*

The **International Tennis Hall of Fame and Museum** at the Newport Casino is a famous venue for tennis. Founded in 1880, the casino (a gentlemen's club) has the oldest continuously used grass courts in the world, where you can serve and volley on the 13 public courts on which the first United States Open was played back in 1881. The museum features video footage of early tennis stars such as Bill Tilden (1920s) and Don Budge (1930s). You can push a button to select a great match to watch, perhaps Margaret Court defeating Billie Jean King in the great 1970

was a city made up of wealthy merchants and ship owners, among them the first two owners of the **Hunter House.** Connoisseurs of 18th-century furniture come here nowadays to see the beautiful work of the famous Newport firm of Townsend and Goddard. Look for their trademark shell and the "undercutting," or space between the claw and ball foot. Don't miss the painting of two spaniels, which was presented to Dr. William Hunter, the father of the 19th-century owner of the house. It is the first work in oil by the American artist Gilbert Stuart. ∎

Wimbledon final. Among the treasures on display are the 1874 patent for a Lawn Tennis Portable Court, granted by Queen Victoria to Major Wingfield (1833–1912), the inventor of the game.

Over a century before the beginning of the Gilded Age, Newport

Above: The Newport Casino's grass tennis courts are still in use after 120 years of play.

Below: The America's Cup, the most famous international yachting trophy

America's Cup

From 1851 to 1983, the New York Yacht Club held a 134-ounce (3.8 kg) silver ewer called the America's Cup. In 1851, John Cox Stevens of the New York Yacht Club took the yacht *America* to England, and won the One Hundred Guinea Cup at the Royal Yacht Squadron's annual regatta. He took the cup to the United States, and presented it to his club. Renamed the America's Cup, it became an international challenge trophy for a match between yacht clubs.

In 1983 the run of 24 successful defenses came to an end when *Australia II* beat *Liberty* by four races to three. The connection with Newport was severed. In summer former America's Cup participants can be seen scudding across the waters of Rhode Island.

For race information: *The Museum of Yachting, Fort Adams State Park, Newport, tel 401/847-1018*. America's Cup Charters run 2-hour sunset sailing cruises *(Tel 401/846-9886)*. ∎

The past glamour of the Astors' ballroom at Beechwood Mansion is re-created in the present.

Newport mansions

When it comes to opulence, the Newport mansions are as magnificent as England's stately homes or France's châteaux of the Loire.

Visit Kingscote *(Bellevue Ave., tel 401/847-1000, closed Oct.–May, $$)* to understand how Newport became the resort of the rich and famous. In 1839, when summer visitors stayed in hotels, George Noble Jones, a plantation owner from Georgia, built the first and simplest of the mansions. It was bought by the King family after the Civil War, who commissioned Stanford White, the architect of nearby Rosecliff, to remodel the house. He added the 1881 dining room, with its walls of newfangled glass bricks, ordered from Louis C. Tiffany for 25 cents each.

Until the Breakers set new standards for ostentation, the 1852 Château-sur-Mer *(Bellevue Ave., tel 401/847-1000, closed Nov.–Jan., Mon.–Fri. Jan.–April, $$)* was the most luxurious mansion in Newport. It reflects the taste of George Peabody Wetmore, who inherited this mansion, aged only 16. It remained in the family until 1966. Architect Richard Morris Hunt began renovations in the 1870s, putting in the Italian Renaissance Revival furnishings in the dining room. Note the footrests under the table: These were not for comfort, but to protect the parquet floor from the sharp heels of ladies' shoes.

When owner Alva Vanderbilt spent 11 million dollars on the 1892 Marble House, *(Bellevue Ave., tel 401/847-1000, closed Mon.–Fri. Jan.–May, $$)*, she signaled the start of the Gilded Age. The mansion, inspired by the Petit Trianon at Versailles, broke all records for cost. The entrance features gold veined, yellow marble from Siena, Italy. In the dining room, the pink Numidian marble was cut from Algerian quarries once used in Roman times, and specially reopened for this project. Weighing 60 pounds (27 kg) each, the bronze chairs were so heavy that a footman was needed behind each one to seat guests. Most breathtaking of all is the Gold Ballroom, where Mia Farrow and Robert Redford whirled in the movie *The Great Gatsby* (1974). The 22-carat gold leaf reflects in the glass doors, French windows, and enormous mirrors that adorn the room.

The grandeur of the Breakers's facade is matched by its interior decor.

The most famous, most visited, and most extravagant of all the Newport mansions is The Breakers *(Ochre Point Ave., tel 401/847-1000, closed Mon.–Fri. Jan–May, $$$)*, an American royal palace. Gilt, marble, and silk proclaim the status of Cornelius Vanderbilt II, head of the wealthiest family in the United States. For him, this was a mere cottage, with its 70 rooms. His real home in New York City had twice that number. The Vanderbilt's favorite architect, Richard Morris Hunt, based The Breakers (1895) on the palazzos of Renaissance Italy. The library boasts a 400-year-old fireplace from Château d'Arnay-le-Duc in France, while the formal dining room soars two storys high above a table that seats 34. The tour also goes behind the scenes. In the galleried butler's pantry, the call board could summon a member of staff to any of 50 stations around the house. Behind glass are the 200 place settings of "everyday" Meissen china, while the silver was locked away in a vault 10 feet (3 m) deep.

Rosecliff *(Bellevue Ave., tel 401/847-1000, closed Oct.–May, $$)*, built in 1902, is the prettiest of the mansions, a fitting backdrop for the legendary parties and dinners staged by society hostess Theresa Oelrichs. The ballroom, the largest in Newport, measures 40 by 80 feet (12 m by 24 m), perfect for moviemakers in search of glamour. As well as Arnold Schwarzenegger's tango scene in *True Lies* (1994), the formal state dinner in *Amistad* (1997) was also shot here. In 1904, the house was the setting for a *Bal Blanc,* an all-white party where guests dressed in white and the flowers were white. When the Secretary of the Navy refused to sail a few white ships past the windows, "Tessie" Oelrichs ordered up her own fleet, decorated with white lights. Designed by Stanford White, the house took four years and two million dollars to build.

A touch of showbiz brings the Astors' Beechwood Mansion to life. You are greeted by a liveried footman before being shown around by a servant, or one of the Astor family. These costumed actors take you back to 1891, and the stories are as much about Mrs. Astor, the "Queen of American Society," as the decor. The music room was originally part of a Paris hotel. Taking a fancy to it, Mrs. Astor had it dismantled and shipped back to Newport.

Eight mansions are run by the Preservation Society of Newport County. Both Chepstow *(Narrangansett Ave.)* and The Elms *(Bellevue Ave.)* require reservations. If you plan to see more than two, buy a combination ticket. Avoid lines by arriving at either end of the day. ∎

A walk through old Newport

With its historic buildings, Newport is a delightful place for a stroll. This route takes you past colonial gems and statues of local heroes. Wear comfortable shoes, since you walk up- and downhill, and the brick sidewalks are uneven.

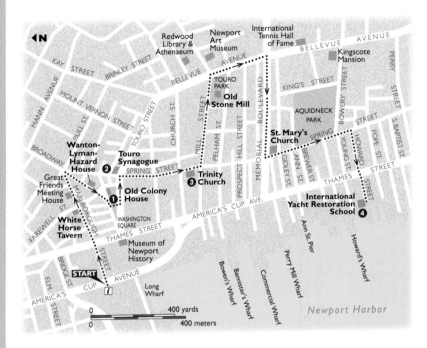

Starting from the visitor information center (*23 America's Cup Ave.*), cross the road and follow Marlborough Street. At the corner of Farewell Street is the **White Horse Tavern** (*Marlborough & Farewell Sts., tel 401/849-3600, closed for lunch Tues.*), which has been dispensing food and drink since 1673. Opposite, set back from the street, stands the Great Friends Meeting House (1699). Turn right on Broadway, pausing in front of the **Wanton-Lyman-Hazard House** (No. 17), with its off-center door. Dating from 1675, this is the oldest house in Newport.

Overlooking the harbor in Washington Square is the **Old Colony House** ❶ (*Tel 401/846-0813, closed Sun.–Wed. Oct.–May, $*). Built of English brick, this was the original seat of the colony's government. Citizens heard about the accession of King George III (1760) from the balcony; they later renounced

their allegiance. Courtroom scenes for the movie *Amistad* (1997) were filmed inside. In the park stands a statue of Oliver Hazard Perry, hero of the Battle of Lake Erie in 1812, while the Brick Market houses the **Museum of Newport History** (see p. 204).

Cross the square to Touro Street, turn left, and walk uphill to Spring Street. Just ahead is the **Touro Synagogue** ❷ (*Touro St., tel 401/847-4794, call for hours*), built in 1763. The first and the oldest synagogue in the United States and designed by Rhode Island's Peter Harrison, the building sits at an angle, so that the Torah faces east toward Jerusalem.

Turn right on Spring Street. Every other house seems to be on the National Register of Historic Places and named for former owners. Peer down side alleyways and lanes, where brick sidewalks front yet more clapboard 18th- and 19th-century houses.

On your right is the 1726 **Trinity Church** ❸ (*Queen Anne Sq., tel 401/846-0660, closed a.m. & Nov.–May*), with its high steeple. Inside is a three-tiered "wine glass" pulpit, the only one of its kind still in its original position: in the center, not off to one side.

Turn left uphill on Mill Street to Touro Park, where the **Old Stone Mill** was supposedly built by Benedict Arnold (1615–1678), not the traitor but his ancestor, the first governor of Rhode Island.

At Bellevue Avenue, you can continue ahead to the **Redwood Library** (*50 Bellevue Ave., tel 401/847-0292, guided tours Mon.–Fri. 10:30 a.m.*). Established in 1747 by Abraham Redwood, it showcases an impressive collection of paintings, antique furniture, and statuary.

Turn right along Bellevue Avenue, and right again on Memorial Boulevard, down to the corner of Spring Street. In 1953, Jacqueline Lee Bouvier married John F. Kennedy in the 19th-century **St. Mary's Church** (*Memorial Blvd., tel 401/846-4926, closed Wed. p.m.*).

Turn left on Spring Street and walk down to Howard Street, where you turn right toward the **International Yacht Restoration School** ❹ (*449 Thames St., tel 401/848-5777*). Here you can watch students building and restoring classic sailboats. ■

The **Old Colony House on Washington Square** featured in the movie *Amistad*.

🅰 See area map p. 197
▶ Visitor information center
🔁 2.6 miles (4.2 km)
🕐 2 hours
▶ International Yacht Restoration School

NOT TO BE MISSED
- Old Colony House
- Touro Synagogue
- Trinity Church
- International Yacht Restoration School

The **Redwood Library is one of Newport's many historic attractions.**

Providence, R.I.

THE CAPITAL OF RHODE ISLAND, 52 MILES (83 KM) SOUTH
of Boston, is a small, attractive city built along the Providence River.
History buffs come here to stroll Benefit Street, the so-called Mile of
History. Art lovers head straight for the Rhode Island School of
Design's Museum of Art, while gourmets rave about the restaurant
scene, a spinoff from the Johnson & Wales University.

If you haven't been to Providence
for a decade, prepare to be sur-
prised. With the opening of
**Waterplace Park and River-
walk** in the 1990s, this resurgent
city has rediscovered its waterfront.
In summer, be sure to see **Water-
Fire,** a magical stream of 80 bonfires along the Providence River
that light up the water and the
buildings along the busy banks.

The city divides into distinct
areas. **Federal Hill,** to the west,
has long had an Italian flavor, exemplified by its cafés and grocery
stores on Atwells Avenue and De
Pasquale Square. **College Hill,**
across the river, is home to Brown
University and the Rhode Island
School of Design. Then there is the
area around the **State House**
(*Smith St., tel 401/222-2357*), a
landmark of the city. Atop the
dome stands the state symbol, the
gilded statue of the Independent
Man. The charter granted to Rhode
Island in 1663 by King Charles II is
on display inside.

Along the river are renovated
old buildings and new shopping
areas, although indoor shopping
malls are nothing revolutionary in
Providence. The oldest in the
United States is **The Arcade** (*65
Weybosset St., tel 401/598-1199,
closed Sun.*), built in 1828. To see
the sights, hop on and off The Link,
the trolley (*fare 50 cents*) that loops
around them all.

In 2002, in a converted power
station, you will be able to follow
Rhode Island's history, from its
founding by Roger Williams in
1636 to the present day.

BENEFIT STREET
The most impressive street in town,
and one of the best preserved in all
New England, is Benefit Street,
lined with historic houses. There
are many reminders of the four remarkable Brown brothers, who left
their mark on Providence back in
the 18th century. Nicholas (1729–
1791) was a patron of Rhode Island
College (now Brown University).
Moses (1738–1836) gave financial

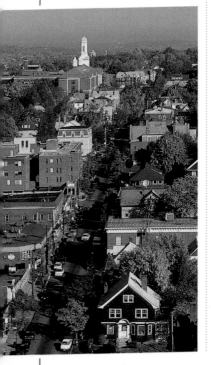

Providence, R.I.
🗺 197 A2
Visitor information
✉ Roger Williams
National Memorial
Park
☎ 401/785-9450

**Thayer Street
cuts through the
heart of town.**

Waterplace Park and Riverwalk anchor Providence's redeveloped waterfront.

John Brown House Museum

✉ 52 Power St.
☎ 401/331-8575
🕐 Closed Mon. & Sun. a.m. March–Dec. & Mon.–Thurs. Jan.–Feb.
💲 $$

RISD Museum of Art

✉ 224 Benefit St.
☎ 401/454-6500
🕐 Closed Mon.
💲 $$

backing to the Slater Mill in Pawtucket (see p. 212), kick-starting the New England industrial revolution. A third brother, Joseph (1733–1785), was an architect, designing **First Baptist Church** (75 N. Main St., tel 401/751-2266) and a mansion for John (1736–1803), now the **John Brown House Museum.** Its splendor suited the "richest merchant in Providence," a fiery patriot who entertained George Washington and Thomas Jefferson.

Brown University is the seventh oldest college in the country. On Prospect Street are the fine wrought-iron Van Wickle Gates, leading to the quadrangle. The oldest building on campus is the 1770 University Hall, used by French and colonial troops in the Revolution. Another lively and creative student body is at the influential **Rhode Island School of Design** or

RISD (pronounced Rɪz-dee). Its impressive **Museum of Art** is spread over three floors and the collection ranges from Egyptian mummies to works by Picasso. Don't miss the 800-year-old Japanese Buddha, alone in a gallery, with benches inviting you to sit and contemplate it. In the Impressionist gallery are scenes of Osny, near Paris, by Gauguin and Pissarro, set next to each other. Other major works are by Cézanne, Monet, Manet, and Renoir. American artists are also well represented, from early painters such as George Innes (1825–1894) and Fitz Hugh Lane (1804–1865) to John Singer Sargent (1856–1925), George Bellows (1882–1925), and Mary Cassatt (1845–1926). The Pendleton House, with period rooms displaying the 18th- and 19th-century American furniture, reopened in late 2000. ■

Harvesting cranberries, New England's signature fruit

More places to visit south of Boston

OCEAN SPRAY CRANBERRY WORLD

Cranberries are big business in southeastern Massachusetts, with both juice and berries exported worldwide. Ocean Spray promotes every aspect of the small, hard red fruit with a blizzard of facts. On your self-guided visit, you will find out that as early as 1683, *The Compleat Cooks Guide* had a recipe for cranberry juice, and that there are 450 berries to the pound (450 g). As for the name, this is attributed to the fruit's pale pink, crane-shaped blooms. Cranberries, you are informed, don't grow on bushes, but vines. The oldest are still fruiting after 100 years. The cooking demonstrations and free samples ensure this is a popular attraction at the new site that opened in 2000.
www.oceanspray.com 🔺 197 C3 ✉ 158 Water St., Plymouth ☎ 508/747-2350 🕐 Closed Dec.–April 🚆 Plymouth (Plymouth & Brockton)

OLD SHIP CHURCH

As well as being the finest example of an original Puritan meeting house, the Old Ship Church is the oldest wooden church in regular use in the United States, where services have continued since 1681. Look up at the ceiling, with its massive oak supports, to appreciate why the church bears its unusual name.
🔺 197 C4 (Hingham) ✉ 90 Main St., Hingham ☎ 617/749-1679 🕐 Open summer Tues.–Fri. p.m.; Sun. service 10:30 a.m. 🚆 Train to Quincy Center, then bus

SLATER MILL HISTORIC SITE

In 1793 the United States industrial revolution roared into action on the peaceful banks of the Blackstone River. Samuel Slater (1768–1835), a clever English mill worker, left home after memorizing the secrets of textile machinery and manufacture. The state legislatures of the new nation were offering bounties for technical information, and Slater and his partners produced the first cotton yarn in the country, breaking the British manufacturing monopoly. Slater's mill ran on the "Rhode Island" system of manufacture, using waterpower and machines. He staffed it with children: seven boys and two girls, all under 12. The process was eagerly copied around New England. Join up with a tour to understand the significance of the three buildings that have been restored to look as they did in 1830.
🔺 197 A3 ✉ 67 Roosevelt Ave., Pawtucket, R.I. ☎ 401/725-8638 🕐 Tours daily 10:30 a.m., 1 & 3 p.m. June–Nov.; closed Mon.–Fri., Sat.–Sun a.m. March–May & Nov.–3rd Sun. in Dec. 🚭 $ ■

A salty mixture of antique stores, cranberries, and seafaring history, Cape Cod and the islands of Nantucket and Martha's Vineyard are also blessed with some of the best beaches on the Eastern Seaboard.

Cape Cod & the islands

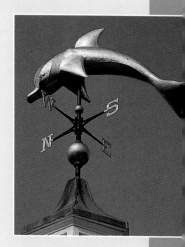

Nautical weathervane in Chatham

Cape Cod & the islands

ONE OF THE MOST FAMOUS VACATION PLAYGROUNDS IN THE UNITED STATES, Cape Cod and the islands of Martha's Vineyard and Nantucket appeal to all ages and all tastes. Families come for seaside holidays; couples get away from it all in romantic bed-and-breakfasts. There are dramatic dunes facing the Atlantic Ocean, and sheltered beaches on Cape Cod Bay. Each of the towns has a distinct character. Despite the inroads of modern development, the charm of Cape Cod and the islands is as strong as ever.

The shape of Cape Cod, or the Cape, is often described as a flexed arm, complete with elbow and bent wrist. Locals use a special code for the different areas of the peninsula. The Upper Cape, closest to the mainland, is the section from Sandwich to Falmouth. The Mid-Cape is a band that includes Barnstable, Hyannis, Dennis, and Yarmouth. Think of the Lower Cape as the area around the elbow: Brewster, Chatham, Harwich, and Orleans, while the Outer Cape is the forearm, including Eastham, Wellfleet, Truro, and on up to Provincetown. So, depending on where you start, you could go "up Cape" to Hyannis or "down Cape" to Provincetown.

The Cape is famous for its sandy beaches, but there are also bike trails, golf courses, and whale-watching trips. Shoppers meander along Mass. 6A, the Old King's Highway,

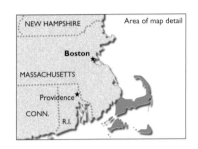

A long tradition of whaling makes the creature a popular motif throughout Cape Cod and the islands.

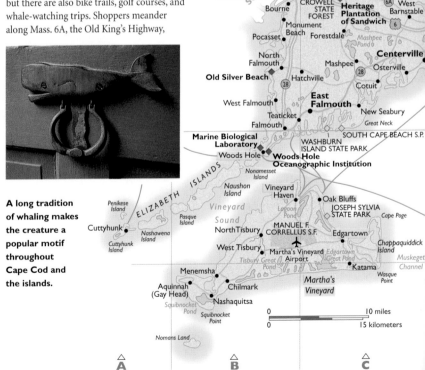

hunting for antiques and locally made crafts. Provincetown, located right at the end of the Cape, is busy, bustling, and fun, long known as an artist's colony and, more recently, for its large gay population.

To the south of the peninsula are Martha's Vineyard and, farther out to sea, Nantucket. Those who have never visited the islands tend to think of them as identical twins. After all, they were both charted by Bartholomew Gosnold (died 1607) in 1602, and together, they were bought 40 years later by Thomas Mayhew (1593–1682) of the Massachusetts Bay Colony for £40 (about $60 by today's rates) and a beaver hat. Today, both are popular as vacation destinations. However, not only do they look different, the islands also have different personalities; think of them as siblings rather than twins. The Vineyard (everyone calls it that) is larger, with more variety in the landscape; its several towns each have their own distinct character. Nantucket, out in the Atlantic Ocean, is flatter, more windswept, and has only one community, Nantucket Town. Each island has its fans, who (somewhat) jokingly disparage the other. See both, then decide for yourself.

On Cape Cod and the islands, summer is the high season, but more and more visitors are discovering the pleasures of the less crowded weeks before Memorial Day and after Labor Day. There are special festivals to provide entertainment, and more inns, museums, and crafts shops remain open. Christmas may be chilly, but candlelit tours of old houses and blazing log fires guarantee good cheer. ■

Sailing is an enjoyable way to explore Cape Cod.

Sandwich

IF YOU GET NO FARTHER THAN THE FIRST TOWN ON CAPE Cod, you will have seen one of the prettiest communities in New England. Sandwich is the oldest town on the Cape, settled in 1637. Today many residents commute to Boston from their white clapboard houses. With its pond, craft shops, and bed-and-breakfasts, this is an idyllic-looking town.

Pick up the walking guide pamphlet from the Chamber of Commerce and stroll down Water Street, stopping by the 1640 **Dexter Grist Mill,** which still grinds flour *(next to Town Hall, closed mid-Oct.–mid-May).* A few steps on is the **Thornton W. Burgess House** *(4 Water St. tel 508/888-4668, closed Oct.– April),* a shrine to the local author (1874–1965) of the Peter Cottontail children's books. Farther along the street is the **Hoxie House** *(18 Water St., tel 508/888-1173, closed mid-Oct.–mid-May),* its interior

furnished as it would have been when the saltbox-style cottage was built in 1675.

Opposite the Town Hall is the **Sandwich Glass Museum.** A visual delight, with its highly collectible colored glass sparkling in the windows, it covers the rise and fall of the town's 19th-century glass-making industry. To understand the background, begin with the audiovisual presentation, then move to Gallery 1 and the portrait of Deming Jarves (1790–1869). After the war of 1812, this Boston businessman decided to make glass

Sandwich

▲ 214 C4

Visitor information

✉ Sandwich Chamber of Commerce, 70 Main St., Buzzards Bay

☎ 508/888-5144

🕐 Closed Sat.–Sun.

instead of importing it from England. He employed glassblowers from Boston and England. A fine example of their superior skills is the sugar bowl and compote (1830) on display. Both beautiful and delicate, the layers of rings are known as "Beehive" glass. The galleries show the evolution of a distinct American glassmaking style, as new technology made pressed glass affordable to most people in the 1830s. The Victorians favored rich colors, such as blue, green, ruby, and amethyst. By 1888, producers in other states undercut Sandwich, and the Boston & Sandwich Glass Company closed for good.

HERITAGE PLANTATION OF SANDWICH

The main attraction in Sandwich is also the largest on the Cape. Situated about a mile (1.6 km) from the center of town, the plantation is subtitled "Americana Museums and Gardens," and it caters to all ages and all interests. Wander at your own pace through the lovely landscaped grounds, or take the little shuttle bus that makes regular rounds of the 75-acre (30 ha) estate, dropping visitors off at the museums, each in an interesting building. Closest to the main entrance is a round barn, modeled after the famous one at the Hancock Shaker Village in western Massachusetts. This one is the showcase for the **J. K. Lilly III Automobile Museum,** a display of antique and vintage cars. Star billing goes to the Duesenburg, specially built in 1930 for Gary Cooper. The film star paid about $14,000 for this Model J Derham Tourister, one of only eight ever made. Its lime green and sunshine yellow look positively flashy next to the first official presidential car, a 1909 White Steamer ordered by President Taft.

At the opposite end of the estate is the **Art Museum,** a diverse collection of American folk art. Climb aboard the 1912 carousel, hand-carved by Charles Looff (1852–1918), better known for his Coney Island merry-go-round. The carousel is now restored to full working order, and you can choose from 29 wooden steeds, all with real horse-hair tails. The other galleries have displays of scrimshaw, cigar store figures, art of the American West, and a rotating selection from the 200-strong archive of Currier & Ives prints. There is also the **Military Museum,** with 50 antique firearms and some 2,000 military miniatures carefully arranged into dioramas. If you are anywhere near Sandwich at the end of May or early June, head for the plantation, where the 125 varieties of rhododendron are at their best. ■

Sandwich Glass Museum

✉ 129 Main St.

☎ 508/888-0251

⊕ Closed Mon.–Tues. Nov.–Mar. & all Jan.

💲 $

Heritage Plantation of Sandwich

✉ 67 Grove St.

☎ 508/888-3300, 508/888-1222 (24-hour recorded information)

⊕ Closed mid–Oct.–April

💲 $$

Over 150 years ago, Sandwich was best known for making glass.

Bay side villages

THE BEST WAY TO EXPLORE THE VILLAGES ALONG THE north side of the Cape is to follow Mass. 6A, the Old King's Highway. Dennis and Brewster were home to daring sea captains; their mansions are a testimony to their skill and wealth.

A popular minister, after whom the town of Dennis was named, lived in the Josiah Dennis Manse.

Dennis

🅰 215 D3

Visitor information

✉ Chamber of Commerce, 242 Swan River Rd., W. Dennis

☎ 508/398-3568 or 800/243-9920

Cape Playhouse Center for the Arts

✉ 820 Mass. 6A

☎ Playhouse & cinema: 508/385-3911 Museum: 508/385-4477

💲 $$

Brewster

🅰 215 E4

Visitor information

✉ Town Office

☎ 508/896-3500

DENNIS

A quiet beach town, Dennis was established in 1783 and named for Reverend Josiah Dennis, pastor of Yarmouth's East Parish. His saltbox home, the **Josiah Dennis Manse,** showcases period decor.

New England in general, and the Cape in particular, have a tradition of summer stock theater. One of the most famous venues, located in Dennis, is the **Cape Playhouse Center for the Arts,** which encompasses a movie house and museum, as well as a theater. In 1927, Raymond Moore persuaded actors that a summer job at his Cape Playhouse *(Closed Oct.–May)* was preferable to a hot, humid New York. Among those who trod the boards of the 600-seat converted meeting house were Henry Fonda, Humphrey Bogart, and Gregory Peck. The Cape Cinema has an equally star-studded history. In 1939 it hosted the world premiere of *The Wizard of Oz.* Actress Margaret Hamilton starred as the Wicked Witch of the West, so her

affluent and appreciative audience were treated to an exclusive preview. They would also have appreciated the spectacular 1930 mural by painter Rockwell Kent (1882–1971) in the cinema, one of only three by him surviving in the United States. In the small **Cape Museum of Fine Arts,** Cape Cod artists, past and present, are represented in an attractive permanent collection, backed by temporary exhibitions.

Two delightful picnic sites are nearby. Take the Old Bass River Road inland, turning onto Scargo Hill Road, to **Scargo Hill Observatory** (1901). This stone tower has 36 steps leading up to views across Cape Cod Bay as far as Provincetown. **Sesuit Harbor** is on the water between Dennis and Brewster. Take a left on winding Sesuit Neck Road for the quiet cove, bobbing with small boats.

BREWSTER

Brewster is famous for the grand houses built by sea captains. Find their graves in the cemetery behind

The indoor-outdoor New England Fire & History Museum in Brewster contains fire-fighting equipment dating as far back as colonial days.

First Parish Church, the "Church of the Sea Captains" *(1969 Main St., tel 508/896-5577).* Brewster also has two small museums. Displays at the **Cape Cod Museum of Natural History** show how the Cape was formed by retreating ice 20,000 years ago, and how it is still changing today. Everyone enjoys the whale gallery, with its video on right whales, and the recorded groans and squeaks of humpback whales having a chat. From an indoor blind, you can spy on northern harriers and great blue herons out on the salt marsh. Not far away is the **New England Fire & History Museum,** with its unusual diorama depicting Chicago's Great Fire of 1871, complete with lights and smoke. Among the 30 working fire engines on display is the world's last remaining bright red, 1929 Mercedes-Benz. ■

Cape Cod Museum of Natural History

🅰 215 D4
✉ 869 Main St.
☎ 508/896-3867
💲 $$

New England Fire & History Museum

🅰 215 D4
✉ 1439 Main St.
☎ 508/896-5711
🕐 Closed mid-Oct.–Mem. Day
💲 $

Old King's Highway

From Bourne to Orleans, the 34-mile (55 km) stretch of Mass. 6A along Cape Cod Bay is known as the Old King's Highway (see pp. 220–21). Winding through seven communities, the road, which was originally a Native American trail, is today lined with historic houses, antique stores, and bed-and-breakfasts. Colonial records reported that the road followed a line "beginning at ye bounds between Sandwich and Barnstable, running for ye most part easterly at a rock lying in Ralph Jones, his fence, ye north side of ye sd way and a heap of stones on ye south side of sd way…" When the writer Henry David Thoreau walked the Cape over 150 years ago, he found that the road was still "a mere cart-track in the sand, commonly without any fences to confine it, and continually changing from this side to that, to harder ground, or sometimes to avoid the tide." ■

Old King's Highway drive

This drive follows Mass. 6A, the Old King's Highway. Winding its way up and down hills, it passes through picturesque villages. One minute you are in woods, the next, you have views of Cape Cod Bay or inland ponds. In fine weather, it also offers an invigorating bike ride.

Start in **Sandwich ❶**, at the Town Hall, a mini-Greek temple built in 1834. The **Sandwich Glass Museum** (see p. 216) is across the street. Follow Main Street, which passes the historic but totally rebuilt **Dan'l Webster Inn** (*149 Main St., tel 508/888-3622, www.danlwebsterinn.com*). The white house next door belonged to Capt. Ezra Nye (1798–1858), captain of a record-breaking clipper ship that completed the Atlantic crossing from Liverpool, England, to Boston in just 20 days back in 1829. Turn left on Jarves Street, then right on to Mass. 6A. Now you are on the Old King's Highway, where every curve brings a new view. Off to the right is Discovery Hill Road, leading to a little world dedicated to author Thornton W. Burgess and his children's books (see p. 216): the **Green Briar Nature Center and Jam Kitchen** (*6 Discovery Hill Rd., tel 508/888-6870, closed Sun. a.m.*). Like the Thornton W. Burgess House, this quiet corner is dedicated to the Sandwich-born author. There are nature walks in the Briar Patch Conservation Area, natural history exhibits, and a kitchen where jam is made in the old-fashioned way.

As you approach the **Barnstable ❷** town line, views open up to marshes to the south and wetlands to the north, with a line of dunes fronting Cape Cod Bay. Everywhere you look the buildings are old. The white clapboard **Olde Colonial Courthouse** (*Rendezvous Ln. & Mass. 6A, tel 508/362-8927, rarely open*) is an 1827 reconstruction of the 1772 original, destroyed by fire. Part of the **Sturgis Library** (*3090 Main St., tel 508/362-6636, closed Sun. July & Aug.*) dates back to 1644, making it the oldest public library building in the country. See a 1604 Bible on display in the Lothrop Room, once used for church services. The library is particularly useful for anyone tracing ancestors who lived on the Cape. Lawyer James Otis, (see p. 27) was born in Barnstable in 1725.

Beyond the junction with Mass. 132, look for historic houses set on spacious grounds on either side of the road. Before you reach the center of **Yarmouth ❸**, you see the **Winslow Crocker House,** dated 1780 on its redbrick chimney, and the **New Church,** built in 1870 by the Swedenborgian sect. As you drive along the Old King's Highway, every other house seems to be a bed-and-breakfast, an antique store, or a craft studio. There are silver- and goldsmiths, glassblowers, potters, and woodcarvers. The star attraction in **Dennis ❹** is the **Cape Playhouse Center for the Arts** (see p. 218), with its theater, movie house, and museum. Near the entrance to the Playhouse is a weathered stone marker, where you can just make out the directions: right to Provincetown 38 miles (61 km), left to Plymouth 39 miles (63 km). Once you are out of town, look to the right for a glimpse of **Scargo Lake,** one of many freshwater swimming ponds on the Cape.

As you come into **Brewster ❺**, you pass the **Cape Cod Museum of Natural History** (see p. 219) and the **New England Fire & History Museum** (see p. 219). To your right is the delightfully named **Brewster Ladies Library,** founded by a

group of young women in 1852 and located in this yellow and brown building since 1868. The town is famous for its handsome sea captains' houses. The **First Parish Church** *(1969 Main St., tel 508/896-5577)* came into being on October 16, 1700, and some 39 shipmasters, of whom 12 died during voyages, are commemorated inside. Many are buried in the graveyard behind the church. At the entrance to **Nickerson State Park** *(Mass 6A, tel 508/896-3491)*, good for camping, swimming, and walking, the **Cape Cod Rail Trail** crosses Mass. 6A. This is a popular cycle route, the paved path being converted from an old railroad line. Mass. 6A comes to an end at the traffic circle outside Orleans. ■

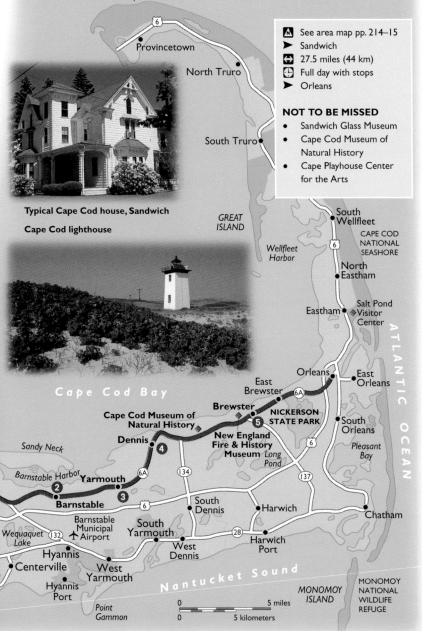

Typical Cape Cod house, Sandwich

Cape Cod lighthouse

🅰 See area map pp. 214–15
▶ Sandwich
↔ 27.5 miles (44 km)
🕐 Full day with stops
▶ Orleans

NOT TO BE MISSED
- Sandwich Glass Museum
- Cape Cod Museum of Natural History
- Cape Playhouse Center for the Arts

Cape Cod National Seashore

THE 40 MILES (64 KM) OF COAST STRETCHING FROM Chatham to Provincetown have been described as the best undeveloped shoreline on the Atlantic Coast. Since the Cape Cod National Seashore was established in 1961, the amount of protected land has gradually increased to its current 27,000 acres (10,800 ha).

Cape Cod National Seashore

www.nps.gov/caco

⬛ 215 E5

✉ Salt Pond Visitor Center, US 6, Eastham

☎ 508/255-3421

Most of the national seashore is on the Outer Cape, and the gateway is generally recognized to be the Salt Pond Visitor Center (see p. 223). From here northward, the Atlantic Ocean powers onto broad sands walled by high dunes and sculpted cliffs rising 85 to100 feet (26–30 m) high. This is the "Great Beach" described by Thoreau in his book *Cape Cod* (1865).

The shoreline is constantly changing, as water surges in from the ocean, displacing and moving sand south toward Chatham or north to the tip near Provincetown. Winds and storms also change the landscape, dredging new canals, filling in old ones, and causing erosion. Lighthouses are particularly vulnerable, and some, such as **Highland Light** (*Highland Rd.,*

off Mass. 6A, closed Oct.–May) in North Truro, have been moved inland to prevent them from falling into the sea. Highland Light (1797), the Cape's first lighthouse, is often called Cape Cod Light. In 1996, it was moved 150 yards inland.

Not all of the national seashore is so dramatic. There are peaceful woods of pine and red cedar, hidden coves, and wetlands such as **Nauset Marsh,** a haunt of birdwatchers. In the neighboring **Salt Pond,** you can see clam diggers bent over, raking for shellfish at low tide on Sundays in summer *(permit required)*. During the winter, you may spot harbor seals as they "haul out," or drag themselves onto the sand bars off **Coast Guard Beach.** As well as land, sand, and sea, the national seashore looks

after an attractive collection of buildings. The **Atwood Higgins House** *(Bound Brook Rd., Wellfleet, closed Sat.–Wed. & Fri. a.m. mid-Oct.–Easter)* in Wellfleet is a 1730s Half Cape that grew into a Three-Quarter and then a Full Cape. Find out exactly how these architectural styles developed in the exhibition at the Salt Pond Visitor Center (see below). In 1868, the grandest house around was the **Captain Penniman House** *(Off Mass. 6 in Eastham, 1.25 miles from Orleans traffic circle, closed a.m. & mid-Oct–Easter)*, built by the whaling captain who took his family along on three voyages.

To get the best out of the national seashore, start at the **Salt Pond Visitor Center.** Orient yourself by looking at the model of Cape Cod, the islands, and the Atlantic Ocean. Then watch one of the regular showings of *The Sands of Time,* a short film that explains how Cape Cod was formed. Don't miss the exhibition, a first-rate background to the flora and fauna, to Cape Codders themselves, and to how they lived. You will learn to identify bayberry, a popular candle scent; the beach pea, with its tiny edible peas; and the white cedar, whose decay-resistant wood is used for shingles on typical Cape Cod houses. Industries such as shipbuilding, whaling, saltworks, and cranberry harvesting are reflected with photographs and tools of these trades.

You can enjoy the national seashore in many ways. Follow the walking and biking trails, swim and surfboard, picnic, or have an evening campfire in designated locations. Some areas and trails are wheelchair accessible, and the **Buttonbush Trail,** starting at the visitor center, is designed for those who are visually impaired. This short path has a guide rope, plus explanations in Braille and in large lettering. During the summer season, there are ranger-led walks and other special activities.

At the tip of the Cape is the **Province Lands Visitor Center.** From the observation deck, you can look over the dunes to Provincetown and also out to sea, where you may spot whales. ∎

Few houses break the line of dunes along Cape Cod National Seashore.

Province Lands Visitor Center

⓵ 215 D5

✉ Race Point Rd., Provincetown

☎ 508/487-1256

Provincetown is known for its relaxed inhabitants.

Outer Cape

AS YOU DRIVE NORTH ONTO THE OUTER CAPE FROM ORleans to Provincetown, the landscape changes. The trees are more stunted, and high dunes on the ocean shore take the brunt of the Atlantic weather. This is the "old Cape Cod" that locals love. Turn off Mass. 6, left down a lane to the bay, or right for the ocean beaches (see pp. 228–29). Even in midsummer, you can still be on your own.

Wellfleet

Ⓜ 215 E4

Visitor information
www.wellfleetchamber.com

✉ Chamber of Commerce, off Mass. 6, South Wellfleet

☎ 508/349-2510

First Congregational Church

✉ 200 Main St.

☎ 508/349-6877

Eastham is the home of the **Salt Pond Visitor Center** (see p. 223), and the Cape's oldest windmill, dating from 1680. Off to the west of Mass. 6 is the unspoiled town of **Wellfleet.** Set on a slope overlooking salt marshes, the town is peaceful, as much of its land is protected by the Massachusetts Audubon Wildlife Sanctuary and Cape Cod National Seashore. Dubbed Port aux Huitres ("Port of the Oysters") by French explorer Samuel de Champlain in 1606, Wellfleet is still synonymous with oysters. The clock in the tower of the **First Congregational Church,** runs on ship's time:

When you hear eight chimes (eight bells), your watch should say four p.m. Old sail lofts have been converted into some 20 galleries, showing jewelry, painting, and pottery.

Blink and you could miss **Truro.** If you want few people, an unspoiled landscape, and fine beaches, you could be in the right spot. Back in 1620, the newly arrived Pilgrims uncovered corn, stored away by the Native Americans, on **Corn Hill.** It helped them through the first winter. Farther north is the **Pilgrim Spring Trail,** leading to the spring where they drew their "first New England water."

**Above right:
Sunset fishing
from a Province-
town jetty**

PROVINCETOWN

Provincetown is at the end of the Cape, protected by a crescent of dunes. Do not try to drive through town; go straight to a parking lot and walk. Although the center is densely packed with small houses and stores, there are only two main streets. **Bradford Street** runs inland; **Commercial Street,** along the waterfront, is a 3-mile-long (5 km) lane that is one-way for traffic, two-way for bikes, and any way for pedestrians. As the name implies, Commercial Street is the business hub of town; here you can buy a T-shirt, rent a bike, order a sandwich, browse in art galleries, and eat in quality restaurants.

Across from the Chamber of Commerce are MacMillan and Fisherman's wharves, where a few boats still unload their catch, and visitors board for tours of the harbor and whale-watching trips. P-town, as it is known, is popular with the gay community, with several festivals (see p. 258) each year.

At the northern tip of the town is the 252-foot-tall (76 m) **Pilgrim Monument.** It is the tallest granite structure in the country: climb 116 stairs plus 60 ramps for a 360-degree panorama. A small museum by the monument chronicles the town's history. As well as the quilts, postcards, and glass, find out about the town's theatrical importance. ∎

Provincetown

 215 D5

Visitor information

✉ Chamber of
   Commerce, 307
   Commercial St.
☎ 508/487-3424

**Pilgrim Monument
and Provincetown
Museum**

✉ High Pole Hill Rd.
☎ 508/487-1310
🕐 Closed Dec.–March
💲 $$

Artistic license

In 1999, Provincetown celebrated 100 years of the Impressionist-influenced Cape Cod School of Art, founded by Charles W. Hawthorne (1872–1930). For some 30 years, he gave weekly painting demonstrations in public, on a wharf. "Make your canvas drip with sunlight," he exhorted his students. The Provincetown Art Association (460 Commercial St., tel 508/487-1750), the focal point of the arts scene today, reflects the work of artists past and present from Provincetown, Truro, and Wellfleet. Theater also has a strong tradition here. The Provincetown Players were formed in 1916, and were soon on stage for Bound East for Cardiff, Eugene O'Neill's first play. Tennessee Williams came here in the 1940s, while he revised The Glass Menagerie, and in the 1960s, actors such as Richard Gere, Al Pacino, and Jill Clayburgh appeared at the innovative Act IV Theater. ∎

Fishing boats still unload their catch at the Fish Pier in Chatham.

Chatham to Woods Hole

CHATHAM AND WOODS HOLE ARE LIKE BOOKENDS FOR the stretch of the Cape facing Nantucket Sound. The straggling villages of Harwich, Osterville, and Centerville are lovely spots, while the Shining Sea Bikepath is a short but pretty route along the shore between Falmouth and Woods Hole. Right in the middle is Hyannis, the commercial heart of the peninsula, where the often garish roadside development and shopping centers seem to be at odds with the picturesque image of old Cape Cod.

Chatham
215 E3
Visitor information
✉ Chatham Chamber of Commerce, 2377 Main St.
☎ 508/945-5199
🕐 Closed Mon.–Fri. off-season

Hyannis
215 D3
Visitor information
✉ Hyannis Chamber of Commerce, 1481 Mass. 132
☎ 508/362-5230
🕐 Closed Sun. Oct.–May

Set right on the Cape's elbow is **Chatham,** which has a well-defined center. The tall steeple of the **First Congregational Church** and the saw-toothed tower of **First Methodist** are landmarks on Main Street, where exclusive stores rub shoulders with the Ben Franklin variety store. Just north of town is "The Provider" statue at the Fish Pier, which honors Chatham fishermen, who still return with catches of lobster, flounder, and scallops. South of town **Chatham Lighthouse** is home of the U.S. Coast Guard and

a base for the United States Weather Service, and also the entrance to the **Monomoy National Wildlife Refuge.** The only wilderness area in southern New England, the two Monomoy Islands were cut off from the mainland by storms in 1958, and remain accessible only by boat. (Visits are organized by the Cape Cod Museum of Natural History, in Brewster, see p. 219).

From Chatham, Mass. 28 leads to Harwichport, a quiet hideaway with good beaches. Just inland is **Harwich Center,** consisting of a handful of white buildings. One is the **Brooks Academy Museum** *(80 Parallel St., tel 508/432-8089),* a handsome mid-19th-century Greek Revival building with displays of old photographs of the community and the history of the cranberry industry. Farther west on Mass. 28 is **Hyannis,** with a mixture of stores and restaurants on Main Street. One Cape Cod institution here is the **Melody Tent,** an outdoor concert stage; the other is the Kennedy Compound. Hyannis and the Kennedys have been linked since 1926, when Joseph P. and Rose Kennedy first rented a house here. During John F. Kennedy's presidency, the compound served as the Summer White House. The story is told through photographs in the small **John F. Kennedy Hyannis Museum** *(397 Main St., tel 508/790-3077).* Hyannis is the Cape's transportation hub, with a small airport and year-round ferry departures for Nantucket and seasonal ferries to Martha's Vineyard.

Farther west, **Woods Hole** is crowded in summer with people getting on and off the ferries to Martha's Vineyard. This picturesque village is perhaps best known for the **Woods Hole Oceanographic Institution,** which discovered the wreck of the *Titanic.* The story of this discovery is told in the Exhibit Center *(15 School St., tel 508/289-2663 or 508/289-2252, closed Labor Day–Mem. Day, $),* with videos of minisub *ALVIN.* Nearby is the **Marine Biological Laboratory** *(Water St., tel 508/289-7423, phone 2 weeks ahead for tours, summer only).* Founded in 1888, it has expanded

its summer program into a year-round study facility, attracting scientists and students from around the world. The one-room exhibition in the visitor center gives only a hint of what goes on in the large brick buildings nearby. If you can, take one of the free weekday tours through the laboratories. Parking in Woods Hole is notoriously difficult, so either bike or take the WHOOSH trolley from Falmouth parking lots. ∎

The imposing exterior of the John F. Kennedy Hyannis Museum

Cranberries

Call them bounce berries, craneberries, or sassamanesh—cranberries are one of the few fruits native to North America. Growing wild on the Cape, they provided food for the Indians and Pilgrims. Sailors ate them to prevent scurvy (they are rich in vitamin C) and used them as ballast on ships. The breakthrough for producers was about 1816, when Henry Hall of Dennis discovered that a fine layer of sand on the vines produced a larger, stronger fruit. Today, Cape Cod grows about 10 percent of Massachusetts' total crop. In September, Harwich, the home of the oldest commercial bogs in the country, hosts a two-week festival celebrating this hard, red, bitter fruit. *(Harwich Chamber of Commerce, tel 508/432-1600).* ∎

Falmouth

🅰 214 B3

Visitor information

✉ 20 Academy Ln.

☎ 508/548-8500 or 800/526-8532

🕐 Closed Sat.–Sun. off-season

Cape Cod beaches

Cape Cod is famous for its more than 300 miles (483 km) of clean, broad, sandy shoreline. In Cape Cod Bay, on the north or bay side of the peninsula, the sea is cold. On the ocean side, where the Atlantic rolls in along the beaches of the Cape Cod National Seashore, the water is even colder. Bathing here in the muggy height of summer is regarded as vigorous refreshment, but the most popular and populated beaches are on the south side, facing Martha's Vineyard and Nantucket Island. Here, the Gulf Stream, curling in from the south, warms the calm water.

There are beaches for all. Windsurfers strut their stuff along the breezy Cape Cod National Seashore, which administers half a dozen beaches between Nauset Beach, Orleans, and Provincetown. One of them is Coast Guard Beach, which was named as one of America's top 20 beaches in 1999, by Florida International University professor "Dr. Beach." Known for its heavy surf, Coast Guard sits below 100-foot-high (30 m) clay cliffs and the Highland Light (see p. 222).

By contrast, families with small children always enjoy Kalmus Beach in Hyannis, or Old Silver Beach in North Falmouth, where the water is clear, calm, and shallow for a long way out. Walkers like to hike Corporation Beach in Dennis, on the bay side, especially at sunset, while the 7 miles (11 km) of dunes on Sandy Neck form part of a 1,300-acre (526 ha) conservation area protruding into Cape Cod Bay from a base near the Barnstable/Sandwich town line. This barrier island is home to a wide range of wildlife. You can also drive out with a four-wheel drive *(permit required)*, then head for the unspoiled easternmost tip, which is off-limits to beach buggies.

Surf fishing runs from May through October, with the very tip of the Cape, at Race Point Beach, Provincetown, particularly fruitful. The shore drops away suddenly, so whales often come in quite close here, as do striped bass and bluefish. Few beaches are firm enough for bike riding, but it's exhilarating to rent a bike in Provincetown to explore the 5-mile-long (8 km) Province Lands Bicycle Trail through the dunes. Off this loop, spurs lead right to the beach for a cooling dip.

Out on Martha's Vineyard, State Beach at Edgartown is as busy as neighboring Chappaquiddick's fine East Beach is empty. On Nantucket, Surfside is popular for its miles of sand plus facilities such as lifeguards, bathhouses, food, and restrooms. Madaket is the westernmost beach on Nantucket, where locals and vacationers go to watch the sunset.

History is everywhere. Walk on First Encounter Beach, Eastham, and you are in the footsteps of the Pilgrims who first met the Native Americans here; bodysurf at Marconi Beach and recall the Italian whose transatlantic wireless station stood here. In 1849 writer Henry David Thoreau hiked to the end of the Cape, noting the flotsam and jetsam from shipwrecks, and wrote, "A man may stand there and put all America behind him." You can do the same today. ■

Tip:
The $20 season pass gives free parking at any national seashore beaches from Provincetown to Eastham. The normal fee is $7 per day. Passes are available from visitor centers, or beach kiosks from May onward. ■

Above: With its high dunes and Atlantic surf, Nauset Beach is one of the best walking beaches on Cape Cod.
Below: At the height of summer, children enjoy a day on the beach at Truro.

Martha's Vineyard

MARTHA'S VINEYARD SITS JUST 5 MILES (8 KM) SOUTH OF Cape Cod. Aboard a ferry from Falmouth or Woods Hole, you can see the low outline of the island ahead. The Vineyard has a Norman Rockwell appeal, with a slower pace than the mainland. Easy on the eye, the beaches are broad, the hills low, the meadows edged by stone walls, the woods thick with black tupelo and red cedar.

Victorian cottages testify that Oak Bluffs has been a popular resort for more than a century.

Martha's Vineyard

🅜 214 C1

Visitor information

www.mvy.com

✉ Martha's Vineyard Chamber of Commerce, Beach Rd., Vineyard Haven

☎ 508/693-0085

With its hidden harbors and high cliffs, the island is only 23 miles (37 km) wide. The main towns are on the eastern shore. The largest is **Vineyard Haven,** the only year-round ferry port and an attractive base for exploring the island.

Farther down the east coast is **Oak Bluffs,** which started out as a Methodist campsite in 1835 and developed into a full-blown resort. Houses still sport frivolous Gothic Revival "gingerbread" decoration. You can ride the Flying Horses carousel, which has been part of the entertainment since 1876, when it competed for trade with a roller-skating rink and theaters. Back then, 30,000 people would ooh and aah as fireworks celebrated the end of the summer season. Many stayed at the **Camp Ground,** just west of Circuit Avenue. Using the same

layout, the tent sites were gradually replaced by the permanent lilac, yellow, and pistachio dollhouse-like cottages that you see here today. Right in the middle is Trinity Park, with the enormous wrought-iron 1879 **Tabernacle,** large enough to hold a congregation 3,000 people strong beneath its 100-foot-high (30 m) canopy. Because the Methodist church was racially integrated, Oak Bluffs was also one of the first vacation resorts open to African-Americans.

Where Oak Bluffs is jolly, **Edgartown** is elegant. Down by the harbor, sea captains showed off their wealth, building handsome houses along North and South Water Streets. Today's affluent visitors stay on private estates out of town, but still come in to shop at the stylish stores. Walk south along

Water Street to admire the 150-year-old pagoda tree; head north for the town dock and the ferry across to the rustic islet of Chappaquiddick (known locally as Chappy), with its long, unspoiled East Beach.

Although the first settlement on the Vineyard was established in 1642, most of what you see is 19th

Vineyard Museum *(School & Cooke Sts., tel 508/627-4441, closed Sun.–Mon. in summer, Sun.–Tues. in winter)* covers the full range of the island's history. In the "Maritime" exhibit, you can see the exotic items brought back from whaling voyages and even the ship's logbooks, some highly decorated, that record the number of whales caught, and how

century, built on the profits of whaling. The grandest house of all is the **Daniel Fisher House** on Main Street, built in 1840 for the then staggering cost of $250,000. A medical doctor and merchant, as well as the owner of a bank, a candle factory, an oil refinery, and the town wharf, Fisher (1791–1876) could afford it. Two years later, the equally splendid **Old Whaling Church** was constructed next door; it is now an arts center. Its 12-over-12 windows soar one story high, while in the 92-foot (28 m) clock tower, the bell still tolls the hours. Behind them stands the oldest house on the island (1672), now the **Vincent House Museum** *(Tel 508/627-8619, closed Sun. in summer)*. Tours of all three properties start at the museum; phone for details. A few blocks away, the small

many barrels of oil each produced. Then, look at the re-created try-works, to see how blubber was boiled down in huge cauldrons.

These towns are "down-island"; if you head west, or "up-island," you find the pleasant hamlets of **Chilmark, West Tisbury,** and, right at the very end of the island, **Aquinnah** (formerly Gay Head). The attractions at Aquinnah are the beach and dramatic cliffs topped by a lighthouse, one of several on the Vineyard. This is a great spot for watching sunsets.

Getting around the Vineyard by bus and taxi is easy, so there is no need for a car. The cycling is fun, too, with over 100 miles (160 km) of car-free bike trails. Only fit and experienced cyclists, however, should try pedaling around the island in one day (see pp. 264–65). ■

The high cliffs at Aquinnah mark the westernmost point of Martha's Vineyard.

"Fifteen thousand pairs of stockings, three thousand mittens and six hundred wigs for seamen were knit annually. It used to be said that when you reached Cape Poge Light, you could hear the knitting needles in Edgartown."
—S. A. Devens, *Sketches of Martha's Vineyard* (1838) ■

Nantucket

SHAPED LIKE A BOOMERANG POINTING STRAIGHT OUT INTO the Atlantic, Nantucket sits 30 miles (48 km) off the mainland. Over the centuries, the island has seen boom and bust, as local industries such as whaling, fishing, trading, and smuggling have flourished and faltered. Today, the mainstay of the economy is tourism. In summer, the population of only 7,000 year-round swells to 40,000 as vacationers from the United States and abroad arrive to experience the charm of what is known as the Little Gray Lady.

It is hard not to be seduced by this island, particularly if you arrive by boat. Whether you take the two-hour-fifteen-minute boat ride or the high-speed catamaran (one hour) from Hyannis, your first view of **Nantucket Town** is of white-trimmed, gray buildings clustered around a sailboat-filled harbor. Behind, the steeples of a few churches higher up the hill stand out against a blue sky. The town itself looks like a film set for a historic drama. You expect to see ladies in hoop skirts swishing along the brick sidewalks, and men in frock coats striding along the cobblestones. Neon lights and fast food chains are banned; there are no traffic lights; and even the signposts are tasteful. It is almost too good to be true. Nantucket is small—only about one-half the size of the Vineyard—so there is no need to

take your own car. Walk around town, take a shuttle bus to the beach, or rent a car if you must. Best of all, bicycle. The system of color-coded bike paths now extends to Siasconset (pronounced Sconset) in the east, and Madaket in the west (see p. 263).

First, explore Nantucket Town, which has some 800 buildings that predate the Civil War. Many are now stylish stores, restaurants, and bed-and-breakfasts. Walk up **Main Street,** the broad boulevard leading uphill from the harbor. This was the first part of town to be rebuilt in brick after the Great Fire of 1846 destroyed about one-third of the buildings in the community. Toward the top is the important-looking **Pacific National Bank,** which stands as a reminder of Nantucket's heyday in the early 19th century, when it was the third largest city in the state, behind only Boston and Salem. A few steps away, on the east side of Main Street, is where R.H. Macy (1822–1877) learned the trade of shopkeeping from his father before setting off to make his fortune in New York, via Boston. A plaque marks the site, now part of Murray's Toggery Shop, home of the faded pink cotton clothing known as Nantucket Reds.

Farther up at 96 Main Street is the **Hadwen House** (*Contact Nantucket Historical Assoc.*), one of several mansions on this block. Its

Nantucket's atmospheric streets (above left) complement its busy and scenic shoreline (above right).

Nantucket

🅰 215 E1

Visitor information

www.nantucketchamber.org

✉ Nantucket Chamber
of Commerce, 48
Main St., Nantucket
Town

☎ 508/228-1700

🕐 Closed Sat.–Sun.

**Nantucket
Historical
Association**

✉ 15 Broad St.,
Nantucket Town

☎ 508/228-1894

🕐 Limited hours
Oct.–May, phone
ahead

💲 Whaling Museum &
Hadwen House: $$$

owner, William Hadwen (1791–1862), was one of the wealthiest men in Massachusetts. Nearby, at 12 Liberty Street, the **Macy-Christian House** *(Contact Nantucket Historical Assoc.)*, dates from a century earlier. The low ceilings and creaking floors show its age, while period rooms are furnished in the styles of the 18th and 19th centuries.

Centre Street, running parallel to the harborfront, was known as Petticoat Row because, in the heyday of the whaling industry, businesses here were run by the women while their menfolk were away at sea. To the right is the **Nantucket Atheneum** *(Lower India St., tel 508/228-1110, closed Sun.–Mon., & Sun. Mem. Day–Labor Day)*, an elegant Greek revival structure dating from 1847. One of the oldest libraries in the country, it is open to all: Settle down and read the newspaper or admire the collection of paintings and ship models. Upstairs is the Great Hall, which has long been a forum. Emerson, Thoreau and abolitionist Frederick Douglass in the 19th century and economist and Harvard professor John Kenneth Galbraith (born 1908) and former NBC news anchorman John Chancellor (1927–1996) in the 20th have all lectured here.

Closer to the harbor, at 13 Broad Street, is the **Whaling Museum** *(Contact Nantucket Historical Assoc.)*, set in a former spermaceti candle factory that was owned by William Hadwen (see above). Regular talks explain the hows and whys of whaling, from the men who sailed the ships to the places they went, and how they hunted their prey. Whalers were the first

Nantucket Lifesaving Museum

✉ 158 Polpis Rd.

☎ 508/228-1885

🕐 Closed Columbus Day—mid-June

💲 $

Nantucket's Whaling Museum, tracing the island's industry, is one of the best in New England.

factory ships, spending three to five years at sea, and in the 1820s–40s there were 88 ships in the island's fleet. It was a dangerous business: Take a look at the small whaleboat on show, then compare it with the 43-foot (13 m) skeleton of a fin-back whale. Sperm whales are even bigger, up to 87 feet (26 m) long. Imagine yourself in a whaleboat, pulled by a harpooned whale desperate to escape; this is what locals called a "Nantucket sleigh ride." As well as harpoons and blubber pikes, the museum has scrimshaw and portraits of sea captains. One was Mayhew Folger (1794–1828), who came across the missing H.M.S. *Bounty* mutineers on Pitcairn Island in 1808. Check out the Navigation Room, where a huge map traces the voyage of a whaler that

left Nantucket in 1846 and returned four years later. By 1860 the whaling industry was dead, overtaken by the discovery of petroleum oil.

AROUND THE ISLAND

When Nantucket Town is busy, head for **Siasconset** on the island's eastern tip. With a post office, a grocery store, and a clutch of tiny cottages, this hamlet is

something out of a fairy story. The white picket fences, handkerchief-size gardens, and front porches all hark back to days gone by. Down on Codfish Park Road, you can see the gaps where severe storms have swept away houses. If you return to Nantucket Town by Polpis Road, you pass by the **Nantucket Lifesaving Museum.** A reconstruction of the Lifesaving Station built at Surfside beach in 1874, this building is small but full of memorabilia. It all comes to life when the enthusiastic volunteers describe how the "Soldiers of the Surf" saved ships stranded on the infamous Nantucket shoals. They will show you the cork life jacket, described in the framed clipping from *Harpers Weekly* of May 19, 1877, that hangs nearby on the wall. They will also explain how the ingenious breeches buoy rescue system worked. Prized exhibits include a rare 19th-century surfboat and the only original beachcart still in existence.

Nantucket prides itself on being separate and different from the mainland. Old-fashioned ways continue, such as the polite request that proper attire be worn in town. That means no bathing suits or bare feet in stores and restaurants. In the evening, men tend to wear jackets and ladies put on dresses or smart trousers. But the island is changing. Those who know Nantucket well talk about the old days, when summer people stayed for weeks or months at a time and became part of island life. Now company presidents and CEOs arrive by executive jet, play golf for the day, and jet out again. New summer houses are being built: enormous mansions that are a far cry from the simple summer places of the past. As always in small resort communities, expansion, development, and conservation are major topics of conversation. ∎

Travelwise

Cycling is a popular way
to explore the region.

TRAVELWISE INFORMATION

PLANNING YOUR TRIP

WHEN TO GO

Boston is a year-round city, always bustling and busy, with plenty to do and plenty to see, fulfilling every interest and every need. It is only the weather that might dictate whether you want to spend more time indoors or outdoors. Age and tastes can always be accommodated, from families to grandparents, large budgets to limited means, from the refined to the raucous. (Note: All towns mentioned in this section are in Massachusetts unless otherwise indicated.)

The first two months of the year are the coldest, so theater comes into its own, along with the rich variety of museums, art galleries, and exhibitions. Thanks to an efficient and reasonably priced public transportation system, it is also easy to get around from one sight to another. Extra attractions Downtown include celebrations of food and wine (see pp. 257–58), reflecting the city's revitalized culinary scene. Since hotel prices plummet at this time of year, winter is an attractive time for those seeking a budget vacation.

In spring, the climate can swing from freezing to balmy in a matter of days, with everyone looking forward to the start of the Red Sox season (see p. 260) in April, along with the Boston Marathon and the annual Patriots' Day holiday (see p. 257), both on April 19. There is nothing like a lawn of bobbing daffodils to cheer you up, and the daffodil festivals on Nantucket and down in Bristol, Rhode Island (see p. 257) are justifiably popular. Although it is still worth wrapping up well, this is also when the cruises on the Charles River (see p. 261) and trips on the Swan Boats (see pp. 108-109) in the Public Garden

reappear. May can be rather crowded as proud parents and relatives flock to the 60 or so colleges in the Greater Boston area to celebrate graduations. The Boston Pops Orchestra season (see p. 258), now well into its second century, opens at the beginning of the month.

New England's music choice is hard to rival, and in summer there seem to be concerts everywhere—often outdoors. You can listen to jazz, chamber music or orchestral classics, all at reasonable prices. August is the time for Italian *festas* (saint's day celebrations), which involve lively processions and floats parading through the narrow streets of the North End. More contemporary is Provincetown Carnival Week (see p. 258), when the gay and lesbian community indulges in parties and lavish costume parades.

New England's fall is justifiably famous, but it is not limited to the countryside. The climate is also perfect for exploring Boston. After Labor Day, hotel rooms can be hard to come by for a few days as students (with anxious parents) return to college. September also heralds the start of another season for the century-old Boston Symphony Orchestra (see p. 258), while October in general, and Halloween in particular (see p. 258), give Salem the chance to exploit its witches to the hilt, with tours of haunted houses and modern-day witchcraft fairs. Similarly, Plymouth is the focus of the limelight around the Thanksgiving period.

The weeks before Christmas are particularly attractive in and around Boston. Apart from the impressive Christmas trees on the Common and outside the Prudential Center, historic houses on Cape Cod, Cape Ann, and in Newport, R.I., are lit by candles, with trees dressed as

they were in Victorian days for the festive season. The year ends in high style, with First Night (see p. 258), a Boston invention, now copied by many towns and cities. Millions of people descend on Downtown Boston to enjoy parades and fireworks, as well as music and shows in pubs, clubs, halls, and even churches on New Year's Eve. Sensibly, the subway system is free after midnight.

See pp. 259–264 for more details if you wish to plan your trip around one of the many artistic, cultural, sporting, and other events that take place in Boston throughout the year.

CLIMATE

New England boasts four distinct seasons. Boston's climate, however, is hugely influenced by the ocean. The locals like to complain about the notorious "nor'easters" that can usher in blinding rainstorms. Then there's also the chance that Logan International Airport might be "socked in" with fog. Although these instances are relatively rare, the weather can be unpredictable, so it is worth carrying some sort of protection from the rain. If you are going out to sea (for whale-watching, for example), take some extra warm clothing.

In winter, Boston can be bitterly cold, while high summer can bring high temperatures and humidity. That is why May and the fall (between September and early November) are particular favorites for visitors. Average maximum daily temperatures between December and February hover around 37°F. Average maximum temperatures increase rapidly throughout the spring (March 46°F, April 56°F, May 66°F) with June through September remaining consistently above 70°F. Temperatures return to comfortable levels in October (63°F) and November (52°F) to round out the year.

WHAT TO TAKE

Casual dress is the order of the day. Medium weight clothes are suitable for most of the year, although lightweight clothing during the months of July and August is essential. A jacket and tie for men is often required in the evening for the more formal restaurants in the city. Ask when you make reservations to avoid any embarrassment.

FURTHER READING

Apart from those authors and their works referred to on pp. 178–79, other entertaining books on the region include:

The Curse of the Bambino (Penguin, 1991) by Dan Shaughnessy, which examines the legend of baseball's Red Sox and their lack of success.
The Rascal King: The Life and Times of James Michael Curley, 1874–1958 (Addison Wesley, 1992) by Jack Beatty, is all about Boston's most famous mayor, and his notorious political machine.
The Complete Guide to Boston's Freedom Trail (Newtowne Press, 1990) by Charles Bahne is exhaustive but entertaining.
The Perfect Storm (W. W. Norton, 1997) by Sebastian Junger; the best-selling novel about the ever present dangers of New England's fishermen.
The Fitzgeralds and the Kennedys: An American Saga (Simon & Schuster, 1987), by Doris Kearns Goodwin, tells the story of the ill-fated Boston dynasty that still fascinates many people.

HOW TO GET TO BOSTON

PASSPORTS & VISAS

Thanks to the Visa-Waiver Scheme, nationals of the U.K., Japan, and most western European countries do not need a visa if they are staying for less than 90 days. A valid passport

and onward/return air ticket are, however, necessary. If you have any doubts about your eligibility, it is essential to check with the nearest U.S. Embassy or Consulate well before you plan to go. Canadian and Mexican visitors need proof of citizenship rather than visas.

BY AIR

Boston is served by **Logan International Airport,** tel 800/23 LOGAN or 800/262-3335, one of the world's major airports. All major international and national carriers fly here.

T.F. Green Airport, tel 401/737-8222, outside Providence, R.I. offers an alternative that is growing in popularity, thanks to the success of low-cost airlines and to its proximity to attractions south of Boston. Boston itself is only an hour away.

Logan airport to the city
Logan Airport is 3 miles (4.8 km) from Downtown Boston. Access is easy, using any of the public transportation, water shuttle, taxi, water taxi, or limousine services.

Massport operates free shuttle buses linking the important terminals and transportation stops. The No. 11 circles between each terminal (A, B, C, D, and E). Bus No. 33 runs between terminals C, D, and E and the T (subway) stop. Bus No. 22 connects terminals A and B and the T.

Taxis charge about $10–$12 to Downtown locations. The T (subway system) costs $1.

Airport Water Shuttle, tel 617/330-8680. A seven-minute ride across the harbor to Rowes Wharf offers spectacular views of the city. Purchase tickets on board: $10 for adults, $5 for senior citizens, children under 12 free. Every 15 minutes, Mon.–Fri. 6 a.m.–8 p.m. & Fri. 6

p.m. to 11 p.m.; Sat. & Sun. every 30 minutes, 10 a.m.–11 p.m. No service on major holidays.

City Water Taxi, tel 617/422-0392. These boats serve 10 destinations in Boston Harbor, from the World Trade Center to Charlestown Navy Yard. Take the No. 66 bus to the departure point. Purchase tickets ($10) on board. Services run April–mid-Oct. 7 a.m.–7 p.m.

Harbor Express, tel 617/376-8417. Boats link the South Shore (Quincy) with Logan and Downtown Boston. Year-round regular service (from $5).

BY TRAIN

Amtrak, tel 617/482-3660, provides swift rail access from New York City (208 miles/325 km), Philadelphia, Pa., and Washington, D.C., with hourly arrivals at South Station.

BY BUS

Greyhound Buses, tel 800/231-2222, arrive at South Station, while most other bus lines arrive and leave from the Trailways Bus Terminal, 555 Atlantic Avenue, opposite South Station (tel 617/482-6620).

BY CAR

Boston is such a walkable city, with an excellent public transportation system, it is not worth renting a car until you leave the city. In any case, parking is always difficult.

GETTING AROUND

IN BOSTON

Boston has the oldest, but still one of the best, public transportation systems in the United States. The **Massachusetts Bay Transport Authority (MBTA),** tel 617/222-3200, www.mbta.com, runs a network of trains, trolleys, buses, and subway trains that stretch far beyond the Greater Boston area. For most visitors, the T (subway system) provides adequate transportation to all the major attractions in the Boston area. A black T on a white circle marks the stations. Booths at each station sell tokens for the rides, which cost $1. Visitors should take advantage of the Boston Passport, which entitles holders to one, three, or seven days of unlimited transport ($6, $11, and $22) on both the T and on buses. You can purchase it on arrival at Logan Airport (Terminal E), or at many T stops, and at the visitor information booth situated on Boston Common.

BY BUS
Although Boston has a cheap and comprehensive bus system, the layout of the T is much easier for visitors to get around. If you insist on riding the bus for the fun of it, ask at your hotel or any of the subway stations for advice on a useful route. Buses run from 5:30 a.m. to 1 a.m. The Official Public Transport Map (from the MBTA, see p. 237) shows routes and schedules.

BY TAXI
As Boston's public transportation is so efficient, taxis are considered a luxury. Once that transportation closes down (between 12 and 12:30 a.m.), however, taxis can be at a premium. Head for a hotel, where they discharge and pick up passengers. In Cambridge, Harvard Square is the best bet.

OUTSIDE BOSTON

BY AIR
Apart from Logan International Airport (Boston) and T. F. Green Airport (Providence, R.I.), other useful airports in the Boston area include:

Barnstable Municipal Airport, Hyannis, tel 508/775-2020

Martha's Vineyard Airport, tel 508/693-7022

Nantucket Memorial Airport, tel 508/325-5300

Provincetown Municipal Airport, tel 508/487-0241

Airlines
Cape Air, tel 508/771-6944 or 800/352-0714, www.flycapeair .com. Serves Hyannis, Martha's Vineyard, Nantucket, Provincetown, Boston, New Bedford, and Providence, R.I.

Continental Connection, tel 800/523-FARE, www.colganair .com. Serves Hyannis, Nantucket, and La Guardia, New York City.

Island Airlines, tel 508/228-7575 or 800/248-7779, www.nan tucket.net/trans/islandair. Serves Nantucket and Hyannis.

Nantucket Airlines, tel 508/228-6234 or 800/635-8787, www.nantucketairlines.com. Serves Hyannis, Martha's Vineyard, Nantucket, Provincetown, Boston, New Bedford, and Providence, R.I.

US Airways Express, tel 800/428-4322 www.usairways .com. Serves Hyannis, Martha's Vineyard, Boston, and New York.

BY SEA
The Massachusetts coast buzzes with a variety of high-speed ferry transportation, linking popular destinations around the coast to each other and to the islands of Nantucket and Martha's Vineyard. As well as reducing the stress and time required for driving, ferries offer unusual vistas.

Bay State Cruises, tel 508/487-9284, www.baystate cruisecompany.com. Operates May–mid-Oct. between Boston and Provincetown. Journey time: 3 hours (2 hours express).

Cape Cod Cruises, tel 508/747-2400, www.province townferry.com. Operates May–Sept. from Plymouth to Provincetown, offering a 95-minute service.

Cape Island Express Lines, tel 508/997-1688, www.mvferry .com. Operates May–early Oct. from New Bedford to Martha's Vineyard, 90-minute journey.

Falmouth Ferry Service, tel 508/548-9400. Runs between Falmouth and Edgartown, Martha's Vineyard, 1-hour journey, May–mid-Oct.

Fast Ferry (part of Steamship Authority, see below), tel 508/495-3278, www.island ferry.com. Runs services from Hyannis to Nantucket in 1 hour, year-round.

Freedom Cruise Line, tel 508/432-8999, www.capecod.net /freedom. Harwich Port to Nantucket in 90 minutes May–mid-Oct.

Hy-Line Cruises, tel 508/778-2600 or 888/778-1132, www.hy-linecruises.com. Hyannis to Nantucket, in 2 hours May–Sept. or 1 hour high-speed ferry, year-round. Hyannis to Martha's Vineyard in 1 hour 45 minutes year-round. Nantucket to Martha's Vineyard in 2 hours 15 minutes, June–mid-Sept.

Island Queen, tel 508/548-4800, www.islandqueen.com. Services from Falmouth to Martha's Vineyard in 35 minutes, late May–mid-Oct.

Steamship Authority, tel 508/477-8600, www.island ferry.com. Hyannis to Nantucket in 2 hours 15 minutes, and Woods Hole to Martha's Vineyard in 45 minutes, both services operate year-round. This company also operates Fast Ferry services, see above.

Yankee Fleet, tel 800/942-5464 or 978/283-0313, www.yankeefleet.com. Services between Gloucester and Nantucket take 4 hours 30 minutes and run from June to September.

BY CAR

Boston is the gateway city to major New England attractions. Nearby, in Massachusetts, are Salem (16 miles, 26 km), Plymouth (37 miles, 59 km), and Hyannis (76 miles, 123 km), while Providence, R.I. (50 miles, 80 km) is also an easy drive. Most of the major car rental companies are represented at or near the airport. Reservations are essential in fall, and are advised year-round.

Within Massachusetts, the speed limit on all major highways is 55 mph. (88 kph). However, on the Massachusetts Turnpike (known as Mass. Pike or I-90), the speed limit is raised to 65 mph (104 kph). Lower speed limits apply in built-up, residential areas. Children under 12 must be strapped in with a safety belt at all times. You are allowed to turn right on red unless signs indicate that this is specifically prohibited. Drunk driving is a serious offense in the state, attracting heavy penalties.

PRACTICAL ADVICE

HOLIDAYS

As well as the usual United States national holidays, Boston celebrates the following state and city holidays:

Evacuation Day (March 17); Patriots' Day (third Mon. April); Bunker Hill Day (June 17). In Rhode Island, Victory Day (Aug. 14) is a holiday.

It is always worth calling ahead where possible to check that the attraction you are planning to see is open on these holidays.

LIQUOR LAWS

In Massachusetts, the legal age for drinking alcohol is 21, so you might need to produce a driver's license or passport as proof of age. Although bars are open on Sundays, beer and liquor stores are closed. It is illegal to sit in a park or square with an open container of alcohol, and any drinking in public is illegal. DWI (driving while intoxicated) is a serious offense, and attracts severe penalties.

MEDIA

Newspapers
Boston has two major daily newspapers. The heavyweight *Boston Globe* is 120 years old, and is often regarded as the voice of the (liberal) establishment, while the rival *Boston Herald* is a tabloid. The *Globe's* Thursday entertainment section is comprehensive in its coverage of what is worth—or not worth—seeing in town. Boston is also the world headquarters of the internationally recognized *Christian Science Monitor. USA Today* and the *New York Times* are also readily available on the newsstands.

OPENING TIMES

Within the city, the most popular attractions are likely to remain open year-round. Outside the city center, most attractions are open seven days a week in summer, but many have reduced opening hours in spring and late fall, and are open only on weekends in the depths of winter. It is always worth calling ahead both to check opening hours and also to find out whether any special tours are scheduled.

SALES TAX

In Massachusetts, a sales tax of 5 percent is added to all goods except for clothing and non-restaurant food up to a value of $175. A levy of 5.7 percent is charged on hotel rooms, in addition to a 4 percent local tax (a possible total of 9.7 percent).

TIPPING

Restaurant gratuities should be given at around 15–20 percent of the bill (as long as your expectations were met). Always take care to ensure that the gratuity has not already been added to the bill automatically. Tip taxis 15 percent, and tip $1 or $1.50 for each bag handled at the airport or by the hotel bellmen. Leave $1–2 a day for the maid who services your hotel room. Remember that a tip is an acknowledgment of good service: don't feel obliged to tip if you feel that you have received unsatisfactory service.

TRAVELERS WITH DISABILITIES

At Logan Airport, the **Airport Handicap Van,** tel 617/561-1769, provides a useful shuttle service between terminals.

Cabs with facilities for the disabled are readily available at each terminal at no extra charge.

Boston hotels and visitor attractions such as museums are all obliged by law to have proper access for all guests. Access to some of the older, historic sights may be restricted due to the design of the buildings. It is worth calling the attraction you are hoping to visit ahead of your trip in order to avoid disappointment.

Access First Travel, tel 781/322-1610 or 800/557-2047, e-mail accessfir@aol.com, is a co-op in Malden, just north of Boston, which offers packages specially tailored to suit the needs of travelers with disabilities. They can also book flights and hotels, and ensure that any specialist arrangements are made.

For visitors to the Cape, the *Cape Cod Disability Access Directory*, tel 508/430-0136, www.capecoddisability.org, is an excellent and wide-ranging publication. It is available from the Cape Cod Chamber of Commerce, local Chambers, visitor centers, and a variety of other outlets.

VISITOR INFORMATION

There are always new packages and discounts available for visitors, so it is worth asking the visitor information office about the current selection. Boston's most recent innovation is the City Pass, a nine-day pass offering savings of 50 percent on entry fees to six of the city's major museums.

The headquarters for Boston's tourism information is at Copley Place. Use this office to obtain information before your visit:

Greater Boston Convention and Visitors' Bureau, 2 Copley Place, Suite 105, Boston, MA 02116-6501, tel 617/536-4100, 888/723-2678, www. bostonusa.com

For information on National Parks and outdoor activities try the **National Parks Service** website at www.nps.gov

Visitor information centers can help with maps, T passes, sightseeing tours, and phone calling cards:

Boston Common, 147 Tremont Street, Boston

Prudential Center Cambridge, Harvard Square, next to MBTA, tel 800/862-5678

Other useful visitor information offices in and around Boston include:

Massachusetts Office of Travel & Tourism, 10 Park Plaza, Suite 4510, Boston, MA

02116, tel 617/973-8500, www.massvacation.com

North of Boston Convention & Visitors Bureau, 17 Peabody Square, Peabody, MA 10960, tel 978/977-7760, www.northof boston.org

Greater Merrimack Valley Convention & Visitors Bureau, 9 Central St., Lowell, MA 01852, tel 978/459-6150, www.merrimackvalley.org

Rhode Island Tourism Division, 1 West Exchange St., Providence, R.I. 02903, tel 401/222-2601, www.Visit RhodeIsland.com

Newport Visitors Information Center, 23 America's Cup Ave., Newport, R.I. 02840, tel 401/845-9123 or 800/976-5122, www.GoNewport.com

Cape Cod Chamber of Commerce, Hyannis, MA 02601, tel 508/362-3225, www. capecodchamber.org

Martha's Vineyard Chamber of Commerce, tel 508/693-0085, www.mvy.com

Nantucket Island Chamber of Commerce, 48 Main Street, Nantucket, MA 02554, tel 508/228-1700, www.nan tucketchamber.org

EMERGENCIES

For police, fire, or ambulance services, dial 911 (free call). Tell the operator the address preferably with a landmark, and the service required. You should stay by the telephone until help arrives. The Massachusetts State Police are at tel. 508/820-2300.

HEALTH

Your hotel will have the name and number of a doctor or dentist in case of an emergency. Boston has some of the world's finest medical facilities.

Hospitals
The best-known hospitals include:

Massachusetts General Hospital, 55 Fruit St., at Cambridge Street, tel 617/726-2000, T: Charles/MGH

Brigham & Women's Hospital, 75 Francis Street, tel 617/732-5500, T: Brigham Circle

Drugstores/pharmacies
The CVS chain of drugstores has branches all over town. This one is conveniently situated:

CVS, 155-157 Charles St., Beacon Hill, tel 617/523-1028. Open 24 hours; pharmacy open 7 a.m. to midnight.

SENSIBLE PRECAUTIONS

The parts of Boston where most visitors go are as safe or safer than most U.S. cities. However, you should take all normal precautions:

• Do not give your bags to anyone in an airport or train/bus station other than authorized personnel, or your taxi driver while loading the trunk.
• Be alert to your immediate surroundings, especially in a crowd.
• Don't carry or flash large amounts of money. Keep your wallet in your front pocket, hold your purse securely with the clasp facing in, or use a concealed money belt.
• Do not use ATMs when there is no one around.
• If you are robbed, hand over your wallet and whatever else is requested without resistance, and call 911.
• Don't leave any valuables in your car. If you do leave any of your possessions in your car, ensure that they are stored out of sight.

HOTELS & RESTAURANTS

HOTELS & RESTAURANTS

As Boston is such a compact and walkable city, with rapid public transportation, location is not as vital as in many cities. There is always some major attraction or another wherever you decide to stay. The waterfront area has a crop of new hotels that provide ready access to many historical sights. Many grand hotels are in the Downtown district. Usually filled with businessmen, these often offer attractive rates on weekends. The Back Bay area is a sophisticated part of the city, with its stylish stores and restaurants. Cambridge, across the river, has a different, slightly Bohemian ambiance. Wherever you go, however, Boston is likely to be expensive. As well as its business market, there is a thriving convention trade on top of the year-round tourism, which peaks for college graduations and fall foliage visits.

ACCOMMODATIONS

It is important to make reservations well ahead of time if you plan to travel at peak times. Between November and April there are more deals to be had, but although special weekend and family-friendly rates are available, make sure you press the reservations clerks to reveal any deals that are on offer.

There are reservations agencies that remove the burden of telephoning hotel after hotel, but they often seem to have more ordinary rooms on their books. For stays of a week or longer, there are agencies that specialize in renting apartments.

A bed-and-breakfast in a private home might be a more affordable option, and certainly gives you a better insight into how folks lead their lives in the city. When calculating the cost of your visit, remember that the price of a room is usually quoted exclusive of taxes, so an additional 12–15 percent has to be added in.

The hotels in this part of the book are listed by area, then by price, in alphabetical order. Unless stated to the contrary, all the accommodations listed have private bathrooms, TV, air-conditioning, and a telephone. Most are open year-round, and, unless they are bed-and-breakfasts, do not include breakfast in the price. Parking in Boston is notoriously difficult; if parking is offered at a hotel or restaurant, expect to pay.

Below are listed some specialized accommodations agencies, grouped by category.

COUNTRY & SEASIDE INNS

Destinnations, 572 Route 28, West Yarmouth, MA 02673, tel 508/790-0577 or 800/333-4667, www.destinnations.com

HOTEL RESERVATION SERVICES

Boston & New England Reservation Service, 61 South Street, Northboro, MA 01532, tel 508/393-7470 or 800/754-7470, www.boston hotelspecial.com

Boston Reservations Inc., 1643 Beacon Street, Suite 23, Waban, MA 02468, tel 617/332-4199, www.bostonreservations.com

Central Reservation Service of New England, 300 Terminal C, Logan International Airport, East Boston, MA 02128, tel 617/569-3800 or 800/332-3026, www.bostonhotels.net

BED & BREAKFAST AGENCIES
A B&B Agency of Boston (and **Boston Harbor B&B**), 47 Commercial Wharf, Boston, MA 02110, tel 617/720-3540 or 800/248-9262 BNB, www.boston-bnbagency.com

ABC: Accommodations of Boston & Cambridge, 335 Pearl St., Cambridge, MA 02139, tel 800/253-5542 or 617/491-0274

Bed & Breakfast Reservations, 11A Beach Rd., Gloucester, MA 01930, tel 617/964-1606 or 800/832-2632, fax 978/281-9426, e-mail info@bbreserve.com, www.bbreserve.com. Established in 1985. Represents carefully inspected accommodations in Greater Boston, Cape Cod, and the North and South Shores.

RESTAURANTS

Boston was long known for its seafood and rather stodgy restaurants, living on past glories and reputations. That has all, luckily, changed. Now the city has many small restaurants and cafés that well merit the description of "trend-setting." The new breed of chefs knows how to use the abundance of fine, fresh ingredients, creating modern New England dishes.

Even the North End, famous for its piles of spaghetti, swamped with meatballs in red sauce, is producing a new wave of sophisticated and authentic Italian restaurants. Asian cuisine was once confined to Chinese cooking, but other ethnic restaurants have made a bigger impact on the city in recent years, from Thai and Vietnamese to Indian. Eating out is popular, so the best restaurants require reservations well in advance.

All in all, Boston's culinary revolution is as welcome to residents of the city today as was its political revolution 225 years ago. Most restaurants serve lunch between 12 and 2 p.m., with dinner served from 5:30 or 6 p.m. until 10 p.m. (later on weekends). Late-night dining is more restricted than, say, New York or Los Angeles. By contrast, early diners can usually get a table at the more fashionable restaurants.

HOTELS & RESTAURANTS

Restaurants are listed by area as set out in the chapters, then by price and in alphabetical order.

L = lunch, D = dinner

CREDIT CARDS

Most hotels and restaurants accept the major credit cards. Smaller ones may only accept some, as shown in their entries. Abbreviations used in this guide are AE (American Express), DC (Diner's Club), MC (Mastercard), and V (Visa).

DOWNTOWN

🏨 HOTEL LE MERIDIEN
🍴 $$$$$
250 FRANKLIN ST., 02110
TEL 617/451-1900 OR
800/543-4300
FAX 617/423-2844
www.lemeridienboston.com
What was once a federal reserve bank is now a luxury hotel. The original Renaissance Revival features were retained to create a sophisticated, polished look. Not surprisingly for a French-owned hotel, the Julien Restaurant and Café Fleuri both serve French food. In the financial district, so guests are mainly business executives.
🛏 326 🚇 State 🅿 Valet
🔁 🚭 🔲 🚱 🛗
🏧 All major cards

🏨 WYNDHAM BOSTON
$$$
89 BROAD ST., 02110
TEL 617/556-0006 OR
800/WYNDHAM
FAX 617/556-0053
www.wyndham.com
In 1928, Boston's tallest skyscraper was this art deco building, now renovated and converted into a hotel. In the heart of the financial district, it is also close to the waterfront and New England Aquarium, Freedom Trail sites, and Quincy Market/Faneuil Hall. The Caliterra Bar and Grill specializes in northern

Californian and northern Italian dishes.
🛏 362 🚇 State, Aquarium
🅿 Valet 🔁 🚭 🔲 🛗
🏧 All major cards

🍴 DURGIN-PARK
$$
340 FANEUIL HALL
MARKETPLACE, 02109
TEL 617/227-2038
Labeled market dining rooms because of their proximity to the old fruit and vegetable market, this 150-year-old restaurant specializes in traditional dishes such as Boston brown bread and baked beans, chowder, and Indian pudding. Legendary for bad-tempered waitresses and communal tables.
🍴 200 🚇 Government Center 🅿 🚭 🏧 All major cards

🍴 KINGFISH HALL
$$
FANEUIL HALL SOUTH
MARKETPLACE, 02109
TEL 617/523-8862
Boston's most famous chef, Todd English (Figs, Olives see p. 247) brings top-class seafood to Boston's most popular tourist attraction. Eat inside or outside, choose simple fish dishes, Cajun, or sushi. Opened in 2000, it has a contemporary look and informal atmosphere; you can listen to live music in the evenings.
🍴 225 🚇 Government Center 🅿 🚭 🔲 🏧 All major cards

🍴 SEL DE LA TERRE
$$
255 STATE ST., 02109
TEL 617/720-1300
Opened in 2000, this is the sister restaurant of top-of-the-range L'Espalier (see p. 246). Its more affordable menus feature French-inspired specialties such as truffled forest mushroom soup and tapenade crusted striped bass. Expect a casual, rustic atmosphere, with brown

leather banquettes, wooden tables, and a slate floor.
🍴 135 🚇 Aquarium 🅿
🚭 🚱 🏧 AE, MC, V

NORTH END & THE WATERFRONT

🏨 BOSTON HARBOR HOTEL
$$$$$
70 ROWES WHARF, 02110
TEL 617/439-7000 OR
800/752-7077
FAX 617/330-9450
www.bhh.com
Don't be put off by the Big Dig construction on the doorstep; the other side of the hotel has stunning views across the harbor. The brass and glass in the lobby set the tone of luxury that continues in the attractive, modern bedrooms. Close to the business district and Freedom Trail attractions. There are two restaurants, one with tables waterside in fine weather. The airport water shuttle docks right outside the hotel.
🛏 230 🚇 Aquarium, South Station 🅿 Valet 🔁 🚭 🚱 🛗 🏧 All major cards

🏨 HILTON BOSTON LOGAN AIRPORT
$$$$$

85 TERMINAL RD., LOGAN
INTERNATIONAL AIRPORT,
02128
TEL 617/568-6700 OR
800-HILTONS
FAX 617/568-6800
www.bostonloganairport.hilton
.com
Airport hotels are usually
practical and bland, but this
10-story hotel is luxurious
and stylish. Opened in 1999, it
has the latest high-tech
facilities, two restaurants, plus
a coffee bar in the lobby. Only
minutes from downtown, this
is ideal for those arriving late
or departing early. Indoor
walkway to terminals.
🛈 600 🚇 Airport 🅿 ⬍
🚭 ❄ 🏊 🎽 🚫 All
major cards

🏨 SEAPORT HOTEL
$$

1 SEAPORT LANE, 02210
TEL 617/385-4000 OR
1-888/892-468
FAX 617/385-4001
www.reservations@seaporthotel
.com
Opened in 1998, this
comfortable high-rise hotel
suits business travelers but
also offers attractive weekend
break packages. Near the
World Trade Center in the
revitalized Seaport District, it
is just four minutes away from
Logan International Airport
via the Ted Williams Tunnel.
No tipping policy, except in
the commendable Aura
Restaurant.
🛈 426 🚇 South Station
🅿 Valet ⬍ 🚭 ❄ 🏊
🎽 🚫 All major cards

🍴 BRICCO
$$

241 HANOVER ST., 02113
TEL 617/248-6800
Opened in 1999 and an
immediate hit, this informal
North End eatery serves
deceptively simple
combinations such as wood-
roasted whole fish with fennel

and grilled quail with figs and
prosciutto. Like the food, the
wine list marries Italy with
California, with a wide choice
by the glass. Tastings, or
antipasti, are served at the bar.
🍴 100 🚇 State, Haymarket
🅿 Valet 🚭 ❄ 🚫 All
major cards

🍴 ANTICO FORNO
$

93 SALEM ST., 02113
TEL 617/723-6733
Perfect for families as well as
couples, this simple restaurant
could have been shipped over
from Italy. It has plain floors
and tables, a mural of the
Tuscan countryside, and a
wood-burning brick oven, built
by craftsmen from Naples,
which is used for roasting
chicken, braising rabbit, and
cooking pizzas.
🍴 40 🚇 Haymarket 🚭
❄ 🚫 AE, MC, V

🍴 LEGAL SEAFOODS
$$

LONG WHARF, 255 STATE ST.,
02109
TEL 617/227-3115
In 50 years, what started as a
retail fish market in
Cambridge has expanded to
an empire of good-value
restaurants extending across
the United States. All
branches serve the freshest of
fish and shellfish, grilled over
wood, fried, or in sauces. This
one also has a fine view of the
harbor.
🍴 260 🚇 Aquarium 🚭
❄ 🚫 All major cards

BEACON HILL & MUSEUM OF SCIENCE

🏨 FIFTEEN BEACON HOTEL
$$$$$

15 BEACON ST., 02108
TEL 617/670-1500
FAX 617/670-2525
E-MAIL hotel@xvbeacon.com
This is the newest boutique
hotel in Boston, and was

opened in 1999 in a
converted, turn-of-the-20th-
century beaux arts building.
From the eye-catching facade
to the specially chosen
artwork inside, everything
appeals to the design-
conscious visitor who wants
to be just steps away from the
Massachusetts State House.
The bedrooms are luxurious,
with working fireplaces. The
hotel's Federalist Restaurant
has one of the best wine
cellars in the country.
🛈 61 🚇 Park St. 🅿 Valet
⬍ 🚭 ❄ 🎽 🚫 All
major cards

🍴 HUNGRY I
$$

71 CHARLES ST.
TEL 617/227-3524
The tiny oil lamps on the
tables set the mood of
romance in this restaurant,
situated in the basement of an
1840s town house at the
bottom of Beacon Hill. The
small dining room evokes the
19th century, with antiques,
cushions on banquettes,
proper tablecloths, and
elegant glassware. Menus of
traditional French dishes
occasionally nod toward Italy,
the United States, and Asia.
🍴 58 🚇 Charles St./MGH
🕐 Sun. D 🚭 ❄ 🚫 AE,
DC, MC, V

BOSTON COMMON & BACK BAY

🏨 FOUR SEASONS HOTEL BOSTON
$$$$$

200 BOYLSTON ST., 02116
TEL 617/338-4400 OR
800/332-3442
FAX 617/423-0154
www.fourseasons.com
Luxury, perfect service and
attention to detail are the
hallmarks of Four Seasons
hotels. Don't expect a historic
atmosphere, as this is a
modern building overlooking
the Public Garden. Its
Aujourd'hui Restaurant is one

HOTELS & RESTAURANTS

of Boston's best—and most expensive—and the Bristol Lounge is a sophisticated spot to take afternoon tea or sip early-evening cocktails. Rooftop swimming pool completes the package.

🛏 288 🚇 Boylston
🅿 Valet 🔁 🔲 🔲 🔲
🔲 🏧 All major cards

🏨 ELIOT SUITE HOTEL
🍴 $$$$$

370 COMMONWEALTH AVE., 02215
TEL 617/267-1607 OR 800/443-5468
FAX 617/536-9114
E-MAIL hoteliot@aol.com
An all-suite hotel handy for Newbury Street and its stores. Each suite has a living room with a foldout sofa bed, as well as a separate bedroom, and a small kitchen. The 75-year-old building has been renovated and redecorated and bathrooms upgraded. Clio, the hotel's street-level restaurant, is currently one of Boston's hottest.

🛏 95 🚇 Hynes/ICA
🅿 Valet 🔁 🔲 🔲 🏧 All major cards

🏨 LENOX
🍴 $$$$$

710 BOYLSTON ST., 02116
TEL 617/536-5300 OR 800/225-7676
FAX 617/267-1237
www.lenoxhotel.com
The Lenox celebrated its 100th birthday in 2000 and is still run by the Saunders family. A complete facelift has restored the luxury, with decoration ranging from exotic Oriental to European. Anago, the highly rated restaurant, nods toward Italy for inspiration. The basement bar is a popular rendezvous. Just off Copley Square.

🛏 214 🚇 Copley 🅿 Valet
🔁 🔲 🔲 🔲 🏧 All major cards

🏨 FAIRMONT COPLEY PLAZA

Movie stars, presidents, and foreign heads of state have all stayed in this grande dame of Boston hotels, which faces Copley Square. Noted for its architecture, it has the marble pillars, crystal chandeliers, and gilt trim that were the hallmarks of turn-of-the-20th-century luxury. The Oak Room has long been the best steak house in town, while the Oak Bar looks as it did in pre-Prohibition days. Happily, the history is matched by modern amenities.

$$$$$
138 ST. JAMES AVE., 02116
TEL 617/441-1414
FAX 617/375-9648
www.fairmont.com
🛏 379 🚇 Copley, Back Bay
🅿 Valet 🔁 🔲 🔲 🔲
🏧 All major cards

🏨 RITZ-CARLTON, BOSTON
$$$$

15 ARLINGTON ST., 02117
TEL 617/536-5700 OR 800/241-3333
FAX 617/536-1335
www.ritz-carlton.com
Old-World elegance and luxury are hallmarks of this hotel, across the street from the Public Garden. Since 1925, the rich and famous have stayed here, but this is not a people-watching place. The lobby is tiny, the bar dimly lit and clubby. The formal dining room is lovely; more fun are the jazz brunches or weekend dinner dances on the 17th-floor roof garden.

🛏 276 🚇 Arlington
🅿 Valet 🔁 🔲 🔲 🔲
🏧 All major cards

🏨 COPLEY INN
$$$

19 GARRISON ST., 02116
TEL 617/ 236-0300 OR 800/232-0306
FAX 617/536-0816
www.copleyinn.com

This 19th-century town house suits families (children under 12 are free) and anyone on a budget. Rooms are pretty but not plush; the kitchenettes and dining tables are a practical feature. On a quiet side street near the Prudential Center, it is minutes from public transportation.

🛏 21 🚇 Prudential 🔲
🔲 🏧 AE, MC, V

🏨 NEWBURY GUEST HOUSE
$$$

261 NEWBURY ST., 02116
TEL 617/437-7666 OR 800/437-7668
FAX 617/262-4243
www.hagopianhotels.com
Located right in the heart of trendy Newbury Street, with its stores, galleries, and cafés, these three 1880s town houses have been converted into a small bed-and-breakfast hotel. Rooms are attractive and comfortable, with useful features such as hairdryers. Those at the back are quieter. Small patio on Newbury Street.

🛏 32 🚇 Hynes/ICA, Copley 🅿 🔁 🔲 🔲
🏧 All major cards

🍴 L'ESPALIER
$$$$

30 GLOUCESTER ST., 02115
TEL 617/262-3023,
E-MAIL info@lespalier.com
One of the best restaurants in the city is in an 1886 town house in Back Bay. Elegant service, surroundings, and food, at undeniably high prices, make this a special occasion place. Chef-owner Frank McClelland applies classic French techniques to New England produce, offering a prix-fixe menu plus three tasting menus, each with seven courses.

🍽 125 🚇 Hynes/ICA, Copley 🅿 Valet 🕑 Closed L, Sun. 🔲 🔲 🏧 All major cards

GRILL 23 AND BAR
$$$$
161 BERKELEY ST., 02116
TEL 617/542-2255
Bartenders mixing an array of cocktails provide free entertainment, but there is also a good choice of wines by the glass. The clientele is more business executives than young trendies, so the atmosphere is rather sedate. With steaks a specialty, this is not the place for committed vegetarians.
🔢 350 🚇 Arlington
🅿 Valet 🚭 ❄ 💳 All major cards

TOP OF THE HUB
$$$$
800 BOYLSTON ST., 02199
TEL 617/536-1775
You can't beat the view over Boston from the 52nd floor of the Prudential Tower. Whether you come for lunch, dinner, or just for a drink and snack at the bar, this is a must. The food is good, too, ranging from tartare of yellowfin tuna to traditional grilled beef tenderloin or lobster.
🔢 180 🚇 Prudential
🅿 Public 🚭 ❄ 💳 All major cards

SOMETHING SPECIAL

HAMERSLEY'S BISTRO
Gordon Hamersley is one of the city's top chefs, but his restaurant is deliberately informal. The large, attractive room is welcoming and the service friendly yet professional; the real focus, however, is the food. Expect modern, seasonal dishes with intense flavors. Highly recommended as an example of the new-style New England cooking.
$$$
553 TREMONT ST. (AT CLARENDON ST.)
TEL 617/423-2700
🔢 120 🚇 Back Bay, Copley
🅿 🕐 Closed L 🚭 ❄
💳 All major cards

FRANKLIN CAFE
$
278 SHAWMUT AVE., 02118
TEL 617/350-0010
A neighborhood restaurant that attracts diners from all over Boston, this tiny, black-painted space is always full. Dave Du Bois, the chef-owner, serves an eclectic choice of starters and main courses. Try the seared, soy-marinated chicken livers with fresh horseradish. No reservations, no desserts.
🔢 40 🚇 Back Bay
🕐 Closed L 🚭 ❄ 💳 All major cards

THE FENWAY & BROOKLINE

ELEPHANT WALK
$$
900 BEACON ST., 02215
TEL 617/247-1500
The concept of serving two menus, one French and the other Cambodian, may sound odd, but it has proved a resounding success. An attractive place, with a happy, buzzy atmosphere, it appeals to all ages and tastes. In 1998 the de Monterio family opened a sister restaurant, Elephant Walk, Cambridge (2067 Massachusetts Ave., tel 617/492-6900).
🔢 170 🚇 St. Mary's
🅿 Valet 🕐 Closed Sun L 🚭 ❄ 💳 All major cards

BETTY'S WOK AND NOODLE DINER
$
250 HUNTINGDON AVE., 02115
TEL 617/424-1950
New restaurants have themes or gimmicks. Here, choose between rice and noodles, select an Asian or Latino sauce, opt for vegetables, meat, or chicken and sit back while it is prepared. Quick, inexpensive, and fun for all ages, this modern eatery is handy for Symphony Hall.
🔢 82 🚇 Symphony 🚭 ❄ 💳 AE, MC, V

CHARLESTOWN

FIGS
$$
67 MAIN ST., MONUMENTAL AVE.
TEL 617/242-2229
Todd English (see below) was one of the first to do gourmet pizzas. This small restaurant replaced the original Olives, and now has sister establishments at 42 Charles Street (Tel 617/742-5385), plus others in Boston and across the country. Great for families, where the adults want to eat proper food.
🔢 25 🚇 Community College 🕐 Closed L 🚭 ❄ 💳 All major cards

OLIVES
$$
10 CITY SQUARE, 02129
TEL 617/242-1999
A decade ago, Todd English put Charlestown on the culinary map with the original Olives (see Figs, above). Now in larger, stylishly minimalist premises, it is always full, despite the no reservations policy for parties under six. Italian inspiration is given a modern twist, with dishes such as caramelized fillet of monkfish, braised barbecued lamb shank on yam mash.
🔢 110 🚇 North Station
🅿 Valet 🕐 Closed Sun. & L 🚭 ❄ 💳 AE, MC, V

CAMBRIDGE

INN AT HARVARD
$$$$$
1201 MASSACHUSETTS AVE., 02138
TEL 617/491-2222 OR 800/458-5886
FAX 617/520-3711
Owned by Harvard University but managed by Hilton, this hotel has stylish bedrooms, with cherry wood furniture, brass fittings, and window seats. The lithographs hanging

HOTELS & RESTAURANTS

on the walls are on loan from Harvard's own Fogg Museum. In the central Italianate atrium, you can browse through the library, play chess, and eat breakfast, lunch, or dinner.

ℹ️ 113 🚇 Harvard 🅿️ 🛗 📺 💳 All major cards

🏨 A CAMBRIDGE HOUSE BED & BREAKFAST INN
$$$
2218 MASSACHUSETTS AVE., 02140
TEL 617/491-6300 OR 800/232-9989
FAX 617/868-2848
www.acambridgehouse.com
With four-poster beds, swathes of fabrics, piles of cushions, and even some fireplaces, this converted family house suits honeymooners and couples celebrating anniversaries. Yet, academics visiting Harvard also book in, because it is small, personal, and within walking distance of the university.

ℹ️ 15 🚇 Davis Square, Porter Square 🅿️ 💳 All major cards

🏨 CHARLES HOTEL IN 🍴 HARVARD SQUARE
$$
1 BENNETT ST., 02138
TEL 617/864-1200 OR 800/882-1818
FAX 617/864-5715
www.charleshotel.com
This comfortable hotel is unashamedly modern, with patchwork quilts decorating public spaces as well as bedrooms. On weekends, families and couples replace the business clientele. Cheerful and informal, Henrietta's Table restaurant caters to all. The Rialto restaurant (managed separately, see below) boasts a star chef, while the Regattabar attracts top jazz names.

ℹ️ 293 🚇 Harvard 🅿️ 🛗 📺 💳 All major cards

SOMETHING SPECIAL

🏨 RIALTO
One of the city's favorite chefs, Jody Adams turns provincial French, Italian, and Spanish combinations into totally contemporary dishes. Try pumpkin cannelloni with clams and smoky bacon or seared skate with lobster-laurel sauce. Desserts are a specialty. Expect ultra-smooth service, flattering lighting and space between tables.

$$$
CHARLES HOTEL IN HARVARD SQUARE, 1 BENNETT ST., 02138
TEL 617/661-5050
ℹ️ 184 🚇 Harvard 🅿️ 🕐 Closed L 💳 All major cards

🍴 UPSTAIRS AT THE PUDDING
$$$$
10 HOLYOKE ST., 02138
TEL 617/864-1933
"Simple food, perfectly cooked" is the credo of chef Deborah Hughes. Her pan-seared salmon comes with a roasted root vegetable purée, the braised chicken is full of flavor, and the apple pie with cider, caramel, and burnt sugar ice cream is a winner. A bonus is the setting: in Harvard's famous Hasty Pudding Club building.

🍽️ 100 🚇 Harvard 💳 AE, MC, V

🍴 CASABLANCA
$
40 BRATTLE ST., 02138
TEL 617/876-0999
The name refers to the film, immortalized in the mural portraying Sam at the piano in Rick's Café Americana. Since 1955, this has been a haunt of professors, who tuck into the well-priced Middle Eastern dishes. Busy bar. A popular place, a short walk from Harvard Square.

🍽️ 120 🚇 Harvard 💳 All major cards

PRICES

HOTELS
An indication of the cost of a double room without breakfast is given by $ signs.
$$$$$	Over $200
$$$$	$150–$200
$$$	$100–$150
$$	$75–$100
$	Under $75

RESTAURANTS
An indication of the cost of a three course dinner without drinks is given by $ signs.
$$$$$	Over $75
$$$$	$50–$75
$$$	$35–$50
$$	$20–$35
$	Under $20

🍴 MR. BARTLEY'S BURGER AND SALAD COTTAGE
$
1246 MASSACHUSETTS AVE., 02138
TEL 617/354-6559
For four decades this has been a fun, busy student hangout. Walls are hung with old advertisements and posters. It is best known for the hamburgers named for the famous and infamous. Also serves chili, spaghetti, or meat loaf. Order a frappe, Boston's version of a milkshake. Take-out available.

🍽️ 60 🚇 Harvard 🕐 Closed Sun. 💳 None

🍴 REDBONE
$
55 CHESTER ST., 02144
TEL 617/628-2200
Located just over the town line in Somerville, this Southern-style rib shack has been popular for over a decade. With 24 beers on tap, and a wide range of bottled beers, this attracts students and the older generation, all of whom enjoy the informal atmosphere.

🍽️ 80 🚇 Davis Square 🛗 💳 None

WEST & NORTHWEST OF BOSTON

CONCORD 01742

🏨 COLONIAL INN
$$$
48 MONUMENT SQUARE
TEL 978/369-9200 OR
800/370-9200
FAX 978/371-1533
www.concordscolonialinn.com
With a prime site overlooking Concord's famous green, this 1716 inn attracts a good number of visitors. Rooms in the original building have historic ambiance; there are more in the modern annex behind. Families like the cottage with its two-bedroom suites. Both formal and informal dining; the Sunday brunch is popular with locals.
🛏 56 ⓟ Ⓢ Ⓢ ⊗ All major cards

LOWELL 01854

🍴 BREWHOUSE CAFÉ AND GRILL
$$
201 CABOT ST.
TEL 978/937-2690
This bustling restaurant at the Brewery Exchange concentrates on the simple things in life: prime ribs, seafood, honey-garlic chicken, and old-fashioned homemade desserts. Informal, with long hours, this is just three blocks from the Boott Cotton Mills Museum.
🪑 180 ⓟ Ⓢ Ⓢ ⊗ All major cards

NORTH SHORE

SALEM 01970

🏨 THE SALEM INN
🍴 $$$
7 SUMMER ST.
TEL 978/741-0680 OR
800/446-2995
FAX 978/744-8924
www.saleminnma.com
Three historic buildings, each

with its own character, have been converted into this comfortable inn, near the harbor and all the sights. The Cuvee Restaurant, open for breakfast and dinner, is in the 1834 West House. A short walk away is the 1854 Curwen House. Latest addition, the 1874 Peabody House, is all-suite.
🛏 39 ⓟ Ⓢ Ⓢ ⊗ All major cards

🍴 NATHANIEL'S
$$
18 WASHINGTON SQUARE W.
TEL 978/825-4311
Across from the Salem Witch Museum in the historic Hawthorne Hotel, this informal restaurant specializes in seafood and enterprising modern New England dishes. For those in a hurry, the hotel's Tavern on the Green is a good lunch spot, but it also has live music in the evenings.
🪑 60 ⓟ Ⓢ Ⓢ ⊗ All major cards

MARBLEHEAD 01945

🏨 SPRAY CLIFF ON THE OCEAN
$$$
25 SPRAY AVE.
TEL 781/631-6789 OR
800/626-1530
FAX 781/639-4563
www.spraycliff.com
E-MAIL spraycliff@aol.com
Views of the ocean are spectacular from this bed-and-breakfast, designed as a romantic getaway for couples. Outside are attractive gardens and a patio; inside, the pale wood makes a change from the dark Victorian look of many New England bed-and-breakfasts. Three rooms have fireplaces, one comes with a private deck. Below is a sandy beach.
🛏 7 ⓟ Ⓢ Ⓢ ⊗ All major cards

🍴 CAFFE APPASSIONATO
$
12A ATLANTIC AVE., 01945

TEL 781/639-3200
With its five different brew coffees served every day, along with lattés and cappuccinos, this has been voted best coffeehouse in town. Near the town's information booth, it is a good place to stop for light meals and snacks. The fruit smoothies are welcome in summer.
🪑 44 ⓟ Ⓢ Ⓢ ⊗ MC, V

GLOUCESTER 01930

🏨 THOMAS RIGGS HOUSE
$$
27 VINE ST.
TEL/ FAX 978/281-4802
Out of town, on the north shore of Cape Ann, this bed-and-breakfast is named for the family who lived here for 350 years. Local history enthusiast Barbara Lambert opened it as a bed-and-breakfast in 1999, retaining the original wood paneling and low ceilings. Two bedrooms have working fireplaces; the third has views of Annisquam.
🛏 3 ⓟ Ⓢ ⊗ All major cards

ROCKPORT 01966

🏨 YANKEE CLIPPER INN
$
96 GRANITE ST.
TEL 978/546-3407 OR
800/545-3699
FAX 978/546-9730
E-MAIL info@yankeeclipperinn.com
www.yankeeclipperinn.com
From its position on a high bluff just outside of town, this family-run hotel has terrific views. The main building dates from 1929; the Bullfinch House is good for families; the modern Quarterdeck is by itself in the garden. Bedrooms vary in size but all are attractive and comfortable; a few have private balconies. See Veranda, below.
🛏 26 ⓟ Closed mid-Dec.–Feb. Ⓢ Ⓢ ☒ ⊗ AE, MC, V

🏨 INN ON COVE HILL
$$$
37 MT. PLEASANT ST.
TEL 978/546-2701 OR
888/546-2701
www.cape-ann.com/covehill
Legend has it that this 200-year-old clapboard house was built with pirate's gold. Just up the hill from the harbor, with a panoramic view from the third floor wooden deck, this is a comfortable bed-and-breakfast, where home-baked muffins are the wake-up call. Budget travelers appreciate the two rooms that share a bath. Otherwise, modern comforts in bedrooms with period antiques.
🛏 11 🅿 🕒 Closed mid-Oct.–March 🔲 🔲 🚫MC, V

🍴 VERANDA
$$
96 GRANITE ST.
TEL 978/546-7795
Located in the main building of the Yankee Clipper Inn (see above), this restaurant has ocean views and an American and Tuscan menu. Many dishes are elaborate and rich: artichokes stuffed with crabmeat and Boursin cheese, shrimp and polenta in a champagne chèvre sauce. Rockport is a dry town, so remember to bring your own wine.
🪑 65 🅿 🕒 Closed mid-Oct.–March 🔲 🔲 🚫AE, MC, V

ESSEX 01929

🍴 PERIWINKLES
$
74 MAIN ST.
TEL 978/768-6320
Two steps from the Essex Shipbuilding Museum. Tom Guertner serves plain down-home food: crabmeat pie, oven-roasted fresh haddock, with warm apple crisp for dessert. Lunch is served until 4 p.m. Dinner is slightly fancier.
🪑 75 🅿 🔲 🔲 🚫MC, V

🍴 WOODMAN'S OF ESSEX
$
121 MAIN ST.
TEL 978/768-6451
Known to all as "Woodie's," this informal, come-as-you-are restaurant proudly boasts that it is the home of the fried clam. It has been run by the Woodman family since 1914. Diners eat off paper plates at plain wood tables and booths. Most people order the fried clams, although there are other specialties offered as well, including crab cakes, lobster, scallops, and New England clam chowder.
🪑 125 🅿 🔲 🔲 🚫 None

NEWBURYPORT 01950

🏨 GARRISON INN
$$$
11 BROWN SQUARE
TEL 978/499-8500
FAX 978/499-8555
E-MAIL services@garrison-inn.com
Built for wealthy rum merchant Moses Brown in 1809, this family-oriented hotel has a modern, rather than Old-World interior. There are three restaurants to choose from: the Kid's Room is for children, who may be left here to eat their meals under supervision, while parents can dine separately at David's Upstairs (gourmet cooking) or Downstairs (casual fare).
🛏 24 🅿 🚪 🔲 🔲 🚫AE, MC, V

🍴 SCANDIA
$$
25 STATE ST.
TEL 978/462-6271
Open for two decades, the Breidenbach family's small, Victorian decor restaurant specializes in well-priced modern New England dishes such as crab cakes aioli, sautéed scallops dijonnaise, seafood linguini, and lobster stuffed with clams, scallops,

and shrimp. It can be busy on weekends, so be sure to make reservations.
🪑 50 🔲 🔲 🚫All major cards

SOUTH OF BOSTON

NEWPORT, R.I. 02840

SOMETHING SPECIAL

🏨 CLIFFSIDE INN
In a quiet neighborhood near the famous mansions, this spacious 1880 house is more than a luxurious bed-and-breakfast. Everywhere you look, the haunting image of Beatrice Turner returns your gaze. The story of this artist (1889–1948), who painted more than 1,000 self-portraits, is fascinating, and adds to the romantic ambiance. Excellent breakfasts, fulsome afternoon tea, plenty of working fireplaces.
$$$$$
2 SEAVIEW AVE.
TEL 401/847-1811
FAX 401/848-5850
E-MAIL cliff@wsii.com
www.cliffsideinn.com
🛏 16 🅿 🔲 🔲 🚫AE, MC, V

🏨 FRANCIS MALBONE HOUSE INN
$$
392 THAMES ST.
TEL 401/846-0392 OR
800/846-0392
FAX 401/848-5956
E-MAIL innkeeper@malbonecom
www.malbone.com
This former merchant's home, set back from busy Thames Street, is agreeably peaceful. Built in 1760, the furniture and color schemes are traditional. Most of the bedrooms have four-poster beds and working fireplaces; all have linens embroidered with the letter M. Four overlook the harbor.
🛏 20 🅿 🔲 🔲 🚫AE, MC, V

KEY 🏨 Hotel 🍴 Restaurant 🛏 No. of bedrooms 🪑 No. of places 🚇 Subway 🅿 Parking 🕒 Closed 🚪 Elevator

BLACK PEARL
$–$$$
BANNISTER'S WHARF
TEL 401/846-5264
Choose from three eating areas, all overlooking the water. On a sunny day, you can sit outside on the patio with a bowl of Black Pearl clam chowder and a beer to admire the view. The Tavern Room is also informal, but the Commodore Room, with its stylish French cooking, demands a jacket (and a deep wallet).
⊞ 150, 50, 50 ⓢ ⓑ
⚑ AE, MC, V

CHRISTIES'S RESTAURANT
$
OFF 351 THAMES ST.
TEL 401/847-5400
Newport's oldest waterfront restaurant is still going strong after 50 years. As well as the raw bar of local seafood, you should expect all the usual nautical trappings in the three dining rooms. Here, you can order an informal pub lunch, or a Chateaubriand steak for two. In high season, reservations are essential if you wish to sit out on the deck overlooking the harbor.
⊞ 600, deck 130 ⓢ ⓑ
⚑ All major cards

PROVIDENCE, R.I. 02903

OLD COURT
$$$
144 BENEFIT ST.
TEL 401/351-0747
FAX 401/272-4830
E-MAIL reserve@oldcourt.com
www.oldcourt.com
This bed-and-breakfast is on Benefit Street, which is known as the Mile of History. Built in 1863, this plain brick building has a Victorian theme throughout, with antique and reproduction furniture in the rooms. Bedrooms at the back are quiet, with views of the floodlit State Capitol. Popular with parents of students at

nearby Brown and RISD. Full breakfast served.
① 10 ⓟ ⓢ ⓑ ⚑ AE, MC, V

ECLECTIC GRILLE
$$
245 ATWELLS AVE.
TEL 401/831-8010
Providence is known for its wide range of restaurants, often staffed by graduates of Johnson and Wales University. This one serves well-executed, contemporary dishes such as roasted corn chowder spiked with chili, and seared tuna with pumpkin seeds. Take a table or sit at the bar watching the chefs at work. In the busy Federal Hill district.
⊞ 150 ⓟ ⊘ Closed L, all Sun.–Mon. ⓢ ⓑ ⚑ AE, MC, V

CAPE COD & THE ISLANDS

SANDWICH 02563

ISAIAH JONES HOMESTEAD
$$$
165 MAIN ST.
TEL 508/888-9115
FAX 508/888-9648
www.isaiahjones.com
Set in the heart of this pretty town, Jan and Doug Klapper's 1849 bed-and-breakfast is true to its Victorian roots, and is filled with handsome antiques and reproductions. Three of the bedrooms have working fireplaces. Unusually, the full breakfast is served by candlelight.
① 7 ⓟ ⓢ ⓑ ⚑ All major

DUNBAR TEA SHOP
$
1 WATER ST.
TEL 508/833-2485
For a taste of Old England, take tea at this British-owned and -run bed-and-breakfast. Order a cream tea with home-baked scones. In winter,

sit by the fire and listen to readings of Dickens. Good soups, quiches, and hearty British plowman's lunches are also on the menu.
⊞ 30 ⓟ ⓢ ⚑ MC, V

YARMOUTH PORT 02675

WEDGEWOOD INN
$$
83 MAIN ST.
TEL 508/362-5157
FAX 508/362-5851
www.wedgewood-inn.com
E-MAIL info@wedgewood-inn.com
A classic among New England inns, this 1812 house has antiques, patchwork quilts, four-poster beds, and polished wood floors. Bedrooms are in the main building and the converted barn. Gerrie and Milt Graham are the experienced hosts. Right on Mass. 6A, the Old King's Highway, it boasts a large garden.
① 9 ⓟ ⓢ ⓑ ⚑ AE, MC, V

ABBICCI
$$$
43 MAIN ST.
TEL 508/362-3501
A far cry from the ubiquitous clam shack, this purveyor of contemporary Italian cuisine has considerable style. As well as familiar pastas (linguine, capellini, and fettuccine) and veal dishes (parmesan, Milanese), there are unusual twists: Try veal nocciole (with hazelnuts) or polenta with melted fontina cheese and wild mushrooms. The roast duck *agrodolce* (sweet/sour) is basted with honey, apricot sauce, and balsamic vinegar. Sunday brunch pulls in diners from all over the Cape.
⊞ 75 ⓟ Valet ⓢ ⓑ ⚑ All major cards

HOTELS & RESTAURANTS

EASTHAM 02642

SOMETHING SPECIAL

🏨 WHALEWALK INN

A whaling captain's 1830s home is now a delightful bed-and-breakfast, just a stroll from Boat Meadow Beach on Cape Cod Bay. Choose from bedrooms in the main house or separate buildings on the spacious grounds. Most have fireplaces; some have small kitchens. Bicycles available.

$$$$
220 BRIDGE RD.
TEL 508/255-0617
FAX 508/240-0017
www.whalewalkinn.com
🛏 16 🅿 🕐 Closed Jan.–Feb., Mon.–Fri. in Dec.
🅂 🅂 🅂 AE, MC, V

WELLFLEET 02667

🍴 AESOP'S TABLES

$$–$$$
316 MAIN ST.
TEL 508/349-6450
Despite the witty name, food is taken seriously at this handsome 1805 captain's mansion next to the Town Hall. Order local oysters (on the half shell or baked), innovative fish dishes such as salmon rubbed with Moroccan spices, and end with one order of Death by Chocolate, with two spoons.
🍴 155 🅿 🕐 Closed mid-Oct.–mid-May & Tue.–Wed. early and late season 🅂
🅂 All major cards

TRURO 02666

🍴 ADRIAN'S

$
535 ROUTE 6
TEL 508/487-4360
Aficionados come to watch sunsets from the deck of this casual restaurant, which is a short drive out of town. Variations on Italian classics include lobster ravioli; the brick oven produces crisp

pizzas, wood-roasted pork loin, even cayenne-crusted salmon. Breakfasts are also imaginative: huevos rancheros and cranberry pancakes.
🍴 200 🅿 🕐 Closed mid-Oct.–mid-May 🅂 🅂 AE, MC, V

PROVINCETOWN 02657

SOMETHING SPECIAL

🏨 COPPER FOX

O pened in 1999, this is a welcome addition to the numerous bed-and-breakfasts in town. John Gagliardi converted the 1856 house at the quiet east end of the main street, putting pretty furnishings and plenty of comforts into the bedrooms. Relax and watch the world go by from the large front porch.
$$$$
448 COMMERCIAL ST.,
TEL 508/487-8583
E-MAIL copperfox@provincetown
.com
www.provincetown.com/copperfox
🛏 7 🅿 🅂 🅂
🅂 MC, V

🏨 WATERMARK INN

$$
603 COMMERCIAL ST.
TEL 508/487-0165
FAX 508/487-2383
E-MAIL info@watermark-inn.com
A perfect spot for those who enjoy the stores and restaurants of Provincetown but want just the sound of the surf at night. A 20-minute walk from the center, this contemporary wood building is right on the water with its own little beach. All the suites have large windows, private decks, and kitchens. Children are welcome.
🛏 10 🅿 🅂 🅂 🅂 AE, MC, V

🍴 MARTIN HOUSE

$$
157 COMMERCIAL ST.
TEL 508/487-1327

PRICES

HOTELS
An indication of the cost of a double room without breakfast is given by $ signs.
$$$$$	Over $200
$$$$	$150–$200
$$$	$100–$150
$$	$75–$100
$	Under $75

RESTAURANTS
An indication of the cost of a three-course dinner without drinks is given by $ signs.
$$$$$	Over $75
$$$$	$50–$75
$$$	$35–$50
$$	$20–$35
$	Under $20

With a waterside terrace for summer dining and cozy rooms with fireplaces for the winter, this restaurant keeps diners happy all year long. The 18th-century house has creaking floors and simple furnishings, but the food is notable. Stays open until 1 a.m. in season.
🍴 56 🕐 Closed L 🅂
🅂 All major cards

CHATHAM 02633

🏨 CHATHAM BARS INN

$$$$$
SHORE RD.
TEL 508/945-0096 OR
800/527-4884
FAX 508/945-5491
www.chathambarsinn.com
Since 1914, this first-class resort has been one of the places to stay on Cape Cod. Choose from bedrooms in the main building or one of the cottages; dine in one of three restaurants. Tennis, boating, fishing, and golf are all available, plus special children's programs. Located on the edge of town, the inn faces the ocean and has a private beach.
🛏 205 🅿 🅂 🅂 🅂
🅂 🅂 🅂 All major cards

🏨 CAPTAIN'S HOUSE INN OF CHATHAM
$$$$
369 OLD HARBOR RD.
TEL 508/945-0127
FAX 508/945-0866
E-MAIL info@captainshouseinn
.com

This luxurious country inn, set on 2 acres (0.8 ha), dates back to 1839. Most bedrooms have the canopy beds, fireplaces, and antiques to match. Breakfasts are bountiful, with a tempting buffet as well as hot dishes, such as French toast and egg nests. Afternoon teas. Bicycles and croquet available for guests.

🛏 19 🅿 🚭 🌀 🂠 AE, MC, V

🍴 CHRISTIAN'S
$$$
443 MAIN ST.
TEL 508/ 945-3362

In what was a sea captain's home, you can choose between two ambiances. In the casual Upstairs at Christian's with its movie and library theme, order homemade pizzas and listen to the pianist. In the slightly more formal Downstairs dining room, the theme is nautical. Both are strong on seafood, straight from Chatham Pier.

🍴 100,100 🅿 Private 🕐 Closed Tue. D & Wed. D Jan.–mid-March 🚭 🌀 🂠 MC, V

HARWICH PORT 02646

🏨 SEA HEATHER INN
$$$$
28 SEA ST.
TEL 508/432-1275 OR
800/789-7809
E-MAIL goldencape@aol.com
www.seaheather.com

Gables and porches decorate this 1850s house overlooking Nantucket Sound. A few steps away is Sea Street Beach, which is public but feels private. Opened as a bed-and-breakfast in 1997, the inn has traditional furnishings in

the main house. An annex, The Court, has plainer, practical, motel-style rooms.

🛏 24 🅿 🚭 🌀 some 🂠 AE, MC, V

🍴 CAPE SEA GRILLE
$$
31 SEA ST.
TEL 508/432-4745

Set right across the street from the Sea Heather Inn (see above), this comfortable restaurant features creative cooking that attracts diners from all over the Cape. Seared orange and ginger-marinated tuna, for example, comes with tempura shrimp and a pineapple, tangerine, and honey salsa. Save room for the desserts.

🍴 110 🅿 🕐 Closed Dec.–March 🚭 🌀 🂠 AE, MC, V

WOODS HOLE 02540

🏨 WOODS HOLE PASSAGE
186 WOODS HOLE RD.
TEL 508/945-0127
FAX 508/540-4771
www.woodsholepassage.com

Halfway between Falmouth and Woods Hole, this five-room bed-and-breakfast makes a good base for cycling, going to the beach, exploring the Upper Cape, or daytripping to Martha's Vineyard. Expect comfortable furniture, not priceless antiques, and bright cheerful colors, such as raspberry or sunny yellow. Bicycles are free for guests to borrow.

🛏 5 🅿 🚭 🌀 🂠 All major cards

🍴 FISHMONGER'S CAFÉ
$$
56 WATER ST.
TEL 508/548-9148

For 25 years, this casual restaurant has been attracting locals and visitors alike. The no reservations policy means that you must arrive early if you want to dine at one of the tables overlooking the

water. Fish is a specialty, served with a modern twist: blackened sea bass with peach salsa or sashimi-style tuna, for example.

🍴 64 🚭 🌀 🕐 Closed D. Tues. & early Dec.–late Feb. 🂠 AE, MC, V

FALMOUTH 02540

🏨 LA MAISON CAPPELARI AT MOSTLY HALL
$$$$
27 MAIN ST..
TEL 508/548-3786
E-MAIL mostlyhall@aol.com
www.mostlyhall.com

In 1999, Bogdan and Christina Simcic (pronounced SIM-CHIK) bought Mostly Hall, one of Falmouth's most distinctive bed-and-breakfasts. Set back from the street and surrounded by gardens, this spacious 1849 mansion has a cupola on top and deep verandas below. Three of the six bedrooms feature whimsical wall murals painted by the Simcics; the others are traditional, with floral wallpapers and antiques.

🛏 6 🅿 🕐 Closed mid-Dec.–mid-March 🚭 🌀 🂠 AE, MC, V

MARTHA'S VINEYARD

🏨 CHARLOTTE INN
🍴 $$$$$
SOUTH SUMMER ST.
EDGARTOWN, MA 02539
TEL 508/627-4751
FAX 508/627-4652

Both the inn and L'Etoile, its gourmet restaurant, are an expensive and sophisticated treat for special occasions. The furnishings match the best of British country house hotels: antique clocks, enjoyable books on the shelves, and vases of fresh-cut flowers. There are three rules: no weddings, no reunions, and no families with small children.

🛏 25 🅿 🕐 Restaurant closed Jan.–mid-Feb. 🌀 🂠 AE, MC, V

🏨 GREENWOOD HOUSE
$$$$

40 GREENWOOD AVE.,
VINEYARD HAVEN, 02568
TEL 508/693-6150
FAX 508/696-8113
E-MAIL innkeeper@greenwood
house.com
www.greenwoodhouse.com
Larry Gomez and Kathy
Stinson are relaxed and
thoughtful hosts. Their
comfortable bed-and-
breakfast is a short walk from
the middle of town, with its
numerous stores and
restaurants. Guests gather at
the long table for breakfast.
ⓘ 5 🅿 ⓢ 🅂 🕭 All
major cards

🍴 ALCHEMY
$$$$

71 MAIN ST., EDGARTOWN,
02539
TEL 508/627-9999
Opened in 1999, this stylish
bistro-bar could be
transplanted from Manhattan.
The cooking is ambitious:
caramelized shallot custard,
pan-roasted monkfish with
buttered lobster, and banana
rice pudding with a rum-raisin
purèe. Casual upstairs, with a
pool table; a sociable bar; and
a more formal style of dining
downstairs.
🍽 170 ⓢ 🅂 🕭 AE, MC,
V

🍴 CAFE MOXIE
$$$

48 MAIN ST., VINEYARD HAVEN
TEL 508/693-1484
This is the sort of small,
neighborhood restaurant
everyone wants to have
nearby: simple decoration,
friendly staff, and excellent
food. Try mussels steamed in
saffron cream or pan-roasted
duck breast with blackcurrant
and walnut barley risotto.
Vineyard Haven is a dry town,
so remember to bring your
own wine.
🍽 48 🕐 Closed Sun.–Tues.
& Oct.–April ⓢ 🅂
🕭 MC, V

NANTUCKET 02554

🏨 HAWTHORN HOUSE
$$$$

2 CHESTNUT ST.
TEL/FAX 508/228-1468
E-MAIL hhguests@nantucket.net
www.hawthornhouse.com
The Carl family are a creative
lot, using their talents for
stained glass, needlepoint,
painting, and hooked rugs to
decorate this 1849-built
house. Centrally located, so
you can walk to stores and
restaurants. It calls itself a
guesthouse since no breakfast
is served; instead, you get a
voucher valid at nearby cafés.
Good value for money.
ⓘ 10 ⓢ 🅂 some
🕭 MC, V

🏨 MARTIN HOUSE INN
$$

61 CENTRE ST.
TEL 508/228-0678
E-MAIL martinn@nantucket.net
This bed-and-breakfast is in a
quiet residential area just up
the hill from the harbor. Take
your breakfast out onto the
porch in summer; when it's
cool, the fireplace makes the
living room and dining room
feel snug. Like an elegant
private home, this has
antiques, interesting artwork,
and four-poster beds.
ⓘ 13 ⓢ 🕭 MC, V

🍴 BOARDING HOUSE
$$

12 FEDERAL ST.
TEL 508/228-9622
Careful cooking and
interesting combinations make
this one of the best
restaurants on the island.
Dishes such as grilled
yellowfin tuna with wasabi
aioli and ginger sautéed
shrimp with jasmine rice
reflect the modern-American
style, spiced with Asian flavors.
Great for a splurge. More
than 200 different wines in
the cellar. Pleasant patio.
🍽 150 🕐 Closed
Sun.–Mon. Dec.–March ⓢ
🅂 🕭 AE, MC, V

SHOPPING

While many cities now have the same familiar stores situated in ever-expanding anonymous malls, Boston is still a delight for shopaholics. The variety of goods available is enormous, from the most exclusive top-of-the-range designer clothes and jewelry right down to the cheapest, trendiest youth fashions, with plenty of one-of-a-kind boutiques. Outside Boston, all the regions covered in this book have excellent shopping. Malls are easy to find, but you should ask at tourist information offices for lists of local antique dealers, artists, and craftsmen. And, wherever you are, remember that museum gift shops are always good hunting grounds for unusual gifts and souvenirs.

BOSTON

Boston's attractions are spread across the city, and so are the stores. Some areas, however, are particularly fruitful.

Back Bay has long been known as a stomping ground for serious shoppers. Boylston Street, near the Four Seasons Hotel, boasts a clutch of international designer names. A few blocks further west is Copley Place (see below), which is linked by a glass walkway to The Shops at the Pru (see below).

Without a doubt, the best way to spend a shopping day is to stroll along Newbury Street. It is well known for its individual shops selling designer clothes and fine leather goods, as well as for its art galleries (www.newbury-st.com).

In and around Charles Street and Beacon Hill you will find an array of antique and specialty stores. At Downtown Crossing most of the stores are unremarkable, aimed at local office workers rather than visitors, although it is still home to the reknowned Filene's Basement (see below) as well as more ordinary stores such as Macy's East (see below), The Gap and Levis Store.

ANTIQUES
Devonia, upstairs at 43 Charles St., tel 617/523-8313, specializes in antiques for dining, especially wine glasses. Good for unusual gifts, as well as cookware.

BARGAINS
Filene's Basement, 426 Washington St., tel 617/348-7974. The most famous basement of all. Be prepared to hunt for gems and to make an instant decision. The "automatic markdowns" system means prices are reduced over four weeks, with unsold goods donated to charity.

BOOKS
Brattle Bookshop, 9 West St., tel 617/542-0210. Catering to lovers of second-hand books since 1825. There are sale-priced books outside, thousands of volumes inside, and antiquarian books in a special room.

Peter L. Stern, 55 Temple Pl., tel 617/421-1880. For collectors of first edition and antiquarian tomes, particularly 19th- and 20th-century American and English literature, detective fiction, plus autographs and manuscripts. Lame Duck Books, on the same premises, specializes in rare European, Latin American, English, and American literature from 1850 to 1960.

CLOTHES
Alan Bilzerain, 34 Newbury St., tel 617/536-1001. Alan creates the menswear collection; his wife, Bé, designs for ladies. The store also sells international names such as Comme des Garçons, Yohji Yuammamoto, and Issey Miyake.

Louis, Boston, 234 Berkeley St., tel 617/262-6100. This is the city's most exclusive clothing

store. Mainly for men, it is housed in a splendid 140-year-old building that once held the Museum of Natural History.

DEPARTMENT STORES
Macy's/East, 450 Washington St., tel 617/357-3000. In 1996 the Boston deparment store, Jordan Marsh, became Macy's/East. You will find the usual Macy's quality in departments ranging from men's, women's, and children's clothes through luggage to housewares.

Filene's, 426 Washington St., tel 617/350-7268. The flagship branch of the New England group of deparment stores, this building has been a downtown landmark since 1912. The six floors have clothes for the entire family, plus textiles, china, silver and glass.

JEWELRY
Shreve, Crump, & Low, 330 Boylston St., tel 617/267-9100. New York City has Tiffany & Co.; Boston has Shreve, Crump & Low. Over two centuries old, the firm is famous for silver, jewelry, watches, and antiques. The exclusive Boston-themed collection includes "Gurgling Cod" pitchers.

GALLERIES
Childs Gallery, 169 Newbury St., tel 617/266-1108. Specializing in paintings, sculptures, and works on paper, from the Renaissance to the 1950s, this gallery has attracted connoisseurs for 70 years.

The Society of Arts & Crafts, 175 Newbury St., tel 617/266-1810. The place to find locally made glass, jewelry, and ceramics.

LEATHER GOODS
Cole Haan, 109 Newbury St., tel 617/536-7826. Come here for hand-crafted men's and women's shoes in styles ranging from casual to business and evening wear. Also belts, briefcases, handbags, and wallets.

SHOPPING

MALLS

Copley Place, Huntington Ave., bet. Dartmouth & Exeter Sts., www.myspree.com. The list of impressive names says it all: Neiman Marcus, Gucci, Ralph Lauren, and Louis Vuitton. The setting is equally impressive, with plants and acres of glass under an enormous atrium. There are more than 100 stores in all.

Faneuil Hall Marketplace, www.faneuilhallmarketplace.com Boston's most visited attraction is also the most commercial. Don't be put off by the fast food, souvenirs, and T-shirts, there are also upmarket clothing and specialty stores here.

The Shops at the Pru, www.prudentialcenter.com, is connected to Copley place by a glass walkway. The mall is anchored by Saks Fifth Avenue. In general, however, stores here are more middle of the range than at Copley Place.

SPECIALTY STORES

Black Ink, 101 Charles St., tel 617/723-3883. Everything from ink and stamps to unusual ornaments and glassware.

Crane & Co. Papermakers, The Shops at Prudential Center, tel 617/247-2822. This company has been making stationery in Massachusetts for two centuries. Papers are still 100 percent cotton; borders are still applied by hand.

Rugg Road Paper Company, 105 Charles St., tel 617/742-0002, has a fine selection of handmade papers and stationery.

Simon Pearce, 115 Newbury St., tel 617/450-8388. Showcasing beautiful glassware, the work of a Vermont-based Irishman.

Stoddards, 50 Temple Pl., tel 617/426-4187. Two centuries old, Stoddard's claims to be the country's oldest cutlery store, selling knives and scissors for every possible use. They have a fine fly-fishing tackle department. Branch at Copley Place.

CAMBRIDGE

With its large student population, Cambridge has an eclectic range of stores, from funky record and clothing stores to upmarket boutiques. Bookstores abound.

ARTS & CRAFTS

Cambridge Artists Cooperative, 59A Church St., tel 617/868-4434. This treasure-trove is much larger than it looks from the street. Several galleries exhibit the work of local craftsmen and women, whose beautiful glass, knitwear, scarves, silver, woodwork, jewelry, and pottery make fine souvenirs and lovely presents.

BOOKS

Grolier Poetry Book Shop, 6 Plympton St., tel 617/547-4648. Since 1927, this shop has been a meeting place for poets and poetry lovers. Visitors included Allen Ginsberg and Seamus Heaney. Photos hang among the 15,000 volumes crammed onto the shelves. Weekly readings Tues., Fri., or Sun.

SOUVENIRS

Harvard Co-op, 1400 Massachusetts Ave., tel 617/499-2000. A sprawling store that caters to more than just the student population, with clothes, books, and household items. For visitors, this is the place to pick up a souvenir with the Harvard University logo.

WEST & NORTH-WEST OF BOSTON

The center of Concord still looks like a traditional New England village, with its selection of small, individual shops. Due to its manufacturing heritage, nearby Lowell has a grittier atmosphere but, it, too, offers good shopping.

CONCORD

Concord Bookshop, 65 Main St., tel 978/369-2405. More than 60 years old, this bookstore boasts an extensive general selection, plus excellent travel and children's sections. Local authors are featured, from 19th-century names such as Thoreau and Alcott, to contemporary writers such as Doris Kearns Goodwin.

LOWELL

Lowell Gallery, 14 Jackson St., tel 978/458-3137. This quality gift gallery specializes in New England-made crafts and Lowell memorabilia. Jewelry ranges from the whimsical to the classic, with pieces by Boston artists, pewter from Connecticut, and coats from Maine.

NORTH SHORE

The North Shore is an ideal hunting ground for antiques, original works of art, or secondhand books.

ESSEX

White Elephant, 32 Main St., tel 978/768-6901. In business for half a century, this is one of the oldest antique stores in town. Silver, china, glass, dolls, and furniture are just some of the collectibles offered.

NEWBURYPORT

Piel Craftsmen, 31/2 Center St., tel 978/462-7012. Models of historic ships include the *Massachusetts,* the first U.S. Revenue cutter, built in Newburyport and launched in 1791. Watch them being made in the adjacent workshop. Also on sale are maritime prints, ships in bottles, and canvas bags.

ROCKPORT

ART & CRAFTS

Rockport Art Association, 12 Main St., tel 978/546-6604.

Exhibitions by members of the association change regularly, so you may see paintings, graphics, sculptures, and/or photography.

Rockport Quilt Shoppe, 2 Ocean Ave., tel 978/546-1001. Owner and collector Gloria White has over 150 antique quilts from all over the United States. She also restores old quilts and takes orders for new ones. The shop is open "by appointment and by chance," so phone ahead.

SOUTH OF BOSTON

NEWPORT, R.I.

Like any other resort, Newport has its share of inexpensive souvenir shops; but there is also a wide choice of fine stores offering a combination of style, high quality, and exclusivity. Explore Franklin and Spring Streets, America's Cup Avenue, Thames Street, and Bellevue Avenue.

ANTIQUES
Armory Antiques & Fine Art, 365 Thames St., tel 401/848-2398. More than 125 dealers display their international specialties.

FURNITURE
Ball & Claw, 55 America's Cup Ave., tel 401/848-5600. Jeffrey Greene faithfully reproduces furniture in the style of the famous Newport craftsmen, Townsend and Goddard.

JEWELRY
J.H. Breakall & Co., 132 Spring St., tel 401/849-0195. Unusual gold and silver jewelry, often using the sea and marine life for inspiration.

MISCELLANEOUS
A mixture of galleries, cafés, and shops pull visitors to **Bannister's Wharf** (20 shops) and **Brick Marketplace** (32 shops), tel 401/846-4733.

PROVIDENCE, R.I.

Providence can boast that it is home to an architectural gem, the country's oldest mall, as well as one of the newest. For quirky, eccentric shops and cafés, head for Thayer Street, haunt of college students.

ANTIQUES
Tilden-Thurber Co., 292 Westminster St., tel 401/272-3200. Founded in 1766, the store sells some of the best antiques in New England, often made by local craftsmen.

BOOKSTORES
Cellar Stories Book Store, 111 Mathewson St., tel 401/521-2665. The largest secondhand bookstore in the state, piled high with first editions and other collectibles.

MALLS
The Arcade, 65 Weybosset St., tel 401/598-1199. A 160-year-old mall with three floors of boutiques and stores offering quality gifts, souvenirs, and food.

Providence Place Mall, Providence Pl., tel 401/454-6410. Opened in 1999, this downtown mall is anchored by Nordstrom, Lord & Taylor, and Filene's.

CAPE COD & THE ISLANDS

Cape Cod is renowned for its antique shops, especially along Mass. 6A, the Old King's Highway.

The 100 members of the **Cape Cod Antique Dealers Association**'s are listed in a booklet (P. O. Box 191, Yarmouth Port, MA 02675, tel 508/362-6875, www.ccada.com).

The Cape also boasts talented artists and skilled craftsmen:

Cape Cod Potters (www.cape codpotters.com) is an association of some 20 potteries making everything from redware and stoneware to sculptures, rugs, and paintings.

As for general shopping, the most concentrated areas of good stores are in Provincetown and Chatham. On Martha's Vineyard, both Edgartown and Vineyard Haven have interesting and varied stores, while Nantucket Town is densely packed with upmarket boutiques and specialty stores.

PROVINCETOWN

Provincetown's artistic community provides the impetus for the town's thriving gallery scene. Commercial Street is the hub around which they are based, but beware: Many art galleries move to new premises from one year to the next.

GALLERIES
Julie Heller Gallery, 2 Gosnold St., tel 508/487-2169. One of the longer-established galleries in town, this gallery (opened in 1980) specializes in exhibiting Provincetown artists, both early 20th century and contemporary.

CLOTHES
Giardelli Antonelli, 417 Commercial St., tel 508/487-3016. Beautiful, elegant, and expensive ladies' goods in fine wools and silk.

CHATHAM

ANTIQUES
Bob's Antiques, 1579 Main St., tel 508/945-4606

JEWELRY
Chatham Jewelers, 532 Main St., tel 508/945-0690. This is a delightfully tempting shop, where the service is old-fashioned, the staff is knowledgeable, and the jewelry, watches, and clocks on sale are all top quality.

Ross Coppelman, 461 Main St., tel 508/945-7722.

EASTHAM

CRAFTS

Eastham Pottery, 105 Gigi Lane, tel 508/255-1556. Brian Brader draws on local flora and fauna for a range of hand-thrown pottery, sculpture, and tiles. His wife Lisa's attractive scarves, rugs, and handwoven blankets are also on display here.

DENNIS

ANTIQUES

Antique Center of Cape Cod, 243 Main St. (Rte. 6A), tel 508/385-4600.

Robert C. Eldred Co., 1483 Rte. 6A, East Dennis, tel 508/385-3116. Eldred's auction house is the most famous name on the Cape for antiques. If you enjoy buying antiques in this way, call ahead for the sale schedule.

CRAFTS

Scargo Stoneware Pottery, 30 Dr. Lord's Rd. South, tel 508/385-3894. Harry Holl exhibits paintings and sculptures, and stages informative pottery demonstrations in season. Open 10 a.m.–6 p.m. in summer, 10 a.m.–5p.m. in winter.

BREWSTER

ANTIQUES

Shirley Smith & Friends, 2926 Main St. , Rte. 6A, tel 508/896-4632.

CRAFTS

Heart Pottery, 1145 Main St., Rte. 6A, tel 508/896-6169. Diane Heart is often to be found at her wheel when you visit to admire her raku, stoneware, and functional porcelain. Scenic nature photography is also on display. Closed Sundays.

SANDWICH

ANTIQUES

Sandwich Antique Center, 131 Rte. 6A, tel 508/833-3600.

YARMOUTH PORT

ANTIQUES

The Town Crier, 153 Main St., tel 508/362-3138.

MARTHA'S VINEYARD

ANTIQUES

C.W. Morgan Marine Antiques, Beach Rd., Vineyard Haven, tel 508/693-3622.

CLOTHES

Dream Weaver, 1 South Water St., Edgartown, tel 508/627-9683. Clothes are often works of art.

CRAFTS

Travis Tuck, 7 Beach St., Vineyard Haven, tel 508/693-3914. Witty weathervanes made to order at his studio.

JEWELRY

Edgartown Jeweler's Studio, 261 Upper Main St., Vineyard Haven, tel 508/627-6820. A cooperative displaying the work of four local jewelers.

NANTUCKET

ANTIQUES

Manor House Antiques Co-op, 31 Centre St., tel 508/ 228-4335.

CLOTHES

Murray's Toggery Shop, 62 Main St., tel 508/228-0437. This is the home of Nantucket Reds, the cotton trousers that faded from deep coral to pale pink. Now the cloth is pre-faded, and comes in shirts, shorts, caps, and bags that are all prized souvenirs of the island.

GALLERIES

Artists' Association of Nantucket, 19 Washington St., tel 508/228-0294. For over half a century, the association has hosted regularly changing exhibits by local painters and sculptors.

ENTERTAINMENT & ACTIVITIES

Boston, along with the North Shore, Newport, Providence, and Cape Cod, offers a wide range of festivals, entertainment, and sporting activities. Whatever the time of year, and whatever your interests, you will find something to tempt you.

ANNUAL EVENTS

JANUARY
Boston Cooks!, tel 617/536-4100, late Jan.–early Feb.

Boston Wine Festival, Boston Harbor Hotel, tel 617/439-7000, Jan.–April.

Chinese New Year, Boston, tel 617/542-2574, Jan. or Feb. Three weeks of partying in Chinatown.

FEBRUARY
Black History Month, Boston, tel 888/SEE BOSTON. Exhibitions, lectures, and special events throughout the city.

Newport Winter Festival, Newport, R.I., tel 401/845-9123 or 800/976-5122, mid-Feb. Dedicated to fun and frolics, from ice-carving and skating and snow sculptures to hot-air ballooning.

New England Boat Show, tel 617/242-6092, Feb. 20–28.

Regatta Bar Jazz Festival, Charles Hotel, Cambridge, tel 617/876-7777, mid-Feb.–late May.

Presidents' Day, Quincy, tel 617/376-1900, 3rd Mon. Celebrations in the home town of two United States presidents.

MARCH
Boston Massacre Reenactment, Old State House, Boston, tel 617/720-3290, March 5. Soldiers and patriots in colonial garb, with muskets and music.

Celebrity Chefs Culinary Program, Fairmont Copley Plaza Hotel, tel 617/267-5300, month-long.

New England Flower Show, tel 617/536-9280, March 17–25.

St. Patrick's Day, tel 617/635-3911, March 17 and nearest weekend. City-wide celebrations.

Women's History Month, tel 888/SEE BOSTON. Exhibitions, lectures, and special events throughout the city.

APRIL
Boston Marathon, tel 617/236-1652, 3rd Mon. The world's oldest annual marathon, run every year since 1897 as part of the city's Patriots' Day celebration (see below). Thousands of spectators line the course to cheer on some 40,000 runners who cover the 26 mile, 385 yard (42.195 km) course from the suburb of Hopkinton to Copley Square.

Daffodil Festival, Bristol, R.I., tel 401/253-2707, all month.

Daffodil Festival, Nantucket, tel 508/228-1700, last weekend.

Patriots' Day, tel 888/SEE BOSTON, the actual date is April 19, but the public holiday is on the 3rd Mon. Parades and celebrations. Venues such as Paul Revere's House and the Old North Church conduct special ceremonies.

MAY
Lilac Sunday, Arnold Arboretum, Boston, tel 617/524-1717, mid-May.

WaterFire, Providence R.I., tel 401/272-3111, all month. A unique experience: 80 bonfires illuminate the Providence River, with accompanying music.

JUNE
Bunker Hill Weekend, Bunker Hill, Boston, tel 617/242-5641, Sun. nearest June 17. Parades and ceremonies commemorate the famous battle in Charlestown.

Cambridge River Festival, tel 617/349-4380, June 16.

Harborfest, Boston, tel 617/227-1528, www.july4th.org. The festival builds up to the Fourth of July. Chowderfest, music, fireworks, and more.

Newport International Film Festival, Newport, R.I., tel 401/848-9443, 1st week.

JULY
Fourth of July, Boston, tel 617/266-1492. Celebrated with the Boston Pops at the Hatch Shell, plus great fireworks.

Hall of Fame Tennis Championships, Newport, R.I., tel 401/849-3990 or 800/457-1144, 2nd week. Straight after Wimbledon, this is the only grass court championship on the men's professional tennis circuit in the United States.

Newport Music Festival, Newport, R.I., tel 401/846-1133, mid-month. Chamber music concerts in famous mansions.

AUGUST
August Moon Festival, Chinatown, Boston, tel 617/542-2574, end of month.

Feast of the Blessed Sacrament, New Bedford, tel 508/992-6911, 1st weekend. Celebrated by the Portuguese community —and everyone else in town.

Festas, North End, Boston, end of month. A series of vibrant and energetic Italian-style religious celebrations.

Gloucester Waterfront Festival, Gloucester, tel 781/283-1601, mid-month. Celebrates the town's fishing heritage with lobster bakes, craft fairs, and boat trips.

Newport Folk and Jazz festivals, Fort Adams State Park, Newport, R.I., tel 401/847-3700, 2nd & 3rd weekends. World-class performers take part in these renowned international outdoor events.

Provincetown Carnival Week, tel 508/487-2313, 3rd week.

SEPTEMBER
Boston Film Festival, tel 617/266-2533, runs for 10 days from 1st weekend.

Harwich Cranberry Festival, Harwich, tel 508/441-3199, mid-month. A country-style celebration of the berry that grows here on the Cape.

OCTOBER
Columbus Day Parade, Boston, tel 617/635-4505, 2nd Mon. Parade with an Italian flavor.

Halloween, Oct. 31, Salem, tel 800/777-6848. The spooky event is celebrated with two weeks of haunted happenings before Halloween itself.

Head of the Charles Regatta, tel 617/868-6200, Oct. 20–21. The Charles River has been a nursery for some of the world's most famous and talented oarsmen and women. In mid-October, thousands pack the banks and bridges of the Charles to watch crews from all over the world.

Nantucket Arts Festival, Nantucket, tel 508/228-1700, 1st week.

NOVEMBER
Nantucket Island Noel Celebration, Nantucket, tel 508/228-1700. The Yuletide flavor becomes intense on the island from Thanksgiving to mid-December.

Thanksgiving, Plymouth, tel 508/746-2334 or 800/USA-1620. A popular celebration and parade in the home of the first Thanksgiving.

Veteran's Day, Boston, tel 617/635-3911, Nov. 11. Many ceremonies.

DECEMBER
Boston Tea Party Reenactment, tel 617/338-1773, Sun. nearest Dec. 16. Marches and speeches at Old South Meeting House and Boston Tea Party Museum.

Christmas in Newport, Newport, R.I., tel 401/849-6454, all month. A series of events mark the approach of Christmas.

First Night Boston, tel 617/542-1399, www.firstnight .org, Dec. 31. The largest New Year's celebration in the United States. Established in 1976, this involves well over 250 performances in around 50 indoor and outdoor venues. Alcohol-free. Disabled access to many shows. The program starts at noon on December 31 with family-oriented events and climaxes with fireworks at midnight. A single badge entitles the wearer to free access to all events for the duration. Children under 4 go free.

ENTERTAINMENT

CULTURAL CENTERS

CLASSICAL MUSIC
Boston Symphony Orchestra, Symphony Hall, tel 617/266-2378 (info), 617/266-1200; 888/266-1200 (credit cards), www.bso.org. The BSO performs at Symphony Hall in Boston (Oct.–April), and at Tanglewood, near Lenox, in western Massachusetts (July, Aug.). Concerts in Boston take place on Fri. afternoons, Sat. evenings, most Tues. and Thurs. evenings, and eight Fri. evenings.

BankBoston Celebrity Series, see local newspapers for details. For more than 60 years the Celebrity Series, sponsored by BankBoston, has been presenting the best of dance, music, and theater to Boston audiences.

Boston Lyric Opera, Shubert Theatre, 265 Tremont St., tel 617/542-4912 or 800/447-7400 (tickets), www.blo.org. The BLO, founded in 1976, showcases exciting young talent. Lectures often precede performances.

Isabella Stewart Gardner Museum, 280 The Fenway, Boston, tel 617/734-1359, www.boston.com/gardner/, Sept.–May, Sat. & Sun. 1:30 p.m. Concerts in the Tapestry Room.

Music Conservatories
Boston has some of the country's finest training grounds for young musicians, which present classical, jazz, and world music programs year-round.

Berklee College of Music, tel 617/266-1400.

The Boston Conservatory, tel 617/536-6340.

Longy School of Music, tel 617/876-0956.

New England Conservatory of Music, tel 617/585-1100.

DANCE
Boston Ballet, tel 617/695-6950, www.boston.com/boston ballet. One of the top five companies in the United States, performing an internationally acclaimed repertoire. Most performances are at the Shubert Theatre (see Boston Lyric Opera, above).

POPULAR ENTERTAINMENT
Cape Cod Melody Tent, 21 W. Main St., Hyannis, tel 508/775-9100, www.ticket master.com. This outdoor arena hosts some of the biggest names

in entertainment for one-night stands through the summer.

Cape Playhouse, 820 Rte. 6A, Dennis, tel 877/385-3911, www.capeplayhouse.com. Operating seasonally, "America's Oldest Professional Summer Theater" has a fine array of plays, comedies, and musicals. Children's Theater Fri. a.m.

The FleetCenter, Fleet Center, Fleet Zoo, tel 617/624-1000, www.fleetcenter.com. Hosts many popular concerts. Check newspapers.

NIGHTLIFE

COMEDY CLUBS

Boston's comedy clubs range from traditional to alternative and from sketches to stand-up. Some clubs specialize in a particular style, others change from night to night.

Comedy Connection, Faneuil Hall, Quincy Market, tel 617/248-9700. Performers vary from star names to amateurs, with tickets priced accordingly.

Improv Boston, Back Alley Theatre, 1253 Cambridge St., Cambridge, tel 617/576-1253. This improv group proudly boasts that it is the region's longest running. Still going strong in Inman Square, it also holds events for children.

IRISH PUBS

Boston's Irish connections are celebrated in Irish pubs. Most are in areas that visitors rarely go to, such as Jamaica Plain. Two in the downtown area have the usual flowing stout, live fiddle music, and loud singing:

The Black Rose, 160 State St., tel 617/742-2286.

The Irish Embassy, 234 Friend St., tel 617/742-6618 .

CLUBS

Boston has a tradition of live music, with some local groups

going on to stardom. The *Boston Phoenix* and Thursday's *Boston Globe* "Calendar" section list pubs and clubs with live music.

Club Passim, 47 Palmer St., Cambridge, tel 617/492-7679. This is the legendary club where Joan Baez and Bob Dylan played, and still has echoes of the 1960s, when Cambridge was at the forefront of political protest.

House of Blues, 96 Winthrop St., Cambridge, tel 617/491-2583. This was the first of the popular chain and has a popular gospel brunch on Sunday mornings.

Lansdowne Street Music Hall, 36 Lansdowne St., tel 617/351-2525. Formerly Mama Kin, and part owned by Aerosmith, this still showcases local talent.

Plough & Stars, 912 Massachusetts Ave., Cambridge, tel 617/441-3455. This is one of the best pubs with live music, and there's hearty food to boot.

The Big Easy, 1 Boylston Place, tel 617/351-7000. Boylston Place, which runs through the Theater District, is also known as the Alley. This is one of a string of nightclubs catering to the affluent young crowd from nearby offices.

MICROBREWERIES

In recent years, Boston has developed a reputation for its special brews, which are often made on the premises of microbreweries. Look for names such as Tremont Ale, Sam Adams, Pilgrim Ale, Ipswich Ale, and Harpoon Ale; and try the specialty seasonal ales, made to secret recipes.

Boston Beer Works, 61 Brookline Ave., tel 617/536-2337. As well as a fine range of brews, there is a restaurant serving lunches and dinners in a cavernous setting.

Brew Moon, 113–115 Stuart St., tel 617/742-2739, and 52 Church St., Cambridge, tel 617/499-2739. These popular pubs, one in the Theater District and the other in Cambridge, serve beers and better-than-average food to their stylish, young clientele.

Cambridge Brewing Company Inc., 1 Kendall Square, tel 617/494-1994. Office workers come here to relax, watch sports on TV, and sip their suds. Pool hall next door.

Commonwealth Brewing Co., 138 Portland St., tel 617 523-8383. The first of the city's microbreweries, started by an Englishman, this cavernous tavern is right by the FleetCenter. It rocks before and after concerts, basketball and hockey matches.

John Harvard Brew House, 33 Dunster St., Cambridge, tel 617/868-3585. Right on Harvard Square, this wood-paneled watering hole pulls in the university crowd. Good food, unusual beers and ales.

Sevens Pub, 77 Charles St., tel 617/523-9074. If you are looking for the atmosphere portrayed in the famous sitcom Cheers!, avoid the touristy Bull & Finch and head for the busy booths and neighborhood ambiance of this popular pub.

ACTIVITIES

FISHING

Both sea fishing and freshwater fishing are popular New England hobbies, with many charter skippers available to guide you. Cape Cod is especially rich with opportunities for game fishing within an hour of the shore. No fishing licenses are required for striped bass, bluefin tuna, bluefish, pollock, and bonito, which are abundant spring and fall. Bottom fishing is also popular, from party boats, the beach, or numerous jetties.

As well as the famous local cod and flounder, you can fish for sea bass and haddock. Fresh water ponds and streams provide trout, perch, pickerel, and bass and the combative "salters," the local name for sea trout, out on the Cape.

GOLF
The 1999 Ryder Cup between the United States and Europe at the Country Club, Brookline was a timely reminder that golf has long been a popular sport in the region. Public courses abound in Massachusetts, with over 40 on Cape Cod alone. Unless stated, all those listed have 18 holes, and are open year-round.

ORGANIZED SIGHTSEEING
Few cities have as many varied and interesting ways to get the best out of the history and culture of the area. Choose from tours aboard a motor coach or a trolley, with a guide on foot or on the water. For the first-time visitor, it is always worth taking one tour to get an overview of the city highlights before setting off under your own steam.

SPORTS
Bostonians are crazy about sports. Whether they watch TV from their armchairs at home, from their stadium seats, or take themselves off to go hiking or jogging, play golf or fish, they make the most of the great outdoors.

WALKING TOURS, RIDES, & DRIVES
The region is well provided with bike trails and self-guided walking tours, often exploring various historical themes. Many come under the auspices of the National Park Service, so it is worth calling to see whether ranger-led tours are planned.

WHALE-WATCHING
Few activities have mushroomed as rapidly as whale-watching,

with boats leaving ports and harbors all along the New England coast, heading for the Stellwagen Bank, where the giants feed. It is important to take warm clothing with you, even in the height of summer, since temperatures can drop suddenly. Wear rubber-soled shoes or athletic shoes. Skin and eye protection against the sun is also essential, as is medication if you are prone to seasickness.

BOSTON

BASEBALL
Boston Red Sox, Fenway Park, 4 Yawkey Way, tel 617/267-9440, 617/267-1700 (reservations), 617/236-6666 (stadium tours May–Sept.), www.redsox.com. The Boston Red Sox are a major topic of discussion, as well as the main summer spectator sport (April–Oct.). Games at 1:05 p.m. & 7:05 p.m.

BASKETBALL
Boston Celtics, FleetCenter Fleet Zoo, tel 617/624-1000, www.nba.com/celtics. The Boston Celtics were once legendary. Today, they still pull in adoring fans at the FleetCenter. College games at Boston College, Boston University, and Harvard are also popular.

GOLF
Putterham Meadows, 1281 W. Roxbury Parkway, Brookline, tel 617/730-2078. Often called Brookline Golf Club (not to be confused with the famous Country Club), this is a friendly spot where the course was renovated in 2000. Flat, but with enough tricky holes to test you. Par 71, 6,307 yards.

HOCKEY
Boston Bruins, FleetCenter (see Basketball, above), www.bostonbruins.com. The one sport in which Boston's colleges command nationwide respect is hockey. Played at the FleetCenter, the annual Bean Pot

(Feb.) is a tournament between Boston College, Harvard, Northeastern, and Boston University. The NHL's Boston Bruins, like the Celtics, have seen better days, but have a hard core of fans who still turn out at the FleetCenter Oct.–June.

TENNIS
The International Tennis Hall of Fame, 194 Bellview Ave., Newport, R.I., tel 401/846-0642. These are the oldest grass tennis courts in the world, and anyone can play on them mid-May–Sept. Make a reservation to serve and volley on one of the 13 courts where the pros have played, or take a lesson.

ORGANIZED SIGHTSEEING
The Black Heritage Trail, tel 617/742-5415, www.afroammuseum.org. See p. 94 Guided tours offered year-round by the Boston African–American National Historical Site. This 1.6-mile (2.5 km) trail, which opened in 1974, starts at the Robert Gould Shaw Memorial (Park St. & Beacon St.). Sites include the 54th Regiment Memorial, Smith Court Residence, and the African Meeting House. Phone ahead Labor Day–Mem. Day.

Boston Duck Tours, tel 617/723-DUCK, www.ducktours.com, are truly amphibious, as you tour in a World War II landing craft, starting on land, then plunging onto the Charles River. It's fun and informative. Tours leave from the Prudential Center, May–Nov.

Boston by Foot, Inc., 77 N. Washington St., tel 617/367-2345 or 617/367-3766 (recorded information), bbfoot@bostonbyfoot.com. These walking tours are deservedly popular, thanks to the enthusiasm and knowledge of the guides. As well as the standard historical walks, there are also architectural and even Halloween themes.

Boston Harbor Cruises, I Long Wharf, tel 617/227-4321, www.bostonharborcruises.com. Specialists in narrated historic tours, as well as informal sunset cruises, etc.

Boston History Collaborative, tel 617/574-5950, Sat. a.m. Half-day trolley tours. Tickets include admission to houses and museums.

Boston's Literary Trail, www.lit-trail.org. A half-day, guided tour covering homes and meeting places favored by 19th-century authors. Includes: Omni Parker House, Harvard College, The Old Manse, and Walden Pond. Reservations a must. If you cannot take the tour, buy the book—*The Literary Trail: A Guide to Greater Boston's Newest Trail Linking Sites in Boston, Cambridge and Concord*—and follow the trail on your own. The book is available from local bookstores or from the Boston History Collaborative (see above).

Boston Spirits Walking Tour, tel 781/235-7149, members.aol .com/nehaunts. Selected evenings at 7:30 p.m. One-hour tour around Boston's most haunted spots, such as the Central Burying Ground and Boston Common.

Boston's Tall Ships, tel 617/742-0333. Explore Boston Harbor in one of two elegant schooners or reproductions of old fishing boats. Tours depart from Long Wharf.

Charles River Boat Company, tel 617/621-3001. The only cruiser on the Charles. The sightseeing trip includes knowledgeable commentary. Departs from Cambridge Galleria.

Minuteman Trolley Tours, tel 617/269-3626. Boston and Cambridge with historical narration. Passengers may alight and reboard when they want to as they tour.

North End Market Tours, L'Arte di Cucinare, 6 Charter St., tel 617/523-6032, e-mail mtopor@aol.com. These tours of the Italian North End, run by Michele Topor, are a food lover's delight, with stops to taste breads, cheeses, wines, and cakes at the authentic Italian stores and delis of the North End. You get an insight into the life, past and present, of the area, along with anecdotes, references to famous folks, and historical facts.

Old Town Trolley Tours of Boston, tel 617/269-7010, www.historictours.com. Provides a variety of specialist tours, from the Kennedy tour to themed chocolate and Halloween tours, including some in Cambridge. Reboarding is permitted.

S.P.N.E.A. Walking Tours, 141 Cambridge St., tel 617/227-3956, www.SPNEA.org. The Society for the Preservation of New England Antiquities organizes 2-hour Beacon Hill walks with expert guides each Saturday at 11 a.m. (mid-May–Oct.). Based on a theme of the year 1810, the walk includes a slide show, a tour of the Harrison Gray Otis House, and both slopes of Beacon Hill.

SELF-GUIDED TOURS
Boston Irish Heritage Trail, tel 888/749-9494 for map, or download it from www.irish heritagetrail.com. This is a self-guided tour highlighting the contributions made by the Boston Irish over the past 300 years. The 3-mile walk starts at the Boston Irish Famine Memorial (see p. 66).

Boston Women's Heritage Trail, tel 617/522-287. Self-guided trails, each 1.5 hours long, cover Downtown, the North End, Beacon Hill, South Cove, Chinatown, and Back Bay. The homes of Julia Ward Howe and Louisa May Alcott are included. A guidebook is available in bookstores and visitor information centers.

The Freedom Trail, Boston National Historical Park Visitor Center, 15 State St., tel 617/242-5642 or 617/227-8800 (tours), www.thefreedomtrail.org (see pp. 58–59). A 2.5-mile (4 km) walking trail through Downtown Boston linking 16 historic sites. Start from the visitor center on Boston Common. Allow four hours, Ninety-minute, ranger-led tours start at the visitor center and end at the Old North Church.

WHALE-WATCHING
Boston Harbor Whale Watch, 50 Rowes Wharf, tel 617/345-9866. From June–Sept., this highly professional operation runs 5-hour trips out to sea. Videos help to explain the life of the mammals.

Boston Harbor Cruises, I Long Wharf, tel 617/227-4321. By using high-speed catamarans, this company has cut the time for a trip to 3 hours (instead of the usual 5 hours). Naturalists aboard.

New England Aquarium Whale Watch, Central Wharf, tel 617/973-5281 or 617/973-5207 (harbor cruises), www. neaq.org, April–Nov. Aquarium experts lead 4-hour trips to see whales. Popular, so reservations are recommended.

CAMBRIDGE

GOLF
Fresh Pond Golf Course, 691 Huron Ave., tel 617/349-6282. A nine-hole course just 5 minutes from Harvard Square, this easy-to-walk course has three par 3s, two par 5s, and four par 4s skirting Fresh Pond Reservoir. Par 35, 3,100 yards.

ORGANIZED SIGHTSEEING
Harvard Yard Tours, Holyoke Center, 1350 Massachusetts Ave., tel 617/495-1573, Mon.–Sat. 10, 11:15, 2, & 3:15;

Sun. 1:30 & 3. Well-informed students lead daily tours of the university.

M.I.T. (Massachusetts Institute of Technology) Tours, Information Center, 77 Massachusetts Ave., tel 617/253-4795, Mon.–Fri. 10 a.m. & 2 p.m. Enjoy a student-guided walking tour of one of the world's greatest scientific educational institutions.

Tory Row: Brattle Street in the 18th century, Hooper-Lee-Nichols House, 159 Brattle St., tel 617/547-4252, Sat a.m. mid-June–mid-Oct. The Cambridge Historical Society organizes a 2.5-hour guided walking tour. (See p. 158–61 for Brattle Street.)

SELF-GUIDED TOURS
African–American Heritage Trail, Cambridge Office for Tourism, 4 Brattle St., tel 617/441-2884, www.cambridge-usa.org. Self-guided brochures highlighting former Cambridge residents such as Harriet Jacobs and W.E.B. Du Bois are available at the visitor information booth on Harvard Square.

Mount Auburn Cemetery, 580 Mount Auburn St., tel 617/547-7105 (see p. 162). Cemetery staff provide free maps, information, and an audiotape driving tour for sale or rental at the entrance gate.

WEST & NORTHWEST OF BOSTON

CYCLING
The Minuteman Bikeway, MassBike, 59 Temple Place, Suite 669, Boston, tel 617/542-2453, www.massbike.org. This is an abandoned rail route, paralleling much of Paul Revere's ride, which is now an 11-mile (17 km) bike trail. It begins near the Alewife T station in Cambridge, and passes through Lexington and Arlington to Bedford.

Pamphlet available at tourist information booths.

NORTH SHORE

GOLF
Cape Ann Golf Course, 99 John Wise Ave., Essex, tel 978/768-7544. With views of the ocean and the surrounding marshes, this is a peaceful spot where the water comes into play on two holes when the tide comes in. Using the two markers on each hole to shoot from, you can play this 9-hole course twice for a full 18. Par 69, 5,900 yards.

ORGANIZED SIGHTSEEING
Footprints, 15 North Rd., Bearskin Neck, Rockport, tel 978/546-7730, 11 a.m., 1 p.m., 3 p.m. daily, Mem. Day–Columbus Day. Call for other dates. Hour-long walking tours around Rockport. Choose from one of three routes.

SELF-GUIDED TOURS
Salem Heritage Trail, www.salem.org (see p. 186).

WHALE-WATCHING
Cape Ann Whale Watch, Main St., Gloucester, tel 978/283-5110. With research scientists aboard, you are guaranteed knowledgeable guides. This operation dates from 1979.

Captain Bill's Whale Watch and Deep Sea Fishing, 30 Harbor Loop, Gloucester, tel 978/283-6995 or 800/33 WHALE. This fleet has five boats, so there is usually a time to suit you. Experienced naturalists are on hand to answer all your questions.

Yankee Fleet Whale Watch and Deep Sea Fishing, 75 Essex Ave., Gloucester, tel 978/283-0313 or 800/942-5464. Another highly experienced company offering both whale-watching and fishing trips.

SOUTH OF BOSTON

ORGANIZED SIGHTSEEING
Newport Historical Society, Museum of Newport History, Newport, R.I., tel 401/846-0813, Thurs.–Sat. mid-May–mid-Sept. Guided walks, starting at the museum, cover the town's colonial and Golden Age eras. The society also publishes self-guided tours.

FOOTBALL
New England Patriots, Foxboro Stadium, 60 Washington St., Foxboro, tel 508/543-1776 or 800/543-1776, www.patriots.com. Foxboro is the home of the New England Patriots. The stadium is south of the city in Foxboro, midway between Boston and Providence. The club has been to the Super Bowl, but never triumphed.

SOCCER
New England Revolution, Foxboro Stadium (see above), www.anyrevolution.com. Soccer team based at Foxboro Stadium.

WHALE-WATCHING
Captain John Boats, Inc., Town Wharf, Plymouth, tel 508/746-2643 or 800/242-2469. As well as whale-watching cruises, this company also offers deep-sea fishing.

CAPE COD & THE ISLANDS

CYCLING
Cape Cod and the offshore islands are well-suited to cycling, due to a network of trails and readily-available bike rental shops. You can cycle around Martha's Vineyard in a day, although this doesn't really give you time to stop and look at places along the way.

Bike rentals
Arnold's, 329 Commercial St., Provincetown, tel 508/487-0844.

Holiday Cycles, 465 Grand Ave., Falmouth Heights, tel 580/540-3549, seasonal.

Rail Trail Bike Shop, 302 Underpass Rd., Brewster, tel 508/508/896-8200.

Young's Bicycle Shop, Steamboat Wharf, Nantucket, tel 508/228-1151.

R. W. Cutler Bicycles, on the corner of Main & Dock Sts., Edgartown, Martha's Vineyard, tel 508/627-405.

Martha's Bike Rentals, 4 Lagoon Pond Rd., Vineyard Haven, Martha's Vineyard, tel 508/693-6593.

Bike paths
Cape Cod has a long-distance trail, while shorter trails can be found at Provincetown, Falmouth, and elsewhere on the cape. Both Martha's Vineyard and Nantucket have cycle paths as well. Ask for maps and routes at the visitor information offices.

Boston–Cape Cod Bikeway, a 70-mile (112 km) route along low-traffic roads and several traffic-free trails, often built on former railroad tracks. At the beginning of the Cape, you can cycle along both sides of the Cape Cod Canal.

Cape Cod Rail Trail, (26 miles, 42km) stretching from South Dennis to Eastham, is the longest and most popular off-road bike path.

Shining Sea Trail, celebrating local writer Katherine Lee Bates. The easy ride runs for 3.5 miles (5.6km) from Falmouth to Woods Hole.

FISHING
Cape Cod Chamber of Commerce, P.O. Box 790, Hyannis, MA 02601, tel 800/ASK-FISH. Can provide you with details and a comprehensive directory.

Ladnav Sports Fishing, P.O. Box 2002, E. Dennis, tel 508/385 8150. Capt. Roger Vandal takes fishermen out into Cape Cod Bay to catch striped bass and bluefish.

Sea Joy Sport Fishing, 209 Old Comers Rd., Chatham, tel 508/945-5014. Bass, cod, and even shark are caught on excursions aboard the *Sea Joy.*

GOLF
For complete information about golf on the Cape, you should contact:

Tee Ball Golf, P.O. Box 37, Bass River, MA 02664, tel 800/TEE BALL, e-mail tball@golfcapecod .com.

Golf courses
Ballymeade Country Club, 125 Falmouth Woods Rd., North Falmouth, tel 508/540-4005. Set on the highest point of the Cape, with wonderful vistas over the water. Tennis, fitness center, and a comfortable clubhouse. Par 72, 6,928 yards.

Bass River Golf Course, 62 Highbank Rd., South Yarmouth, tel 508/398-9079. With its short but scenic front nine, and longer open back nine, the oldest municipal course on Cape Cod has character, thanks to the design genius of Donald Ross. Par 72, 6,129 yards.

Bayberry Hills Golf Course, 635 West Yarmouth Rd., West Yarmouth, tel 508/394-5597. With plenty of trees, testing doglegs, and bent grass fairways, this is a modern-style challenge for golfers of all abilities. Five sets of tees. Par 72, 7,172 yards.

Cranberry Valley Municipal Golf Course, 183 Oak St., Harwich, tel 508/430-5234. Voted one of the country's best public golf courses by *Golf Digest,* expect 18 challenging holes, with thickly wooded fairways. Par 72, 6,296 yards.

Dennis Highlands Golf Course, 825 Old Bass River Rd., Dennis, tel 508/385-8347. Right in the village of Dennis, this course has matured beautifully since opening in 1985. the terraced tees, 42 bunkers, and undulating greens ensure a thorough but enjoyable test. Par 71, 6,464 yards.

Dennis Pines, Mass. 134, Golf Course Rd., East Dennis, tel 508/385-8347. Set on 170 acres (69 ha) of pine forest, this championship course has been a favorite with locals and visitors alike since 1966, thanks to the high standards of maintenance as well as the scenic beauty. Par 72, 6,500 yards.

Hyannis Golf Club, Mass. 132, Hyannis, tel 508/362-2606. A public championship course, that hosts prestige events such as the Cape Cod Open and the Cape Cod PGA. Large driving range, four pros, and a full service restaurant, this is justifiably popular. Par 71, 6,711 yards.

Holly Ridge Golf Club, 121 Country Club Rd., South Sandwich, tel 508/428-5577. this is an executive par-3 course, which is particularly suited to juniors, seniors, and those wanting fun rather than a stiff challenge. A lovely, lush setting. 2,952 yards.

Kings Way Golf Club, Old King's Hwy., Yarmouthport, tel 508/362-8820, April–Nov. this popular executive par-3 course is always kept in immaculate condition by friendly staff. King's Way Restaurant is open to the public. Par 59, 4,023 yards.

Ocean Edge Resort and Gold Club, 832 Village Drive, Brewster, tel 508/896-5911. Set on Cape Cod Bay, this is one of Cape Cod's finest resorts, and its championship golf course is rated one of the best in the East. Expect 64 Scottish-style pot bunkers and five freshwater ponds along the way. Soft cleats required. Special packages available for tennis as well as golf. Par 72, 6,667 yards.

Quashnet Valley Country Club, 309 Barnstable Rd., Mashpee, tel 508/477-4412 or 800/433-TOFF. Meandering along the river valley, this is a pretty as well as testing natural course. The clubhouse has been renovated. Restaurant. Pro shop. Par 72, 6,602 yards.

HORSEBACK RIDING
Moon-A-Kiss Farm Stables, 809 Sandwhich Rd., Falmouth, MA, tel 508/548-5570. Open year-round, with a large indoor arena for show jumping and trail riding in the surrounding woods. Teaching youngsters is a specialty at these family-friendly stables.

ORGANIZED SIGHTSEEING
Cape Cod Duckmobile, tel 508/362-1117 or 888/225-DUCK. An amphibious landing craft tours the streets of Hyannis before plunging into the harbor. Witty narration.

WHALE-WATCHING
Hyannis Whale Watcher Cruises, 269 Mill Way, Barnstable, tel 508/362-6088 or 800/287-0374. Using high-speed boats, this company operates from the Mid-Cape. Naturalists on board.

Portuguese Princess, Commercial St., Provincetown, tel 508/487-2651 or 800/442-3188, April–Oct. With a 99-percent success rate, this fleet guarantees whales. Portuguese-style food served on board. Leaves from MacMillan Wharf.

Published by the National Geographic Society

John M. Fahey, Jr., *President and Chief Executive Officer*
Gilbert M. Grosvenor, *Chairman of the Board*
Nina D. Hoffman, *Executive Vice President,*
                      President, Books and School Publishing
William R. Gray, *Vice President and Director, Book Division*
Elizabeth L. Newhouse, *Director of Travel Publishing*
Barbara A, Noe, *Senior Editor and Project Manager*
Allan Fallow, *Senior Editor*
Cinda Rose, *Art Director*
Caroline Hickey, *Senior Researcher*
Carl Mehler, *Director of Maps*
Joseph F. Ochlak, *Map Coordinator*
Gary Colbert, *Production Director*
Richard S. Wain, *Production Project Manager*
Larry Porges, *Editorial Coordinator*
Keith R. Moore, *Contributor*

Edited and designed by AA Publishing (a trading name of Automobile Association Developments Limited, whose registered office is Norfolk House, Priestley Road, Basingstoke, Hampshire, England RG24 9NY. Registered number: 1878835).

Rachel Alder & Marilynne Lanng, *Project Managers*
David Austin, *Senior Art Editor*
Victoria Barber, *Editor*
Mike Preedy, *Designer*
Inna Nogeste, *Senior Cartographic Editor*
Richard Firth, *Production Director*
Steve Gilchrist, *Prepress Production Controller*
Cartography by AA Cartographic Production
Picture research by Zooid Pictures Ltd., & Carol Walker, AA Picture Library
Drive maps drawn by Chris Orr Associates, Southampton, England
Cutaway illustrations drawn by Maltings Partnership, Derby, England
Whale illustration drawn by Ann Winterbotham

Library of Congress Cataloging-in- Publication Data
Wade, Paul.
        The National Geographic traveler. Boston & environs / Paul Wade & Kathy Arnold.
        p. cm.
        Includes index.
        ISBN 0-7922-7926-3
        1. Boston Region (Mass.)--Guidebooks. I. Title: Boston & environs.
II. Arnold, Kathy.
        III. Title.

        F73.18 .W33 2001
        917.44'610444--dc21   00-069201

Printed and bound by R.R. Donnelley & Sons, Willard, Ohio.
Color separations by Leo Reprographic Ltd., Hong Kong
Cover separations by L.C. Repro, Aldermaston, U.K.
Cover printed by Miken Inc., Cheektowaga, New York.

Visit the society's Web site at http://www.nationalgeographic.com

THE NATIONAL
GEOGRAPHIC TRAVELER

A Century of Travel Expertise in Every Guide

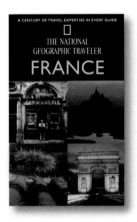

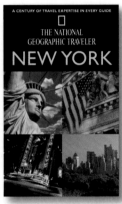

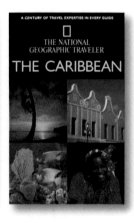

- **Australia** ISBN: 0-7922-7431-8
- **Boston & Environs** ISBN: 0-7922-7926-3
- **California** ISBN: 0-7922-7564-0
- **Canada** ISBN: 0-7922-7427-X
- **The Caribbean** ISBN: 0-7922-7434-2
- **China** ISBN: 0-7922-7921-2
- **Costa Rica** ISBN: 0-7922-7946-8
- **Florence & Tuscany** ISBN: 0-7922-7924-7
- **Florida** ISBN: 0-7922-7432-6
- **France** ISBN: 0-7922-7426-1
- **Great Britain** ISBN: 0-7922-7425-3
- **Greece** ISBN: 0-7922-7923-9
- **Hawaii** ISBN: 0-7922-7944-1
- **Italy** ISBN: 0-7922-7562-4
- **Japan** ISBN: 0-7922-7563-2
- **London** ISBN: 0-7922-7428-8
- **Los Angeles** ISBN: 0-7922-7947-6
- **Miami and the Keys** ISBN: 0-7922-7433-4
- **New Orleans** ISBN: 0-7922-7948-4
- **New York** ISBN: 0-7922-7430-X
- **Paris** ISBN: 0-7922-7429-6
- **Rome** ISBN: 0-7922-7566-7
- **San Francisco** ISBN: 0-7922-7565-9
- **Spain** ISBN: 0-7922-7922-0
- **Sydney** ISBN: 0-7922-7435-0
- **Thailand** ISBN: 0-7922-7943-3

AVAILABLE WHEREVER BOOKS ARE SOLD